SLIGHTLY OUT OF TUNE

IDIR N. AITSAHALIA

NORTHPORT BOOKS

Published by Northport Books, Princeton, New Jersey 08540, U.S.A

Copyright © 2014

www.northportbooks.com

ISBN 978-1-942175-01-8

First Paperback Edition: September 2014

Photos by Sophie Meunier and Yacine Aït-Sahalia

Cover designed by Idir N. Aitsahalia

To my father, for giving me my taste in traveling.

To my mother, for giving me my taste in writing.

PART I

1. OVER THE RAINBOW

MONDAY, FEBRUARY 11, 2013

BOROUGH OF QUEENS, NEW YORK CITY

Northport University: US News & World Report Best College ranking: #3; admission rate: 6.9%; living Nobel laureates: 22; nationalities represented: 70; date of founding: 1762; undergraduate enrollment: 6,407; tuition fees: $40,180; endowment: $18,421,099,000.

Zhang Haitun rehashed these statistics in his head as he stared out at the blurry spectacle sweeping across the rear bus window. The teenager was exhausted after a long and bumpy plane ride across the Pacific Ocean two days before and still disoriented by the jet lag. It did not help that he had left Manhattan at six in the morning in the coach bus now ferrying him and forty other Chinese tourists across Long Island. Yet, he repressed his sleepiness to look at the unfathomable beauty in front of him.

As the driver guided the bus away from New York City, the urban shades of gray of the Manhattan skyline turned to a bucolic palette of colors. Blue ponds and coniferous trees in an array of greens scattered the sides of the roads. Brown deer chased black squirrels into the yellow daffodils poking through the white snow. It was unlike anything he had ever seen in his native Tianjin,

2

where a smoggy haze blanketed buildings in a cloak of invisibility.

He knew, though, that the true beauty of the place lay not in color but in fame. When his parents had at last been granted a break from their civil service jobs for the Chinese New Year, they had finally taken their first trip overseas to the United States, for which they had saved up for so long. The travel brochures in Tianjin advertised Washington D.C.'s government monuments, California's beaches, and Utah's canyons, but Zhang Chenxu and Yuan Zuoya had instead chosen an increasingly popular tour package of America's national treasures: that of the most prestigious institutions of higher education.

`Haitun stopped looking out the window for a moment when the tour guide, introducing himself as Xie Jianqing, took the microphone. "We are arriving in the town of Northport, New York, home of the world-famous Northport University," Xie told them in Mandarin. Haitun could barely keep from screaming with joy. The 2009 edition of US News & World Report's college rankings had positioned Northport third in the country, behind Harvard and Princeton and ahead of Yale. News of Northport's rapid rise to prominence had reached Tianjin in the 2010 Shanghai Ranking, which had placed Northport second only to Harvard, the next stop for the tour bus.

The campus was marvelous. On the other side of the wide boulevard from the downtown area, picturesque Gothic towers lined the streets, and groups of students strolled through the snowy grass to the side of manicured flowering forsythias. Haitun had never seen anything so beautiful in his life. Here, in Long Island, he had reached the mythical land over the rainbow.

The coach bus skidded to a stop on the side of the road. Haitun smiled gratefully at his parents, overjoyed at the prospect of exploring the blissful town. Xie Jianqing explained their arrival in downtown Northport and rounded up the passengers near a white stone building. An enormous sign on its columned facade showed an image of an ancient Egyptian mummy, which Haitun understood to be an advertisement for a museum exhibit.

The Zhangs followed the rest of the pack, listening as Xie Jianqing used his megaphone to describe the long and rich history of Northport University, from its foundation when New York was still a British colony to its prescient embracing of the Information Age. "Some of the world's most influential electronic inventions, including those used by millions in China today," Xie explained, "Trace their origins back to groups of students at Northport." Xie held up his cellphone. "Before becoming a multinational corporation, Grape Electronics was based in a Northport dormitory." Zhang Haitun smiled. He had always admired this country for its fostering of creativity. Would such innovation one day be possible in China?

"Northport boasts twenty-two living Nobel Prize laureates on its faculty," Xie continued. "It's not unusual for undergraduates to interact with them on a first-name basis."

Haitun stared in awe at a statue of a figure whom he guessed to be the university's founder. "Haitun!" his mother called. "Stand there for a picture!"

His father broke in, "Go ahead—I'll be staying behind." Zhang Chenxu grabbed a camcorder from his backpack and walked slowly behind the rest of the group, filming them as well as the Northport students throwing frisbees on the snowy grass. His father's habit of recording every detail of noteworthy events had annoyed Haitun for his entire life, but he had stayed silent out of respect for his parents. This visit to Northport certainly qualified as such a momentous event.

Soon, however, it was clear that the Zhangs had taken one too many pictures. Haitun's father had caught up with his wife and son, but the rest of the group was nowhere to be seen. If Haitun wanted to be at the admissions office at eleven o'clock to hear the secrets of how to claim this paradise as his home for four years, he was in trouble. "Baba, Mama," he asked, "How do we find the admissions office now?"

"The map won't be of any help; it's only in English, and the drawings are so complicated," his mother pointed out. "We should ask someone."

Haitun looked around. The campus was a maze. Right in front of him was a massive white edifice with turquoise glass panels, where the few students who passed zipped by on their bicycles.

Suddenly, a student in long green pants, a yellow coat, purple gloves, orange sunglasses, and a blue backpack appeared out of nowhere, staring down at his shoes as he walked past them. The rainbow man was their only hope of making it to the admissions office before the official information session started.

"Please, where is admish house?" Haitun asked the rainbow man. His pronunciation would not have won his school's foreign language contest, but now he just hoped that the man would be able to understand his question and get him and his parents there in time.

After scanning all three of the Zhangs' faces, the rainbow man replied in perfect Mandarin, "The admissions office, Webber Hall? Walk to your right until you get to a dead end, turn to your left, and walk forward until you reach a strange-looking silver building. It's hard to describe, but you can't miss it."

Haitun was stunned. The rainbow man had not mispronounced a single syllable. When his father prodded him on the back with his camcorder, though, Haitun finally spoke. "Th-th-thank you. Where did you learn to speak such perfect Chinese?"

"Well, I studied it for a year or so in Australia and three years here. Northport's Mandarin program is great!"

Unsure whether the rainbow man was joking, Haitun stopped for a few moments. He was still flabbergasted by the fact that a white man with four years of experience could not only pronounce the words so eloquently, but with greater grammatical accuracy than Haitun himself. Speaking Mandarin that way would require learning it from birth. But what could he say? Such was the nature of Northport.

Haitun's mother, Zuoya, broke the silence. "You are such an amazing young man. Thank you so much for helping us! We would love to talk with you longer, but we really need to run to the admissions office. Can we find you there in two hours maybe? We have so many questions!"

Zhang Chenxu frowned, as if to reprimand his wife for bothering the young man, but they had struck a local who was not only brilliant, but also friendly. "Well, madam, I can't make it before twelve fifty-five," he replied. "But I will see you then and there."

✈ ✈ ✈

WEBBER HALL, NORTHPORT UNIVERSITY

Alizeh Khorsandi scanned the room. "Well, that concludes today's admissions session. Thank you very much for visiting Northport. Now, any last questions?"

His parents and the other visitors were already exiting, but Zhang Haitun stayed and approached the young woman. "And your name is?" she asked.

"Gary," Haitun responded, using the name his English teacher in Tianjin had arbitrarily bestowed upon him.

"Well, hello, Gary. Where are you visiting us from today?"

"China," he answered.

"Welcome to Northport, Gary! How are you enjoying your visit to campus?"

"I love it so much! I want to study here for next four years!" he replied enthusiastically.

"I really hope you get to, Gary! So, how can I help you?"

Haitun hesitated, terrified to make a poor first impression and potentially ruin his chances of getting into Northport. "In China, we have very hard exams, so which grade do we need to admit to Northport?"

Alizeh sighed. She had been an admissions officer at Northport for only two years, yet she had already begun to hate the eleven o'clock session. It fit best with the most popular Chinese tour, and her superiors insisted she proctor it every other day in addition to her usual office work. It was very frustrating to explain to the pushy Chinese parents without being rude that their preconceptions about the admissions process were wrong. No, there was no magic formula for getting into Northport. No, being the lead violinist in their town or captain of their Model United Nations team was no guarantee of admission. No, it wasn't worth the trouble flying over an ocean trying to find the Holy Grail, because they would be sorely disappointed.

The Chinese visitors reminded her of her own Iranian parents when she had gone through that phase herself, though every year the Ivy League admissions process became more ruthlessly competitive. The intangible factors that made or broke an individual application were often inscrutable, even for her.

"Well, we consider applications holistically, which means we look not only at grades but also essays, extracurricular activities, leadership, community service, passion, and dedication."

Haitun was very surprised by the admissions officer's response. He would need time to decipher and process all of it. He simply answered, "Thank you," then rushed out of Webber Hall to find his parents waiting. They did not seem displeased with his disappearance, assuming that anything he asked would help his chances of admission into Northport. Haitun took one long, last look at the gleaming building, with its silver steel sails jutting out of a blue prism. If luck favored him, perhaps he would lay his eyes on the strange edifice again in three years.

Haitun turned around when his mother gleefully whispered in his ear, "Look who came back!"

"Well, I'm impressed," Zhang Chenxu told the rainbow man. "I would never have thought such a busy young man would take the time to talk to a few lost tourists!"

"And you're so polite!" Yuan Zuoya added.

Haitun silently agreed with his mother's comment. Following a summer in the United States, one of Haitun's classmates had returned decrying Americans' utter lack of courtesy and manners, especially towards elders. Now that he had met the rainbow man, however, Haitun wondered how his classmate could ever have made such an insane observation.

"May I please have the honor of learning your name?" Haitun inquired.

"Jiecun," the rainbow man told Haitun and his parents. Haitun smiled. Of course he had adopted a Chinese name.

"Do you have a business card?" Chenxu asked.

"Well, um, I can write my email down. I don't have a Facebook account, though I know you don't use Facebook in China anyway," he replied. Jiecun asked Haitun for a pen and jotted down his email address on a torn piece of paper from his pocket.

Haitun waited for Jiecun to ask him for his name, but he did not, so his father interfered. "His name is Haitun."

"I have an American name too," Haitun added. "Call me Gary!"

"Nice to meet you, Gary," Jiecun told him, grabbing the card where Haitun had written his own contact information.

"Oh, one last thing, please, Jiecun!"

"Yes?"

Taking a cheap red watch out of his pocket, Haitun whispered to Jiecun, "Could you please keep this for me in your room? Some people in China say if you leave a watch in a place, it will give you good luck, and you can come back to this place later. I really want to study here in three years. This is utopia."

"Happy to!" Jiecun replied, placing the watch in his own pocket. "Now, sorry to leave you, but I need to go wash my hands before going to class. Enjoy the rest of your visit, and email me if you want me to explain Northport's history or if you have any other questions."

Zhang Haitun waved goodbye to Jiecun, then stared around for a second. He still wondered if the whole scene had been a dream, which might very well be possible given his jetlag and general sleepiness. But then again, at Northport it was no surprise, he thought. Heaven was the home of the gods.

2. HOW INSENSITIVE

FRIDAY, FEBRUARY 15, 2013

MAÇKA PALAS RESTAURANT, NORTHPORT

Aurélia Chitour sat at the table, observing the room. Cheap but tasty ethnic restaurants like Maçka Palas were endemic to Ivy League university towns. To her right dined a family with a bored-looking teenage son who barely stopped his frantic texting to acknowledge his parents' presence. To her left sat a group of mostly Indian and geeky-looking older students, engineers if she had to take a wild guess. Absent from the restaurant were the professors from the nearby McCartney School of Business or Ciccone School of Law. They had probably chosen the New American farm-to-table concept across from Maçka Palas, better suited to a professional school budget. It was a real shame, she thought, that most Northport students saw the town outside the all-inclusive campus as a no-man's land not worth venturing to.

The man she was waiting for—she could not accurately refer to him as her "date"—had not arrived yet, though he had said seven o'clock, and it was six fifty-nine. He had suggested, or rather insisted, that they choose a Turkish restaurant for dinner. Why? Well, it was hard to figure out Jason Curran, even for her.

Jason opened the door. Most Northport students walked around in the university's officially licensed turquoise garb, but not Jason. He pulled off his coat and sweatshirt to reveal his signature look, a green shirt with a dolphin motif, probably purchased during one of his travels.

"Good evening, Jason," Aurélia greeted him sweetly in Portuguese as she rose from her seat.

Jason was clearly taken aback by her early arrival, but his voice seemed rather dull and condescending to her. "Oh, you came ahead of time." So much for Portuguese being a romantic language, Aurélia thought. Then again, he had not paid much attention to the fact that he was taking her on a pseudo-date the day after Valentine's Day.

She considered commenting on his blunt remark, but there was no reason to ruin the evening. She had little free time in her frenetic student life, so she did not want to waste a single minute of it.

The waiter walked to their table and asked, "May I take your order?"

"I'll start with the hummus, please," Aurélia began, before Jason interrupted her.

"I'll order for us both so I can practice my Turkish," he told the waiter in the latter's native language. "One stuffed grape leaves for me please, then a zucchini pancake. For her, a hummus and—" he stared back at Aurélia, waiting for her to decide on her main course.

"Roasted eggplant, no garlic," she completed. Several dinners ago at a French restaurant, she had learned the hard way that he was strongly bothered by pungent odors, so this time she settled on something relatively inoffensive.

"Any drinks for the two of you?" the waiter asked, switching to English.

"Just a glass of water with lemon, no ice, please," Aurélia replied.

"A sour cherry juice for me, please," Jason told the waiter, switching back to Turkish. He saw every restaurant meal as an opportunity for linguistic practice, though he had not missed out on chances to do that this week. Outside the Spanish and Hebrew language dinner tables at Schumann College and his ongoing conversation with Aurélia in Portuguese, he was currently planning his next language immersion visits to the Venezuelan pupusa hut and the new Israeli falafel bar.

"Great, I'll bring those right up. Enjoy your evening," the waiter told them as he left for the kitchen.

"Nice Turkish," she told him. "How many languages do you speak, again?"

"Fifteen," he said surprisingly modestly.

"Awesome! Which ones?"

"English, Greek, Portuguese, Chinese, French, Spanish, Arabic, Italian, Japanese, Turkish, German, Korean, Hebrew, Russian, and Cambodian."

"Wow, it seems like the list gets longer every time I ask you! Some of those are really original, like Cambodian and Turkish! Why did you choose to learn them?"

"Well, I spent several months in Cambodia."

"Right, you told me about that during Orientation. I'm sorry, it was such a long time ago."

"And as for Turkish, the Middle East is fascinating with all the ancient civilizations there. Knowing a language helps you understand the culture better. Farsi's next on my list."

"Awesome! Do you speak all of those fluently?"

"Not completely. I mean, I only started learning Russian last year."

"Wow, just wow, Jason. You're brilliant."

"Just a day in the life," he said.

Aurélia noticed Jason's failure to pay her a compliment in return. She was, after all, a Northport student in her own right, with commendable accomplishments in her English major and charity work, plus a fine-tuned psychological intelligence. However, she had hypothesized over the years that Jason's lack of polite reciprocity was not the product of arrogance. Jason had always been slightly out of tune with the social conventions of the surrounding world. While most others repudiated him for his abrasive style, she knew that he made a constant effort to interact better with those around him and therefore cut him some slack. Once again, Aurélia, bothered but not offended, let his lack of attention to her slip.

"So, what did you do this week?" she asked, changing the subject.

"Well," Jason began, "On Monday, I woke up at half past eight and went to my Portuguese class in Mancini Hall. Then, I stopped by the post office to send my package to Chengdu and went to the White Dolphin Café for an açaí smoothie. At eleven or so, I was about to go to my 'Neural Computation and Coding in Microcircuits' class in Armstrong Hall when I ran into a high schooler from China looking for Webber Hall with his parents."

"Again?" Aurélia interjected. "How many times per week does that happen?"

"As many times as the campus maps are indecipherable. This one's name was Gary. He and his parents seemed so happy to hear someone answer them in their native language! We later exchanged contact information, and he emailed me a list of questions not long after. I told him all about Northport, and he explained to me why he really wanted to study here instead of in China. This reminds me, I was reading a fascinating article in *The Economist* on the gender imbalance in China and what it meant for..."

Aurélia placed her elbow on the table, held her chin, and tilted her head. When Jason began on a topic he enjoyed, there was no end unless she intervened. She just waited until he finished his sentence and caught his breath. "That's great! It's so nice that you can use your languages like that! I was actually talking to my Arabic professor today, and she thinks you're the most amazing and motivated freshman she's ever had. She said you reminded her of the guy in that movie..."

As Aurélia continued to talk, Jason stayed fixated on her face. Her skin color, like that of many Brazilians, revealed a mélange of Mediterranean, African, and likely West Indian blood. When he had first met her in his freshman year introductory Arabic class, she had mentioned that she was learning the language to better connect with her Lebanese roots. He had never thought it polite to ask what her ethnic makeup was, and his failure to figure it out in three years had bothered him for that long.

Soon, though, Jason reprimanded himself for that thought. He had more important things to figure out than Aurélia's exact ethnicity. She was doing the head-tilted-over thing again. She was definitely trying to tell him something. Was she drawing his attention to something in the room? Was she disinterested by what he was saying and thinking about how to tackle her upcoming English paper instead of listening to him? Or was this movement meaningless, one she made instinctively without intending to communicate any subliminal messages?

Ironically, for all his linguistic aptitude, Jason had always struggled to make sense of body language. He could easily deal with the fact that German had a byzantine sentence structure simply because it was consistent. Grammatical exceptions might abound in French, but they were clearly noted on paper. All he had to do was memorize them. However, all that Jason had learned from therapists, online articles, and awkward life experiences had failed to show him a regular formula for body language. Was shaking a sign of ecstasy or trepidation? He wondered what the world he knew would look like if anything could also mean its opposite. How could one program a computer in binary code if 0 and 1 could sometimes signify the same thing, or a bracketed command changed its meaning depending on how the software felt that day?

"So anyway, Jason, at the end of the movie, he discovers that the whole time, his friend has actually been..."

Aurélia looked at Jason. He was obviously not listening to her. In three years of knowing him, she had grudgingly accepted that he was slower than others when it came to picking up on those subtle signals. She had no intention of throwing a fit or using other immature methods to seek his attention.

She reached for a tissue, blew her nose, and sipped some water from her glass, buying a few moments of time with her diversions until she had thought of a different conversation topic. "Did you hear what happened to Azbine Khoumlès?" This time, she initiated the conversation in English. She wanted Jason to aim his single-minded focus on talking to her, not trying to remember the details of Portuguese grammar.

Jason thought for a moment to see if that name rang a bell. What seemed like a lifetime ago, he had created a Facebook account to follow the news and rumors of the

Northport Class of 2013 but had deactivated it soon after. Reading the faces of people in front of him was already a Herculean enough task, so he was doomed to fail if he tried to gauge emotions from others' decisions to "like" statuses, delays in response times, or choices of punctuation at the end of one-word answers. Not much later, Jason had realized that trying to keep up with all that happened on campus without a Facebook was like trying to sing while deaf, so he had officially given up on trying to make new friends in or beyond his classes.

"No, who is he or she?" Jason inquired.

Of course he did not know her, Aurélia thought. He probably knew the names of ten students on campus. "Azbine is, or I should really say *was*, a student in our grade. She was expelled yesterday, for—hear this, now—taking five extra minutes to complete a three-hour test! She told us that Northport's policies punish this the same way as plagiarism! This is so unfair!"

Jason shook his head. He ignored much of what happened on this side of Garvarentz Boulevard, the highly symbolic border between Northport University and the town of Northport. "Where is she from?" he asked Aurélia.

"Algeria, if I remember correctly. Actually, wait, no. Tunisia."

"Ah. And what was she majoring in?"

"Philosophy."

"Where did this happen?"

"Ginsburg Hall, the philosophy department," Aurélia replied, trying to figure out where Jason was going with his cryptic, clinical questions.

"And when?"

"Azbine said last Wednesday. It took the administration a little over a week before they finally decided to expel her."

"What time of day? Early morning, noon, afternoon, evening..."

Aurélia was getting tired of Jason, who was beginning to sound seriously like a detective leading an investigation. "How do *I* know? Why are you asking me all these questions, Jason?"

"Well, it might make a difference. I haven't thought it out yet. Besides, I like being precise."

"All right, but the details don't matter."

"I have to disagree, Aurelia. Until we know exactly what happened, we can't draw any conclusions about what was fair or unfair."

"Jason, if I wait until I know everything, I'll be waiting for a lifetime. They keep all their proceedings secret."

"Then go ahead and wait. What happened to this girl shouldn't matter to you, no?"

"I'm just trying to be nice and empathize with Azbine! That's why I signed the online petition to have her readmitted to Northport."

"Why? On what factual basis? You're getting all emotional instead of listening to logic."

Aurélia grunted. Sometimes she wondered why Jason had so little empathy. Had his parents decided to raise him that way? Had he suffered a trauma in the past that had changed the way he looked at life? The two of them held very stimulating conversations, but they were always on classes, politics, travel, music—just nothing deeply personal. She opened her mouth to retort but kept it still for a few seconds as the waiter brought the appetizers. "What logic? That you don't think what I'm telling you is logical?"

Jason stared for a few seconds as Aurélia snapped off a piece of pita bread and used it to scoop some hummus off her plate. His elementary school classmates had labeled him a "weirdo" for eating the Mediterranean chickpea dip directly with a spoon, though to him Aurélia's behavior of eating with bread was a cumbersome and illogical social custom.

"Jason?" Aurélia called out. It was so annoying how he sometimes blanked out for a few seconds, perhaps because he had seen something esoteric in the presentation of her hummus.

"I heard you. I think her story doesn't make sense."

"Why? Because you're such a perfect, honest student? You'd never think of breaking any rules because rule-breaking is some weird, alien concept?"

"If it were, I'd have studied rule-breaking as a foreign language."

Aurélia was not feeling Jason's brief attempt at humor. "Why don't you believe the story I told you? She even wrote a farewell message to our class on Facebook."

"Look, Aurélia, no university would ever kick out anyone for something as trivial as what she claims."

"Then what do you think she was expelled for? It's not like she tried to murder President DiTancini!"

"Yeah, but what if it's something much bigger, like a pattern of cheating, and the extra time incident helped the administration discover a pattern that had been going on for three years?"

"Jason, how insensitive!"

"Well, it's possible. I'm not saying she did it, but it's probably a complicated situation. The administration wouldn't throw someone out for no reason. They've definitely looked into everything in detail already."

"Well, they must have investigated wrong. That, or they have some hidden agenda."

"Aurélia, it's never a good idea to jump to conclusions without evidence. In this case, we can't just guess that she's innocent and that the administration is overreacting for fun."

"Why? You're the one jumping to conclusions here, with your wild theory that she's some sort of serial cheater! I'm sure she's telling the truth. The university administrators aren't the nicest people out there. If she'd broken a rule on paper like taking a few extra minutes for a test, they wouldn't show her mercy. How would you feel if they'd done that to you?"

Jason ignored her jab at his emotions. It was not subtle at all, which was probably why he had actually been able to notice it. "Why do you think she's honest? She has to be making at least some things up. Didn't you read the series of articles on the cheating policies in *The Daily Deer* two years ago?"

"No, I don't recall, but why does it matter? This is so unfair!" she yelled.

"The administration changed their policy to say that taking extra time to complete a test was a much milder offense than other forms of cheating. Besides, even if the offenses were technically the same in the Northport Honesty Code before, it was just a technicality. It wasn't ever enforced. Come on, cheating and taking five extra minutes are *not* the same thing, not even remotely."

Aurelia thought about Jason's revelation for a second, then looked at the table and assessed her situation. Jason had not even finished his appetizer yet. If she were to kill the time of a still lengthy dinner without getting into another argument, her best bet was probably to close the discussion, then let him ramble for an hour on a topic that obsessed him and feign interest for that long.

Before she finished, however, Jason interrupted. "Tell me one thing, Aurélia. I can see that you're upset. Why do you still put up with me? Now, by senior year, most other students on campus have given up on even trying to approach me unless they need help with their assignments. Look, you know I'm not an expert when it comes to guessing people's emotions, but I'm sure if you just wanted to try new ethnic foods every week, you could find someone else to do it with."

Aurélia, while taken aback by Jason's question, had no reason to be embarrassed or lie. "The truth is, Jason, unlike most people at Northport, I really couldn't care less about who's popular or cool. Most people just brush you off as a jerk, but I don't. I find you so smart and original. I respect the fact that you focus on your passions, even if you rub most people the wrong way. You need to be pretty brave to ignore the way others see you. Most importantly, though, I know you're a good person who never tries to hurt anyone. Because of that, I'm willing to put up with the fact that—yes, I'll say it—sometimes you can be very annoying. Very, very annoying. But I always tell myself that it's fine, because, well, you're Jason, and you can't help it."

Jason's mother had always instructed him to be wary of those who had and masked malevolent motivations. Yet, despite the difficulty he had seeing beyond the literal meaning of people's words, he could sense no malice at all in Aurélia. He already knew how he would have answered the same question had she asked him it. Though he certainly considered Aurélia beautiful, what really attracted him to his best—and only—consistent female friend since freshman year was the fact that she had stood by him for so long. Now that he finally knew her motivation for doing so, he planned to see a good amount of her for the rest of his senior year.

Before he could find a way to phrase his response, Aurelia spoke again. "Now, tell me, Jason, what are your travel plans for the rest of the school year? Venturing to Antarctica over Spring Break, since you've probably been everywhere else by now, and learning Swahili while you're at it?"

Jason breathed a sigh of relief. This would not turn out to be such a bad evening, after all.

3. TIME AFTER TIME

WEDNESDAY, FEBRUARY 20, 2013

GUATEMALITA, EAST NORTHPORT

They called it "the ghetto." Juan Ravénto laughed with pity whenever he heard that name. Sure, the small homes in East Northport's "Little Guatemala" neighborhood were not as glamorous as the mansions in Fort Salonga and Asharoken, but to imply that there was any danger walking at night near the commuter train station was a gross exaggeration. Maybe the area could be considered a bit seedy for a slightly inebriated, single female Northport student strolling obliviously in the street while holding her phone, but by Juan's standards, the neighborhood seemed perfectly fine.

Perhaps he had just seen too much. In 1983, Juan evacuated his native Guatemala with his father and seven siblings while still a boy, in the midst of a brutal civil war where government agents had killed his mother as part of a massive genocide against the Ixil Maya. In the land of opportunity, even the so-called "ghettoes" like Guatemalita seemed very safe by comparison. Juan had willingly accepted his long work hours as a janitor at Northport University for a chance to reside in one of them.

Juan Ravénto stepped off the bus and walked alongside the Puccini School of Medicine for about ten minutes until he reached Mancini Hall, a massive stonewalled building with exquisite fountains on one side and modern art sculptures on the other. The students at Northport knew it as the site of their Romance language classes; Juan knew it as the site of his first shift of the day.

Walking down a small flight of stairs on the side of one of the ramparts, Juan pulled out his key, then grabbed the bucket, mop, and cart he had left in an exiguous cabinet. He tugged his materials across the hallway to the basement-level men's restroom, then placed his cart on the floor and began cleaning the stall closest to him. He sprayed the disinfectant and restocked the toilet paper, then repeated the process. Juan Ravénto did not have the most glamorous job in New York State, but it was sufficient for him to buy a standing house, food for his family, and soccer equipment for his son.

Juan sighed. He had only one stall left. He walked towards it and unsuccessfully tried to pry it open. Every other day or so, that stall was locked. He had only started morning custodial work in Mancini Hall at the beginning of the calendar year, gladly accepting the slight salary raise for the extra shifts after the firing of the previous janitor. Despite that, he had noticed that time after time, this stall in particular was not only occupied, but also a hotbed of conversation with a voice on the telephone in a language that was neither English nor Spanish. As he had done the last few times he had been in this situation, Juan stayed put, staring at the ceiling and humming merengue tunes for about ten minutes.

Finally, Juan looked in relief as the student in the stall walked out. Unfortunately, he had decided to wash his hands for two minutes on end. Yes, it was true that Northport's Arlen Health Center had recommended that everyone wash his or her hands after the recent gastroenteritis outbreak, but this was overkill. Juan did not want to bother the serial hand-washer, though, so he went to clean the previously occupied stall. After he came out, Juan looked around. A huge mess of water and soap engulfed the floor.

Juan Ravénto could no longer hold his annoyance. "*Ay, Dios Mio!*" he shouted.

✈ ✈ ✈

THURSDAY, FEBRUARY 21, 2013

**WILLIAMS GYMNASIUM,
NORTHPORT UNIVERSITY**

Jason Curran executed one last sidekick, then placed his hands on his waist and performed the closing salutation, facing first the instructor and then the black-and-white photograph of Bruce Lee. Most of the other students generally rushed the last element of any martial arts class, but for Jason, getting every detail correct was an obligation, out of a desire to both respect the tradition of the art and do everything to the fullest without cutting corners.

He walked off the red and blue mats and placed his boxing gloves in his bag. He had reconverted his father's sturdy old duffel bag into his martial arts bag before coming to Northport. Its bright orange color made it stand out among black suitcases in airports and now the turquoise equipment bags sold by Northport's martial arts program. Jason glanced at the room before leaving one of his favorite places on campus. Pictures of legendary practitioners such as Chuck Norris and Muhammad Ali, numerous trophies, and Japanese katana swords lined the walls.

Northport did not know his native Sydney's warm climate, so he bundled up in his sweatshirt, coat, gloves, scarf, and hat. Over the years, he had learned to live with the nauseating stench of the men's locker rooms, but he still made a habit of rubbing sanitizer onto his hands. As he pressed on the dispenser, Derek Park punched him lightly on the shoulder. "Well, that was a fun class, wasn't it?" he asked.

"Yeah! Thanks for helping me out with the headlock on that last drill! That was a tough one!"

"No problem, bro!"

Jason smiled. He had begun training in Chinese jeet kune do in Sydney, when he was still in middle school, yet he often required help on some of the more advanced techniques. Three and a half years ago, Derek had generously offered to serve as his training partner whenever he could and correct his form. The two had then become friends during the first quarter of their freshman year, when they were together in both jeet kune do and a First-Year Seminar, a twelve-student, discussion-based class named "COS 195: Enigmas: Using Computers to Code and Decipher Secret Languages" taught by the most recent winner of the Rota Award, a yearly accolade bestowed upon Northport's most beloved faculty member.

This year, Derek lived across the hall in Lauderdale College and occasionally came to keep Jason company. By now, he was, along with Aurélia and practically no one else, one of the only students who still bothered to converse with Jason.

The two walked back the well-lit path from Williams Gymnasium to Lauderdale College. "Yo, Jason," Derek asked, "Are you going to the Iota Nu Alpha bash tomorrow night?"

"Is that a frat?" Jason asked, proud to have picked up on the Greek letters.

"Yeah, man. My friend Eugene Seth's throwing a rad party in Ulvaeus Rink, with the theme 'Fire and Ice.' No pun intended, but it's gonna be super chill!"

"Me? No, you know, I rarely go to any events, except when Lauderdale takes us on a free trip to the Metropolitan Opera. I'm really not a fan of parties—I mean, college social life is already such a minefield for me. When you add the blaring music, it's impossible to hear what anyone is saying! Plus, I'm way too busy with my project."

"Oh, right, your project! How's that going?"

While in high school, Jason had begun developing an idea for a groundbreaking neurotechnological invention dear to him. His parents had initially been dismissive, saying that the technical challenge was insurmountable, but after a while they had chosen to support him, whatever he decided. The summer before leaving Australia, preparing the extremely stressful transition to living with complete strangers at the other end of the world had preoccupied him far too much to focus on his project. Since he had arrived at Northport, however, the pursuit of this idea had consumed him.

"Oh, it's going really well!" Jason replied gleefully. "I'm taking all but one of my classes in my two majors, Neuroscience and Engineering, so I can get lots of inspiration for my project. And when I'm not doing classwork, I pretty much focus all my energy on it."

"Sweet! Anything new since last time?"

"Yeah, I'm going to a computer science talk in two weeks. Hopefully it'll give me the missing element of my project."

"Awesome, dude! Hey, remember what I told you last time? If you need any help with the business part, just hit me up!"

For years, Jason had barely given any thought to marketing; recognition and profit were less than secondary goals. He only hoped that the finished product would help him correct some of his own flaws. Besides, he needed to prove to himself that he could make a breakthrough in neurotechnology, and after starting to pursue the idea, he had vowed never to give up.

"You know," Derek continued, "As Student Council President, I can market the project to all of Northport!

And being from Palo Alto, I have tons of contacts in Silicon Valley. I actually go back there often to help my friends with the startups they're trying to launch, so I can hook you up with them so you can talk venture capital or advertising when you're ready."

Typical Derek, Jason thought. Only he could be friends with literally everyone at Northport and clearly beyond campus as well. Jason harbored no illusions about the real motive behind Derek's affability towards him: an omnipresent need to sympathize with every single constituent. "Wow, thanks a lot, Derek!"

"Yeah, bro!"

Before Jason could respond, Derek turned to wink at a student walking by, no doubt heading to Williams. "Hey, girl! So, I'm seeing you later tonight?"

The girl giggled. "Yeah, of course! Your place or mine?"

"Either's fine, as long as I get to see you, Vanya!"

Vanya—if Jason had heard her name correctly—grinned, then waved goodbye to Derek. Sometimes, Jason wondered how it would feel to be like Derek, how popularity would revolutionize his life. Would the entire campus grovel at his feet and fulfill his every desire? Would he finally be invited to the parties he only knew of from vague rumors, or even better, have the power to choose which guests to accept and which to reject?

However, cultivating interpersonal relationships on a large scale was far too difficult, time-consuming, and unrewarding for him, so he had not waited long at Northport to give up on any ambitions he might originally have entertained of rivaling any other student on campus in terms of popularity, especially the Student Council President. Jason just wondered how Derek had climbed to the top of the food chain. Did he simply have a way with people that Jason completely lacked, despite all his efforts and improvements over the years?

Jason played back through his first encounter with Derek during Northport's Freshman Orientation Week. When Derek had inquired about his hobbies, Jason had described the electronic circuitry project he had completed right before leaving for college, and Jason had thought—even though it was always very difficult to pick up on those things—that Derek was only pretending to understand the scientific explanation. When the conversation had inevitably shifted to Jason's remarkable language aptitude, Derek had mentioned that in addition to English and Korean, he spoke basic Spanish, which their quick Spanish conversation revealed was indeed quite basic.

Was this because making nice with every student on campus was a full-time job that left Derek no time to become an expert in science or languages, or rather because Derek had tried to tackle these domains and been unable to progress? Perhaps, Jason thought, these differences in skills were the only thing allowing everyone to survive in an environment as ruthless as Northport. Everyone was king or queen of something. Jason would never be king of the student community, and he had learned to accept, even to embrace, that fact.

Derek turned back to face Jason. "Sorry about that, bro!"

"It's fine, Derek. I feel like I'm watching a magic show." The fact that, for once, he was not telling the truth stung Jason. He had only seen a magician once in his life and found the performance not fascinating but frustrating. Insatiably curious about the inner workings of everything around him, he had thrown a tantrum upon realizing that the sorcerer did not plan to explain his method.

A more accurate analogy to Derek's bravado would have been Jason's frequent childhood visits to Sydney's Taronga Zoo. Though observing the animals' interactions and trying to figure out their social dynamics mesmerized Jason, he was still very glad to stand outside the cage. That being said, Jason still thought the magic show comment more appropriate than, *"I feel like I'm watching the orangutans at the zoo; you're the king of the jungle."* More than enough times, Jason had felt shock when what he took to be an innocuous comment on his part had come off as racist, sexist, or otherwise unwelcome.

Derek chuckled. "Really, man, don't worry about the networking part, really. Once you're ready for the next step, just tell me, and I'll talk to everyone I know. I'm sure it'll work out great!"

"Thanks!" Jason turned to pull out his cellphone and opened his Internet browser. His electronic funds transfer from China should be coming in anytime.

Trying to start a friendly conversation, Derek asked Jason, "What're you doing, bro?"

Jason passed his cellphone to Derek, then began to explain before they reached the dorm. He might only have two real friends at Northport, but at least he had chosen them well.

✈ ✈ ✈

MONDAY, FEBRUARY 25, 2013

SONDHEIM CENTER FOR CHEMICAL RESEARCH, NORTHPORT UNIVERSITY

Elena Zarabić had left Serbia only five months ago, yet sometimes she joked to herself that she had seen more strange occurrences in five months at Northport than in over twenty years of chaos in her native land. Perhaps the trying life of a graduate student working until two in the morning in a laboratory emitting putrid fumes brought along hallucinations.

Then again, even from her skewed perspective, what she saw seemed very real. Elena looked through the turquoise windowpane on the wall, the distinguishing architectural feature of the Sondheim Center for Chemical Research. With her view of the outside world obstructed by tall bottles of liquid chemicals piled up, it was difficult to make out exactly what was happening, and she did not spend most of her time in the laboratory staring at the scenery.

After observing this very scene happen nearly every other day for five months, however, she had become intrigued. A pattern started to emerge in the behavior of the four shadowy figures she could discern through the glass. The three on the left were different every time she saw them—sometimes the gender of one of them would change, for example—yet they almost seemed built on the same model, products of the same factory. The man on the right was the same every time, though. He always came to exchange various objects with the three others.

After less than two academic quarters, Elena was not yet versed in local customs, but she still thought this was strange. What could be going on between them? Drug dealing, possibly, or exchanges of stolen tests as part of a cheating ring? Should she say something? Should she do anything? She had no idea whom to contact or what Northport's procedures were.

Elena called out the undergraduate who assisted her in the research laboratory.

She removed her eyes from her laptop and looked at Elena. "Yes?" she replied.

"Time after time, I have witnessed some strange behaviors happening outside that laboratory window. Come and watch. Do you see these people over there?" Elena asked, gesturing at them. She explained why this worried her, though without diving too deeply into speculation. "Is this normal? What do you think is going on?"

"That is very strange indeed. I know exactly who to tell," her undergraduate assistant replied with confidence. "My friend will be able to figure out who's involved in this and what it's about. I'm sure he'll know what to do."

"Thank you," Elena replied. At least she would be at peace about these worrisome encounters. If the man on the right thought he could hide his meetings with his shadowy associates by coming to the small tree-lined alcove near the Sondheim Center, he had underestimated Elena Zarabić.

4. ANYTIME, ANYWHERE

TUESDAY, MARCH 5, 2013

CAMPUS POST OFFICE, NORTHPORT UNIVERSITY

Jason Curran pulled the straps on his backpack, then sprinted across campus. He feared that the stop at the post office would delay him, so he had to rush through a stampede of bicycles to arrive punctually. At least he did not have to waste time checking the GPS on his cellphone, as he had memorized the entire campus map over three years ago during Freshman Orientation Week. He just needed to turn right before reaching the Shantytown, the self-deprecating name many graduate students used to refer to their concrete apartment blocks on the edge of campus.

Finally, Jason approached Silicon Woods, the grove housing Northport's Shankar School of Engineering and a cluster of university-founded technology companies. The startups were split into two distinct groups: those operating from refitted log cabins and those whose headquarters were modeled after—there it was! Jason had reached the copper and orange block that was Baerwald Auditorium. Catching his breath, he leaned his hand against a burgeoning maple. The Northport Undergraduate Handbook he had read before entering mentioned a widespread superstition that any Northport student who touched a maple tree on campus would not graduate.

Some students avoided even the maple leaves that lay on the ground during the fall, but Jason could not care less about Northport's archaic traditions.

Jason opened the door, then straightened his hair and used his shirt to wipe off the sweat dripping from his face. He had come to Baerwald in the hope of making significant progress on his project. The last thing he wanted to do was look like he had just left the gym, or a gutter. He walked through the foyer and into the auditorium, where visitors still filled the narrow red seats. Perfect, he thought. He would not make a bad impression by coming in late. Jason was clearly the youngest among an audience composed of professors, visitors, postdoctoral scholars, and graduate students from the Shankar School of Engineering. The topic was very technical, so the elderly members of the community with more time on their hands than students who usually patronized talks on politics were not here today.

When roughly a quarter of the hundred or so spots were occupied, the older male at the podium stood up and picked up the microphone. "Good morning!" he told the small but rapt audience. "Thank you all for joining me here today. I am Rashiv Shroff, Chair of the Northport's Shankar School of Engineering. Today, I am delighted to introduce a very special guest speaker, Lars Børgensen. After leaving his native Denmark to study for a Ph.D. at the University of Chicago, Professor Børgensen taught at Northport until 2005, when he left to work for Bechtel Corporation in Reston, Virginia."

Rashiv Shroff drank some coffee from his cup, then continued. "Professor Børgensen's most recent work has focused on nanotechnology, particularly the field of implantable devices, for which he and his team have had contracts from several United States government agencies. It is an honor and a pleasure to welcome my friend Lars back to Northport. Now, please join me in welcoming Lars Børgensen!"

As the audience clapped, a towering middle-aged man in a gray suit came to the podium. "Well," he began, "I must say, it's good to be back. I'm so glad that my daughter, Melissa, chose to come to Northport last year, so that I have more excuses to return to the campus I love. I always adore seeing the smiling faces of students who have a real passion for their subject, which is why sometimes I miss academia, along with the fact that back when I taught, my boss"—he pointed at Rashiv Shroff—"just stayed at home and never actually told me what to do."

The audience laughed heartily. "Should I take that as a compliment?" Rashiv Shroff asked jokingly.

"Since you've kept this job instead of working in the industry, yes," Lars Børgensen replied lightly. Jason chuckled, though he hoped that he could soon hear what he had come for rather than the banter.

"In all seriousness, though," Lars Børgensen continued, "I should get down to business. In the last few years, I have been working with Bechtel to develop electronic devices that can be implanted without surgery into the body. Now, much of my work has involved contracting for the U.S. government, so I can't disclose all the details. Instead, I'll discuss the manner in which over the course of only a few decades, this technology will be able to perform a variety of everyday functions. Imagine if you could swallow your cellphone! You'd be completely connected to the world, anytime, anywhere."

Jason listened closely as Lars Børgensen explained the manner in which a tiny chip implanted in the tooth could send vibrations directly to the ear and brain and how the silicon casings of nanotechnology devices could actually disintegrate once placed in the body. Thankfully, this was not one of those talks where the speaker oversimplified the subject matter—on the contrary, the material was so technical that even the graduate students asked for clarifications at the end. Jason had come here to find the right path to technical expertise for his project from one of the world's experts in the field, and he would be certain not to walk out without it.

★★★

BAERWALD AUDITORIUM, NORTHPORT UNIVERSITY

"Well, Jason, we've been talking for almost half an hour, and I need to leave to fly back to Washington soon, but it's been great meeting you!" Lars Børgensen told Jason, shaking his hand. "It's almost unheard of for undergraduates to come hear me speak. The subject is far too specialized for them. Well, unless they're here for the free food, of course."

Jason chuckled. Two weeks ago, he had heard other attendees at a talk on the American political prisoners exported to Palau complain about the absence of free food, an easy escape from the restrictive fifteen-a-week meal plan common for underclassmen.

"Speaking of which, I'm actually going to get something else, if you don't mind," Jason said. He placed another warm stick of tofu satay in his plate, then dipped it in the spicy sambal ulek paste. He was glad that the organizers of Lars Børgensen's talk had decided to order from the new Indonesian restaurant in downtown Northport, Balisayan. Normally, Jason would have rushed toward the grand opening last Saturday night, but instead he had lingered in Schubert Street until five in the morning in an unsuccessful attempt to make progress on his neuroscience research.

"Thank you very much, Professor Børgensen. I have many more questions for the project I mentioned; could I please send them to you?"

"Sure, Jason, here's my email," Lars Børgensen said as he handed Jason a business card. "Good luck with your project, whatever it is!"

"Thank you very much! I will be sure to let you know in due time."

As Jason walked out of Baerwald Auditorium, he made a mental note to try Balisayan with Aurélia sometime. However, that would have to wait. For now, he had a very long email to write.

✈✈✈

MONDAY, MARCH 11, 2013

LAUDERDALE COLLEGE,
NORTHPORT UNIVERSITY

Jason Curran checked his email inbox. *"No new messages,"* the banner at the top of Northport's webmail service read. Almost a week later, Lars Børgensen had still not responded to Jason's extensive list of questions. Jason had talked to enough professors in his career at Northport to understand that they had other tasks in life than responding to overeager undergraduates, but he desperately needed Lars Børgensen's help.

After the original email he had written to Børgensen on Tuesday, Jason had sent him two follow-ups in order to grab his attention. He now began to type up a third but quickly deleted the draft. That was not the way to approach things. During his talk, Børgensen had mentioned that he had a daughter at Northport. If Børgensen did not see the urgency of responding to a random undergraduate, perhaps he would think differently when he received a message from his own child.

Jason opened the online directory for the Northport campus community, then typed in *"Børgensen"* in the *"Last Name"* box. He looked down. *"Børgensen, Melissa D. Undergraduate, Class of 2015. Andersson College."* Perfect, Jason thought. It was almost too easy to find information about everyone online.

Jason took his cellphone, wallet, and keys with him, then walked out of Lauderdale and across a grassy path in the chilly evening breeze. The newest of Northport's residential colleges, Andersson had been completed less than ten years ago in a fervent backlash to the Brutalist style of architecture that had overtaken the eastern portion of Northport's campus, including Jason's own Lauderdale College, about fifty years ago. Jason mused that the building should be classified as Neo-Neo-Gothic. It was not an imitation of the medieval colleges at Oxford and Cambridge, but rather an imitation of Northport's own eighteenth-century Rodgers, Walker, and Joel Colleges, which were themselves imitations of the original Gothic style.

As he walked through Andersson's lobby, Jason asked the first student he saw in the foyer, "Where's Melissa Børgensen?"

"Uh...how would I know?" she replied, walking towards the dining hall. "Are you just coming here to find random people? You're such a weirdo..."

Jason hit himself on the arm. He really needed to be more careful. He made blunders like that far too often. Replying, *"Sorry, but I have a bit of trouble figuring out what's appropriate to say in a given situation, and even though I've been trying to observe how all of you do it, it's really hard to make a mental manual of it, maybe you can talk to me at some point and walk me through what is and isn't socially acceptable by most people's standards?"* would have been another mistake, however, so he was better off just letting bygones be bygones.

He shot off a curt, "Okay, right," then turned his eyes to a wide bench by the entrance. On it sat a student whose muscular body and turquoise Northport Deers football sweatshirt made no attempt to conceal his main extracurricular activity.

This time, Jason phrased his question in a manner that might be slightly less awkward. "Hey, excuse me. Do you know Melissa Børgensen?"

The athletic type laughed, then whispered in Jason's ear, "Yeah dude, are you looking for a nice body tonight? She's sexy."

"No," Jason replied, annoyed. "I just need her help with a project."

"Oh, what kind of project?" he asked. "Crossing every hot chick on campus off your list?"

"No, no, not at all."

Thankfully, the irritating football player was friendly. "Well, I can show you to her room if you want." He guided Jason up a flight of wide marble stairs. "Her room's 228, first one on the right, if I remember correctly— though I was pretty dead when I walked out of there last time, so I might be wrong."

It took him a second, but Jason understood the joke and chuckled. "Thanks!"

"Yeah, dude! See you! Hey, good luck on your, erm, *project* with her. I'm curious to know how long it takes you!"

"I mean, I'm just going to—ah, forget it. Goodbye, now!" As sociable and humorous as the athlete was, Jason did not want to waste a single second of his mission. It was far too important for the success of his project.

Jason knocked on the door and was quickly greeted by a tall blonde in tight black yoga pants and a hot pink tank top with loose-fitting straps.

"Hi, are you Melissa Børgensen?" Jason asked.

"Um, yes. Who are you?" she inquired in a bizarre tone of voice.

Jason tried not to appear too exasperated. Had he really messed up again? Was this something that people actually did, walking into someone else's room, especially a girl's, without prior notice? After nearly four years at Northport, he still could not provide a definite answer to that question. Learning what was and was not acceptable in Australia had been difficult enough; replicating that in a new country, particularly an environment where people came from everywhere, geographically and socially, bordered on impossible. Jason's conversation with Melissa's father had focused unilaterally on science; Jason had not had the chance to even begin to wonder how socially conservative or traditional a background she hailed from. Besides, how closely would an adult college student like Melissa adhere to the customs she had been raised to follow? Now, if Jason explained that his reason for coming here was absolutely not what the football player had more than just implied, would she cut him some slack for his awkward entrance? This was all so exhausting.

"I'm Jason Curran. I'm here because I heard that—"

"Wait, don't tell me," she interrupted in an almost exasperated tone. "Did DaVon send you here?"

"Who?"

"Oh, don't play dumb," she replied condescendingly.

"Really, I don't know who that is."

"You know, DaVon Willison. Tall, black, muscular," she said, carefully enunciating every syllable as if she took him for an idiot rather than a social fringe-dweller who only knew ten people on campus. "Some douche on the football team. I met him at a party last Wednesday night. I was totally blacked out, you know, so I invited him back to my room. I obviously regretted it the next morning, so I posted an embarrassing picture of him making a monkey face with his shirt off on Facebook. He wasn't happy, as you can imagine, so now he's been sending every loser guy in Andersson to my room and telling them they can get an easy girl for the night. So, I guess DaVon told you about me?"

Jason lifted his eyebrows, then chuckled. That was definitely the athlete who had sent him.

"Why are you laughing?" she asked in a rather aggressive tone.

"It's a very funny story, that's all. But no, no guy named DaVon told me about you." It was not a lie, after all. Jason had already known of Melissa before, just not the fact that she was in Room 228. "And I'm not into that sort of thing anyway."

"Oh." The tense lines on her face disappeared. "So what are you doing here?"

"Well, I need to contact your father, so I need your help."

"Uh…why? How do you know him?"

"See, he came to Northport to give a talk on nanotechnology, and I need his help for a project I'm doing. I've tried sending him a few emails, but he hasn't responded, so I thought I'd try to contact him through you instead since he mentioned you were at Northport. He must be traveling or busy with work, but I assume he'll be quicker to respond if his own daughter writes to him."

"Oh, okay. Sure, send me a friend request on Facebook, and you can let me know which questions to ask him!"

"The thing is, I don't have Facebook account," Jason told her, sincerely hoping that she did not judge him for that fact. "Can you give me your email?"

"Yeah, it's M-Borgensen, with a normal O instead of a slashed O, at Northport-dot-E-D-U."

"Cool, thanks!"

"Mhm, and if you give me your phone, I can add myself to your contacts, since I don't check my email religiously."

Jason passed her his cellphone, then waited for her to type in her name, email, and mobile number. "Thanks a lot, Melissa!"

"Yeah, no problem! So you said your name was Jacob?"

"Jason, actually. Jason Curran."

"Oops, sorry! Well, it was nice to meet you, Jason! Send me your questions, and I'll write to my father as soon as I can."

"Great, thanks a bunch! Have a nice evening!"

"Yeah, you too!"

Jason exited her room, then walked back down into the foyer. As he opened the door to leave Andersson College, DaVon Willison was still sitting on the same bench where Jason had originally found him, though a girl in gym shorts and a sports bra had appeared since Jason had last seen him.

"Yo, dude! You're back already? Darn, man! I would have given you at least half an hour!"

"Well, things were a lot easier than expected," Jason replied.

DaVon laughed hysterically. "Duuude, good job! I'm proud of you!"

"Thanks. I hope it pays off," Jason told him, silently cursing at himself for the unintended double entendre.

Jason waved goodbye to DaVon, then opened the door and left Andersson Hall. He had nothing more to do here. This was not and would never be his turf.

5. HOW LONG WILL IT LAST

THURSDAY, MARCH 14, 2013

BERNSTEIN HALL, NORTHPORT UNIVERSITY

"Well, that concludes today's class," Marta Solis López told the twelve students sitting around the rectangular table. "Make sure you've read all four hundred pages for next Tuesday, and check the course website on Suxeed for details on our Spring Break trip to Belize! You don't need to pay for anything, of course, but there are some important medical forms to fill out."

Of all the classes that she taught, "BIO 397: Tracing the Development of the Jaw" was by far her favorite. It was not that the subject matter interested her more—especially at this stage in her academic career, she only taught the subjects for which she had a genuine passion—but rather the class size. The intimacy of a seminar fostered far more engaging intellectual discussion than the massive auditorium in Dalla Hall where she introduced four hundred freshmen every Autumn Quarter to human biology.

As Marta's students grabbed their backpacks and left the room, one who was not her own opened the door and walked in. Normally, she would not recognize a student whom she had only talked to once for ten minutes in her life, but this one had certainly made a unique impression

51

on her. Upon coming to her office several weeks ago, he had told her that he needed to find the best and brightest evolutionary biology student for a confidential project, for which she had referred him to Cayley Thompson. That reminded her, she still needed to write Cayley a recommendation letter for the Newton Fellowship, a prestigious all-expenses-paid Northport summer program to study evolutionary biology in Ecuador's Galápagos Islands.

When Jason had inquired into Marta's ethnicity out of curiosity and she had responded that she was Peruvian, he had conversed with her in fluent Spanish and mentioned without modesty yet free of bragging that it was one of the fifteen languages he spoke. That was impressive, even by Northport standards.

"Jason Curran!" she greeted him. "I assume you're here to find Cayley?"

"Yes, I am. Thank you, Professor Solis López," he responded in Spanish, grateful to her for placing him in contact with someone so qualified for his project.

"Cayley!" Marta called.

A tall brunette in jeans and a white top walked to her desk. "Yes, Professor?"

"Jason wants to speak with you."

"Oh, right," she answered, frowning slightly.

Marta noticed Cayley's apparent discontent, but she realized that it was not her responsibility to figure out the reason. College students had enough pressures and issues to deal with; any reason was fair game. Besides, she had a massive pile of belated referee reports to write. She sat at her desk and let the two students walk out of Bernstein Hall together.

Jason followed Cayley as she walked frantically down Meyer Street. "So, Cayley, did you manage to finish the research on the cortex I sent you three weeks ago?" he asked, hoping she had some insights to offer on auditory stimuli in the sensorimotor area of the brain's cortex.

"No, I haven't, sorry. I'm just so busy!" Would he ever stop? She had told him she was busy the last three times he had badgered her about it.

Jason sighed. He was no longer the seven-year-old who assumed that everyone else cared about everything that he did, so he understood that Cayley had other things to do. This time, though, her procrastination was really becoming ridiculous. The research he had asked her to do should not take very long for an evolutionary biology specialist, he thought. Besides, he was paying her quite handsomely for the task.

"Come on, it really shouldn't take you long!"

"I know, Jason, but I told you, I'm so busy!"

"Doing what?"

"Well, you know, everything! Classes, assignments, and then all the clubs I'm in!" Today, she still had to attend tennis practice, a rehearsal with her a capella group, a charity fundraiser for orphans in Ghana, and a meeting for students intending to study abroad in Ecuador over the summer. Tonight, she would consider herself lucky if she could salvage four hours of sleep, and Thursdays were not even the worst. She wished Jason had not reminded her of her insanely packed schedule, then tried to envision the next time she could get a break from it all. She was certainly thrilled about her biology trip to Belize over Spring Break, but even then she would have to deal with a massive amount of social and academic pressures.

"All right, but you promised me you would get me the research by the beginning of last week! Why didn't you keep your word?" With still no response from Melissa Børgensen, he was growing very tired of empty promises.

Cayley begin to walk faster, wondering why Jason had to be so pushy. He had rubbed her the wrong way from day one; could he not try to compensate for that instead of making things worse? "I told you," she said, "I got overwhelmed and had other, more important things to do!"

"Other things more important than making money and contributing to a grand scientific project?"

Hoping there was still use arguing with a fanatic, she clarified, "I care about my extracurricular activities even more than my classes, Jason! They keep me insanely busy, but I love being in every single one of my clubs!

"Why? Do you think they will help you in your future beyond Northport?"

"I don't want to stress about 'beyond Northport' now, Jason! I have enough to stress about this week!"

"Still, do you *really* like your activities, or do you just think they make you look cool and meet people?"

Cayley had put up with Jason's intense arrogance for a while, but now it was really getting to her. "You're such a jerk, Jason!" she screamed. Normally, she avoided being so abrasive, but this time she thought that she needed to fight fire with fire.

Jason was taken aback by the ferocity of her response. "Wow, I'm sorry. I was just trying to be helpful. You clearly need help sorting out your schedule."

"Wait, so now you're volunteering to help? Do you think this is some kind of joke?"

"No, I'm being serious. You need to set your priorities—"

Cayley had never met anyone so haughty. "How would *you* know my priorities, Jason? It's not like I ever see you in any of these activities!"

"You're right, you don't see me because I'm never there," Jason conceded. "I practice martial arts a few times a week to stay in shape, and that's it. I just don't see the point."

"Don't you like to follow your friends and meet new people, though?"

"Why would I need to? I don't need others. If I enjoy doing something, I'll do it by myself. I sometimes go to the Jobim Sculpture Garden in the middle of the night and sing to the stars. At least the stars don't holler if I sing too loud or off-key."

Cayley wondered how or if she could even begin to explain her motivations to someone so out of tune with the way things worked in college, but she still tried to do so. "Don't you want to share that pleasure with other people, though? Remember that Northport's about 'living and learning,' not just pure learning!"

"I don't care what others do or think, and I don't want my interests to be decided by others."

"So you really love being forever alone? You sound like such a sad, pathetic loner!"

"Yeah, and so what? I enjoy it that way. I have two real friends, and that's enough for me."

Cayley could not believe her ears. *Two?* She quickly remembered her pride in exceeding thirteen hundred Facebook friends. "Wait, only two friends? You're such a loser! Though, you know, since you're so pushy and socially awkward, it makes sense!"

"It's not a crime, you know."

"Still, you're such a creep, chasing after me with your crazy mystery project. Why do you care so much about it?" Were he working on it for a class, she thought, he would have had to do it independently, or at least with classmates, so he would not have had a reason to enlist her aid.

"Because I can," Jason replied. Fearing that his response might have come off as arrogant, he clarified, "Look, I'm in love with the idea, and I'm never going to give up on it."

"Well, if you at least told me what it was..."

"I'm sorry, Cayley, but I can't say."

"See, Jason, that's what makes you creepy. Always by yourself, with dark secrets to hide." With a bit of luck, he would pick up on that hint. She might even be able to help him that way, since she could not deliver the research.

"I mean," she asked, "When you're alone at night, do you ever chat with people online or something?"

Jason was beginning to feel uneasy. She was not just deriding him; she was attacking his lifestyle. "No, I don't, as a matter of fact. I want to spend the time I don't keep for myself talking to people I know I can trust, not learning about who started dating whom over the weekend or digging up some embarrassing high school prom photos to comment on how pretty or ridiculous their dresses looked."

For a second, Cayley wondered whether Jason had a point. Perhaps she could save some of her time to sleep enough for her body to not constantly feel debilitated, or finally be able to look for a fulfilling romantic relationship after cycling through a string of jerks. Why did everything always have to be so complicated? Was that just the price to pay for those whose Ivy League education was heavily subsidized? Her parents had never even dreamed of having access to all the opportunities she now had under her belt in their small Kansas hometown, but they still happily managed their local plumbing company together after their twenty-fifth wedding anniversary. Maybe in Northport's environment, Cayley could find some way to get away from all the pressure, all the rushing, all the noise...No! That was not the way things worked nowadays! She needed to leave immediately, lest he continue to pester her with such radical ideas.

"Well, I need to go now, Jason! I'm going to go find my friends! Have fun going back to your cave!"

As she marched out, Cayley wondered whether she had acted too rashly. Had she spoken so loudly that she could not listen to him? Then again, did someone who behaved so strangely and condescendingly deserve any respect whatsoever? No!

Cayley looked back at Jason for a second, hoping that she had not crossed him so badly that he would plan to get his revenge. He might try, but she would make sure that never happened.

"Have a nice day," Jason told her.

When she was far enough from him, he scoffed. So much for her only being busy with work and extracurriculars. It had taken him a while to realize that in college, hanging out was a full-time job. Well, there was no purpose in agonizing, Jason thought. If everyone else was conforming to the bizarre social rules on campus, no one could force him at gunpoint to do the same. He might not be a clone of the socially typical Northport student, but at least he lived in a community that embraced diversity.

Jason was generally slow to read social cues, but he did not need to expend much mental energy today to realize that he should probably look for another evolutionary biology specialist. That should not be too daunting a task, he thought. A potentially Nobel Prize-winning professor like Marta Solis López had no dearth of star students in her classes. He walked back to Bernstein Hall, intending to open the door and ask Solis López for more student recommendations.

Suddenly, Jason stopped in his tracks. What was the point of that? Every Tuesday and Sunday night, he studied in the Chamfort Library of Sciences. He would try to find the information he needed on evolutionary biology there. No, he did not need Cayley or any other biology major for his research. There was no reason to outsource his passion to others. Like the Little Red Hen in his younger sister's beloved story, he would do it all by himself.

✈✈✈

FRIDAY, MARCH 15, 2012

**ANDERSSON COLLEGE,
NORTHPORT UNIVERSITY**

Melissa Børgensen swiped her card and entered Andersson College's dining hall. She placed her turquoise Northport sweatshirt on the side of a chair next to other section editors of *The Daily Deer*, Northport's student-run newspaper. She walked over to the buffet, where she grabbed a plate from the pile and explored the evening's offerings. In addition to the mainstays of dining hall food, particular areas displayed vegan, gluten-free, Kosher, and peanut-free food, as well as the legendary Friday night Vietnamese specials, for which many students from other residential colleges at Northport came all the way to Andersson.

Melissa placed a few leaves of salad on her plate, then returned to the table. It was somewhat socially acceptable for students to gain weight during their first year due to the inevitable "freshman fifteen" that resulted from no longer being constrained by their parents' dietary diktats, but then again the campus community always expected freshmen to make idiotic decisions. However, she would definitely be shunned if she suffered what her friend had nicknamed the "sophomore sixteen," so she now ate little more than salad, especially on party evenings, when she could not afford to look unattractive.

As she picked up the leaves with her fork, Melissa listened as the other editors of the *The Daily Deer* discussed changes in the age of electronic news. They debated whether it was necessary to start a technology section and if paying to print paper copies every day and distributing them for free was an antiquated and environmentally unfriendly custom. Melissa only spoke to give her approval of the unanimous decision to immediately discharge the staff writer who had vehemently criticized the idea of racial affirmative action in a recent opinion article. She shuddered at the idea that some people could be so grossly intolerant. On a Friday night following a grueling week, though, she was too exhausted to discuss such serious topics.

"I'm going to grab dessert," she told the others, then returned to the buffet and took a banana. She considered bringing back an orange to her room to give her energy for the nights when she finished writing papers instead of sleeping, but she finally decided against it. The card-checkers in Andersson were notorious for enforcing the rule against taking any fruit out of the dining hall, despite the residential colleges' practically unlimited budgets. She wondered whether she should hide the orange in her sweatshirt pocket but soon shot that idea down as well, not wanting to appear fat.

Before she could make it back to the table, however, Melissa Børgensen noticed two students she did not know with the emblem of Northport's improv comedy troupe on their sweatshirts conversing on a topic that piqued her interest.

"Did you hear that Vanya Lakshmi and her boyfriend broke up?" the Hispanic female with magenta-dyed hair asked.

"Yeah, like two days ago!" the Asian female with yellow lemon-shaped glasses replied. "No one talks about it anymore. The new buzz is about my a capella group's leader, Lilly Suzuki. Apparently she has a *girl*friend now."

"Whatever. Vanya and Mike broke up three hours ago!" Magenta Hair countered.

"Oh, certainly not," Lemon Glasses retorted. "These past few weeks, every time I go to the gym, I see Vanya flirting with Derek Park! They always arrange to meet up in each other's rooms!"

"Sleeping with Derek doesn't count as cheating, though," Magenta Hair opined. "He's the Student Council President and super hot. If I were Vanya's ex and heard that she was with him, I'd think she was, like, a normal person, not a cheater, an infidel, for being seduced by Derek."

"Well, now you're sounding like you're falling for his charms too!" Lemon Glasses said, chuckling. "Good luck with that. He's a senior, and you're only a freshman."

"So? It's only weird between a *junior* and a freshman. When you're a senior, you can do whatever you want. Besides, it's not like I can get past the long waitlist. He's so popular with every single girl at Northport!"

"No, I'll rephrase that," Lemon Glasses added. "Not just every girl on campus goes crazy for Derek. *Everyone* does. Every *guy* on campus has a secret man crush on Derek."

Melissa found the argument between the two very entertaining, so she would have continued, had she not heard the loud boom-boom of her cellphone's One Direction ringtone. When she saw the name displayed on the screen, however, she quickly pressed the red *"Decline"* button. Jason Curran was at it again. When she had given Jason her mobile number, she had not expected him to call her with this intensity.

Ever since he had sent her a deluge of questions the hour after she had met him, Melissa Børgensen staunchly regretted having been friendly in agreeing to help Jason. By now, he had called four times, emailed her three times, and texted her twice. Could he not understand that she was busy? If she did not respond the first time, why did he persist? It was not like she talked to her father very often anyway, and she would certainly not contact him to transmit Jason's message now that he had acted like such a pushy creep.

Was this some trick to try to gain her attention and then her affection? No, he seemed too socially inept to even consider that, she thought. If he actually was so desperate to talk to her father, what was this mystery project? The questions she had peeked at were written in incomprehensible technical jargon, and she knew her father was involved in some confidential government work. Was Jason planning anything really bad? What could she do about it?

"How long will it last?" she muttered under her breath.

However, she had no reason to be like Jason and obsess over something stupid. She had more pleasant things on her mind tonight. She transited through the foyer and climbed the stairs up to her room, then changed into very short shorts and a loose-fitting tank top before applying a heavy dose of lipstick and makeup.

Finally, Melissa Børgensen walked back down into the foyer, where her friends, all dressed in even more revealing versions of her clothing, waited in a pack of seven other sophomores and five juniors.

"You're late," the leader of the squad admonished Melissa, combing her black mane with her hand.

"Better late than sober!" Melissa shouted. "Let's get wasted!"

6. I COULD HAVE DANCED ALL NIGHT

ELTON HALL, NORTHPORT UNIVERSITY

It was funny that they referred to Elton Hall as "The Barn," Melissa Børgensen mused as she skipped across the dance floor in a half-drunken stupor. On nights like these, the Barn's occupants were far wilder than domesticated farm animals. As a break between the two most grueling weeks of the Winter Quarter, Dark Week and Exam Week, it was time to blow off steam. On Wednesday, the seniors had thrown the underclassmen in four-year colleges into the showers; on Thursday, the student dressed up as Northport's deer mascot for sports games had stampeded across all the dining halls; today, it was time to carouse.

The tables and chairs of the barn-red recreational building in Fort Salonga had been pushed aside to reconvert the floor into a massive dance space, and hundreds of Northport students of all classes agglutinated themselves into a mass in the center, waving their arms riotously in the air as the loudspeakers blared deafening pop music into Elton Hall's cavernous interior.

Long ago, Northport's administration had given up on trying to regulate what happened inside the walls of the Barn and other party venues. An upperclassman had once told Melissa that according to a loophole in university policies, the buildings hosting the parties she loved so much operated independently, and therefore the flow of alcohol was controlled—or in this case, encouraged—by the seniors who hosted the events. Melissa would certainly not complain. She felt very safe knowing that the Northport campus police could not arrest her there for underage drinking. She had also heard that the campus police did not enter the Barn precisely so that students could be safer. If a student went into an ethylic coma, their friends could contact Arlen Health Center without fearing that the police would become involved.

Melissa looked around for her friend. At the end of a tiring week of schoolwork and tests, she and Cayley Thompson, a junior living across the hall from her in Andersson, put into practice Northport's motto—not the official *"Discere et Vivere,"* but rather the more popular *"Work hard, play hard."* Both students had joined a company of eleven other females from Andersson College to attend the quarter's most hyped event.

Melissa lazily tapped her friend on the shoulder. "What's up, Cayley?"

"Epiiiiiiic!" Cayley responded, more inebriated than Melissa after her third glass of beer. "That DJ, Dol, is sooooooo hot! I could have danced all night!"

"Well, go, my little biaaatch! You still have the whole night!"

"Woooooo!"

Before her friend left, Melissa had one small request for her. "Selfie?"

"Suuure," Cayley said as she tried to find the cellphone she had placed between the strap of her dress and her breast, then snapped a very grainy self-portrait of the two holding red, beer-filled plastic cups and opening their mouths wide into a puckered-lip duck face.

"Instagram the pic!" Melissa told her, giggling.

"All riiiighteeee! Byeeee, Melissssssssa, I'm going to go grind with some duuuuuudes!"

Melissa Børgensen stared at her friend as she left and wrapped her arms around the first male she saw, then began kissing him on the mouth not long after. It was not fair, Melissa thought. Tonight, all her friends except for Cayley had already hooked up, and the way things were going, she could soon delete the "except for Cayley" caveat from that thought.

On days when she had gotten lucky herself, Melissa considered hooking up to be the greatest invention to reach college campuses. By allowing students who had never met before to sleep with each other without even the promise of a night together, casual sex with strangers provided Melissa and her friends a refuge from the pressures of romantic relationships, for which they had neither time nor energy.

Yes, there were those who found this behavior despicable on the part of either or both sexes, but the university administration was more focused on the institution's reputation than on the private morality of its students. Like her friend Cayley, Melissa was too busy writing papers, participating in extracurricular activities, and figuring out her future in the unforgiving world beyond college to invest so much time and attention in a romantic relationship. Besides, what was the point of the exhaustion involved in impressing and getting to know a person if she would inevitably get her heart broken in the process?

She would have time to focus on all that later, when she was working in the real world. For now, all Melissa Børgensen wanted to do was go wild and enjoy herself. She had worked hard in her classes and clubs all week, so she deserved the fun. It was so ridiculous that some dinosaurs stated that women like her should use college as an opportunity to find husbands!

Melissa finished all the beer in her cup. When she was sober, she always found it difficult to rationally convince herself that hookups were the best course of action for her own future. But now that she was dancing with the buzz that came from being drunk, it felt so right. She looked around, wondering how long she would wait before giving up on the idea of spending the night in an unknown male's room. Maybe thirty more minutes...

Finally, a figure came from behind and rubbed the area right under his waist on Melissa's backside. He began to caress her chest under her loose-fitting tank top with his bulky hands, and she waved her arms in the air in arousal, shaking her rear end from side to side to the tune of the deafening party pop the DJ was diffusing across Elton Hall. Of all dance styles, it was by far grinding that she preferred, and she thought it for the best that it was essentially the only one practiced in contemporary college parties, assuming that the erotic frottage qualified as dancing.

After a few minutes of grinding, Melissa turned to face the man who had been rubbing his genitals against hers in order to see him for the first time. He was a sweaty, unintelligent-looking pile of muscle in a lacrosse tank top and a gym short whose color she could not exactly determine in the scintillating lights. Well, if she wanted to end up in his room over the next fifteen minutes, now was her only chance. She began to angle her face forward as he moved his closer and positioned his mouth for a kiss. Almost...

"Melissa!" yelled a voice from the side. "Here you are! I finally found you!"

Even in her drunken stupor, Melissa could recognize the unimposing figure of Jason Curran. "Jason!" she asked him, startled. "What are you doing here?"

"I've come for you," he replied with fierce determination.

The lacrosse player she was dancing with lifted his muscular arm, probably in order to teach the intruder a lesson. However, Melissa pressed his hand down and said, "I'll take care of him." Five seconds later, the athlete was grinding with another target, and she was stuck with the most uncool male in all of Northport. Well, there went her chance of a hookup tonight, she thought.

"Melissa, I'm so glad I found you," Jason told her, panting. "I really need to speak to you."

Melissa turned her head away in disgust, wondering if this Jason ever gave up. "Leave me alone! You embarrass me! Couldn't you see I was busy dancing with my friend?" she asked, noting to herself her liberal use of the word "friend."

"Well, I'm sorry, but it was urgent."

What could be so pressing, to the point of ruining her hookup? "Why bug me now? Couldn't you wait and call me or something?"

"Because you wouldn't respond to any of my emails, text messages, or phone calls! I looked all around campus for you! I went to the libraries, the residential colleges, and the gym."

The alcohol was beginning to climb into Melissa's brain. "Wait, why did you have to find me again?" she asked, confused.

"I absolutely need to reach out to your father. It's really important, since it concerns the project I'm working on."

"Why didn't you ask him directly? Why bother me?"

"The thing is, he didn't reply to my emails either. It must be genetic! But now that I found you, please be sure to tell your father I need to talk to him as soon as possible."

Melissa began to edge away. This was only her second, and still very short, in-person encounter with Jason Curran, and if she could have her way, it would be her last. "Yeah, I'll be sure to tell him."

"Thanks."

"And by the way, you jerk, don't ever call me or interrupt me like that again!" she yelled.

She staggered back into the horde, breathing a sigh of relief as she saw—or thought she saw, as her senses were dulled by all the shots she had drunk—Jason's figure walking towards the door. She backed up, looking to see if any potential hookup partners were still around. The lacrosse player might be gone, but his clones were a dime a dozen on the dance floor. She bumped into someone, turned around to check if she had found the one who would take her back to his room, then let out a small cry of surprise.

"Melisssssa!" Cayley Thompson yelled.

"Caayley! You're baack!" Melissa felt proud knowing that at this rate, if she did not have any pictures of a hookup partner to post on Facebook the next day, neither would her friend.

"Am I waaasted, ooor did I just see youuu talking with Jason Curran?"

"Ooooh. That was Jason Curran, poor me."

"Soo youuu know him too?" Cayley exclaimed. "He's soooo annoying! Can you believe what a weirdo he is?"

"Ugh, he's suuch a creep! He's totally been harassing me for, like, the past week! He won't leave me alone. Emails, texts, phone calls...I never respond, and he never stops!"

"He's suuuuuuuch a stalker!"

"Yeaah," Melissa responded. "A stalker. Thaat's it. Do you knooow who he reminds me of?"

"Naaah."

"The spy cam duude! You knoow?" Melissa asked, wishing Cayley read *The Daily Deer* more often.

"Naoaah, whooo?"

"That duude who got sent to jail for installing spy cams in all the girls' bathrooms! They say he was the worst creeper eever to set fooot on caampus!"

"Ooh, yeaah. Riiiight. Even worse, Jason's a weird loner. Whooo knooows what he could be preparing? Wheneever he tells me about his mystery project, he freaks me out."

"Whateever. I don't want to worry about this now. I'm going to go grind with some other duudes."

"Waaaait, Melisssssssa," Cayley interjected. "I need to go to the bathroom! Can you come with me? You got me aaaall scared now. I hope I didn't cross him when I told him to go to helllll with his stupid mystery project."

"Suuure, let's gooo!"

Melissa and Cayley walked off the dance floor behind a pack of four girls they did not know to the women's room. It was a common practice for all of her friends to go to the restroom in packs. She did not know why her friends did it, but she had learned to do as they did. As Melissa and Cayley followed the quartet in the hallway leading to the women's restroom, a smooth voice stopped them for a second.

"Hello, ladies," a handsome young man greeted them, quickly analyzing their worried facial expressions. "Is anything wrong?"

✈✈✈

SATURDAY, MARCH 16, 2012

LAUDERDALE COLLEGE,
NORTHPORT UNIVERSITY

Jason Curran sat at the desk in his room and opened his laptop, revealing an image of a wooden totem from Vanuatu, one of the many desktops that rotated every two hours on his screen. Launching his Internet browser, he began searching for a professor in a similar field of study to Lars Børgensen who could help him if Børgensen never replied. However, Jason was not in the mood today. He had had enough of chasing unresponsive people, and unlike what Cayley Thompson believed, he frequently took breaks from his work.

Instead, he reached behind the pile of watches left behind by countless Chinese tourists who had heard the urban legend that it was good luck to drop watches off. He flipped over a wrinkled sheet of paper to reveal the map he had been drawing on earlier in the week, then labeled an area *"NÅ-ÏTÏČÏHT."* While in high school, he had printed a blank world map from Wikipedia and begun searching for where to place these arcane titles, but he had persistently been unable to find a location that seemed suitable for Nå-Ïtïčïht. In order to remind himself of his failure, he had brought the map with him to Northport and hung it across from the pillow on his bed every time he moved to a new room.

Yesterday night, however, upon returning from Elton Hall, he had watched a travel documentary about a woman who had trekked alone across the Central Asian steppes. As painfully monotonous as it was, the show had finally given him the answer to his puzzle of so many years. As a result, he had pulled the map off his wall and started marking it. He drew a circle extending roughly from the Aginsky District in southeastern Siberia to Bayandun in northeastern Mongolia, then placed small points and designated them as *"Dnålkårb," "Êllivyöt," "Åilåtşêröf," "Öröbêltşåč," "Ïêrågnåhw," "Nwötrêvlïş," "Ïånöötkïê," "Åilånïb," "Şûrkïşûl,"* and *"Dnålşï-Şşêčnïrp."*

One element, though, was missing for Jason to truly feel at peace. He scrolled through the music he had recently downloaded. The week before, while participating in an online music forum discussion, he had discovered the song "A Vava Inouva," sung by the Algerian Idir in the Kabyle language. His Pandora radio had indicated that Idir was popular among the same audience as two of his favorites, the Cape Verdaean Cesária Évora and the French-Armenian Charles Aznavour, so Jason took the recommendation to heart. He opened the music file, then let the soft rhythms of the Sahara Desert flow through his heart. Even if he notoriously sang off-key, he was gifted with a very musical ear. He was immensely grateful of that fact, because if he could not understand the subtleties of social interactions, at least he could appreciate the beauty surrounding him.

Jason enjoyed this type of music infinitely more than the noise that had boomed from speakers at last night's bizarre party in Elton Hall. By now, he was not bothered much by not being in tune with the tastes of most other Northport students. Did it matter if his room was decorated with pictures of Frank Gehry buildings and classic Boeing 747SP aircraft instead of rock bands and football stars, if the only similarity between his living quarters and theirs was the ubiquitous Swedish furniture? He found it quite hypocritical, though, that most of Lauderdale College's residents complained when he sang opera in the shower while they blared hideous pop in their rooms on Friday nights and constantly shouted for the most random reasons.

Soon, however, the sound of Idir's music drowned under the blasting overture of the opera *Carmen*. Jason picked up his ringing cellphone.

"Hello, Jason, this is Ares," the voice on the phone began in Greek. "Long time no talk! How are you?"

Jason recognized the name. Ares Dimitropoulos lived in the Greek city of Piraeus, right outside Athens, and worked as a manager at a section of the Port of Piraeus that had been recently purchased by a Chinese state-owned company. "Good," Jason answered in Greek. "It's been ages! Was there something particular you needed to talk to me about?"

"Actually, yes, Jason. Here, I'll explain. I hope you have a little bit of time. Sorry for the short notice!"

"Ares?" Jason asked. "I can't really take international calls on my cellphone because they're so expensive. I'll call you from a dorm phone. What's your number? It's appearing as a blocked number on my cellphone."

"Oh, sorry about that. When the Chinese bought our part of the Port of Piraeus, they did that to all our phones. Here, it's 21-4-021-1991."

"Thanks, and please remind me of the calling code for Greece."

"Right. Plus-30."

"Thank you! I'll call you back in a few minutes."

Jason hung up, then heard someone knocking on his door.

"Who is this?" he asked the visitor.

"Aurélia," a gentle female voice responded.

Jason could not say he was surprised. There were very few people who would actually take the time to visit him.

"How are you, Jason?" she asked, wagering that he would not ask her that question first.

"I'm great."

"Always good to hear," she responded. As she had guessed, he did not ask her. "So a Sri Lankan friend just gave me a box of sweets, and I came to see if you wanted a couple," she replied.

"Great, thanks! Actually, I just received my transfer of money from the software company in Chengdu. I'll be able to invite you to the Ethiopian restaurant that opened in East Northport—I read about it in the *Deer*."

"That's very sweet! I look forward to it." For all his originality, it was ironic that Jason did not have more creative ideas for outings than going to the thousandth ethnic restaurant, she thought. Taking matters into her own hands, she proposed, "You know, Jason, I was wondering if you wanted to go for a run to burn all the calories from the sweets."

As much as Jason would have enjoyed a run in the pleasant weather, his responsibilities had to interfere right now. "I have to make a call right now, but I'll find you here at eleven, all right?"

"Sounds good, Jason. Don't you want to open the door to see me, though?"

"Oh, right." Jason opened it slightly, then quickly darted out. He did not want anyone at all, even a friend as close as Aurélia, to intrude on his privacy.

Aurélia frowned. Why was Jason so childish about the whole privacy thing? She did not see what he had to hide. The times he had dropped some hints as to what his mystery project was and finally revealed the name to her, it had not sounded sketchy. Maybe he enjoyed being in an isolated space when he was by himself but preferred the more open atmosphere of a restaurant when he saw her, just as a break from his solitude. After all, considering where they usually met, he probably did not even know where her room was.

Pushing all those thoughts aside, she just hugged Jason tightly.

Usually, Jason did not feel comfortable being touched in certain intimate ways. However, he was becoming closer to Aurélia as senior year dragged on, so thought it imprudent to say anything about it.

"I'll see you soon, Aurélia."

No, there was nothing to stress about, Jason thought as he went to Lauderdale College's computer lab and grabbed the phone. After three years of a difficult social experience at Northport, he had learned to live in his niche. Everything was finally settling down.

PART II

7. TIME TO SAY GOODBYE

SATURDAY, MARCH 30, 2013

KINGSFORD SMITH AIRPORT, SYDNEY

Jason Curran stood in the security line at Sydney Airport, intermittently checking his watch as he stared impatiently at the frozen exodus of travelers. If the security screening process did not accelerate, he might miss his flight to Los Angeles and onward connection to New York. Not that he would be too unhappy if he did. At the end of Spring Break, he was not particularly looking forward to the final rush of work preceding the preparation for Commencement. He would gladly have spent another night, or another month, at his parents' home in Sydney, where he did not have to deal with navigating the cutthroat social dynamics of the Northport campus community.

Jason waited for a few more minutes, then finally gave in to his irritation and pulled out his cellphone. Normally, it was prohibited and punishable by a fine, but the screening personnel seemed too busy to care about one innocuous-looking traveler checking his email. Besides, nearly four years of flying back and forth between Sydney and New York had taught him that airport employees in Australia were more lax than those in the United States.

He stared at the email icon on his phone. He had fifty new ready-to-read messages in his inbox, and new ones would pile up quickly. He needed to ask Derek Park about a funding strategy for his project, maybe reach out again to Lars Børgensen for the first time in a month, and keep his promise to his parents to update them on the progress of his journey back to Northport.

Jason began to comb down the messages. An extraordinary-seeming but condition-laden promotion from a language learning software he no longer used? *Delete*. An advertisement from Slovenia's Adria Airways, which he had flown once ten years ago? *Delete*. A plea for donations from a candidate in New South Wales's state Legislative Council? *Delete*. Sometimes, he wondered if the email sending system knew the meaning of the word "unsubscribe," which he clicked at the bottom of earlier emails every time but to no avail.

His parents had sent him a few articles on Brooklyn's best new hip restaurants and the rumors of a new epic film from his favorite director. He made a mental note to read those on the fourteen-hour flight to California. The email sorting process had been ten times more rapid than he had ever imagined. He was about to close his inbox and switch to his last resort for killing time, a game on his phone where he guided a cartoon dolphin through an asteroid field filled with robotic turtles.

There was, however, one last message, this one from Tony DiTancini. Jason assumed it was like the other mass emails Northport's president sent every so often to the entire campus community along the lines of, *"This morning, one of our most beloved professors announced that he would retire by the end of the year,"* followed by a summary of his accomplishments and an invitation to a farewell dinner.

Jason opened the message, then scrolled down. Strangely, the message was in fact a formal letter emblazoned with Northport's logo, two Gothic towers branching from the top of a turquoise letter N. Why would President DiTancini want to write to him personally and without waiting until classes resumed in two days? Had he somehow learned of Jason's project and found him some appropriate contacts or resources among Northport's faithful and well-connected alumni?

Jason scanned a few words with his eyes, then almost felt his lungs collapse. He held his chest with one hand and his carry-on suitcase with the other as he tiptoed out of the security line—the last thing he needed now was to be arrested for shrieking with horror and sprinting out, though then again, talking to the police might be a welcome distraction. He came to a sudden halt near a bench, sat down with his bags to the side, and read the entire message more calmly, if that was even possible.

"Dear Mr. Curran,

In the past month, Northport has received some information regarding your activities that requires your undivided attention. Several members of the campus community have complained about your behavior and the immediate threat it represents to Northport and possibly the United States of America as a whole. The allegations against you are extremely severe.

Given the harshness of your alleged misconduct and Northport's precautionary principle, you will have to speak with Dr. Nathalie

Washington, Dean of Students at Northport University, who is conducting our internal investigation and will present her findings to the other members of the administration. She will soon send you a time to speak with her and explain your perception of the situation. Do not contact her until you receive a message from her.

In accordance with the guiding principles of the Northport system, you are immediately suspended from the university and will remain so until Dean Washington, the Provost, the Board of Trustees, the Department of Public Safety, the Department of Psychological Services, and I review the findings of the internal investigation of the allegations brought forth against you. Your student privileges are immediately revoked, which means that you will not be allowed to sit in any Northport classes, eat in Northport dining halls, be a member of any Northport student organization, or speak to any members of the Northport community without our explicit permission to do so.

Until the matter is resolved, you are prohibited from returning to campus under any circumstances. As you are not a citizen of the United States of America, we strongly advise you to remain outside the country until the appropriate federal authorities have finished conducting their own investigation of the matter. We, by which I mean the entire administration of Northport, believe that this is the best course of action for the university, given the extenuating circumstances.

In any case, do not engage in any actions that could be interpreted by anyone as acts of vengeance towards those involved in bringing forth and/or acting upon the allegations against you. If you decide to do so, you will be expelled permanently from Northport and turned entirely over to the federal government authorities.

Please understand that we have not made any of our decisions without very careful consideration of their impact on the Northport *community as a whole. Once we have determined the best course of action, we will contact you with our verdict.*

Sincerely,

Tony DiTancini

President of Northport University"

For a moment, a stunned Jason looked out at the window. If he tried, never mind the logistics, he might be able to charge past security, throw himself under the crushing weight of a taxiing jet, and end all his problems right there. Quickly dismissing the idiocy of that idea, he tried to digest the contents of the letter, but somehow his stomach refused to do so. With no idea of what the letter was referring to, he read every sentence over, attempting in his utter shock to analyze their meaning as best as he could.

"Dear Mr. Curran,

In the past month, Northport has received some information regarding your activities that requires your undivided attention."

That was strange. In the past, no one had seemed to care enough about any of his activities to talk about him.

"Several members of the campus community have complained about your behavior and the immediate threat it represents to Northport and possibly the United States of America as a whole. The allegations against you are extremely severe."

Which members? He could count all the people he knew well enough to greet—students, professors, and dining hall chefs alike—on two pairs of hands. And the

United States? He had never involved himself directly in any political organization. Was this a cruel farce?

"Given the harshness of your alleged misconduct and Northport's precautionary principle, you will have to speak with Dr. Nathalie Washington, Dean of Students at Northport University, who is conducting our internal investigation and will present her findings to the other members of the administration. She will soon send you a time to speak with her and explain your perception of the situation. Do not contact her until you receive a message from her."

His perception? Versus what? Jason had never found it easy to understand the way others viewed him, but understanding something unidentified would be impossible even for a social butterfly.

"In accordance with the guiding principles of the Northport system, you are immediately suspended from the university and will remain so until Dean Washington, the Provost, the Board of Trustees, the Department of Public Safety, the Department of Psychological Services, and I review the findings of the internal investigation of the allegations brought forth against you."

Principles? Not even being told what the allegations against him were hardly qualified as due process.

"Your student privileges are immediately revoked, which means that you will not be allowed to sit in any Northport classes, eat in Northport dining halls, be a member of any Northport student organization, or speak to any members of the Northport community without our explicit permission to do so.

Jason had always made a point of following the rules, but not allowing him to even set foot on campus seemed unfair even to him.

"Until the matter is resolved, you are prohibited from returning to campus under any circumstances. As you are not a citizen of the United States of America, we strongly advise you to remain outside the country until the appropriate federal authorities have finished conducting their own investigation of the matter."

The *federal* authorities? Was this part of a new witch hunt? Well, until he knew the answer, he would certainly not be setting foot again in that damned country. How blessed he was to be an Australian citizen.

"We, by which I mean the entire administration of Northport, believe that this is the best course of action for the university, given the extenuating circumstances."

The *university*? Was the impact on him not significant? Was his humanity being ignored in the process against him?

"In any case, do not engage in any actions that could be interpreted by anyone as acts of vengeance towards those involved in bringing forth and/or acting upon the allegations against you. If you decide to do so, you will be expelled permanently from Northport and turned entirely over to the federal government authorities."

How could he engage in acts of vengeance when he did not know who was responsible? President DiTancini had failed to identify the plaintiffs.

"Please understand that we have not made any of our decisions without very careful consideration of their impact on the Northport

community as a whole. Once we have determined the best course of action, we will contact you with our verdict."

What would they decide was the best course of action? If this letter was their definition of justice, he could not look to a much better verdict. He was utterly screwed.

Still unsure whether any of this was true and not just a figment of his wildly creative imagination, Jason read the letter from start to finish a few more times, then pondered what to do. He had never been a fireball of emotions, and he would certainly not start now. He drew on whatever strength had not poured out of him in the last ten minutes to stand up from his seat and pull his suitcase and backpack up. He limped over to the row of taxis for downtown Sydney, then gave his bags to the driver of the nearest one.

"Take me to Mosman, please. 32 Prince Street."

When he had sat in his father's car in the opposite direction an hour ago, Jason had known that it was time to say goodbye. He just had not known to whom.

8. YESTERDAY

BRADFIELD HIGHWAY, SYDNEY

Yesterday, Jason Curran would have admired the view. The buildings of the New South Wales's state capital glimmered in the sunlight. The golden point of the Sydney Tower kept a watchful eye over the city's innumerable bays from its observation deck. Intrepid hikers walked on the black arches of the towering Harbour Bridge, and the white sails of the iconic Opera House faced out, greeting the commuters and tourists alike who rode the green and yellow ferries to the Central Business District's wharf.

Jason always took advantage of the ride to and from Sydney Airport to admire his hometown's majestic skyline, except for today. Right now, he could focus on nothing but that horrid letter from Northport. What was this all about? Could the letter somehow be a fluke? Had a secretary somehow mixed up his name with another's during her Spring Break shift? Jason shook his head. With a gigantic endowment and massive workforce, Northport was one of the largest corporations in the country. Such amateurism seemed impossible.

Perhaps another student impersonated President DiTancini as a cruel prank. Maybe a clever Computer Science major had hacked into the system. Jason briefly wondered but soon realized how unlikely that theory was.

Unless he or she had sent the hoax letter to every single name in the student directory, there would have been no reason to target Jason specifically. He was the center of his own universe, but when it came to Northport's social scene, he was completely on the edge of it.

No, however insane it seemed, the letter was genuine and destined for him. What had he done, though? He was not superstitious, so he did not think it was merely because he had touched a maple on campus. Was this somehow related to his project? Why would Northport not tell him? Why did he have to go through this? Would anyone at Northport try to save him? He seriously doubted anyone would start an online petition, as with the Tunisian student Aurélia had mentioned.

Now, Jason had already told himself that he was not exactly suffering the worst fate in the history of humanity. He was sure that many people would kill to have the life he had today, even without being at Northport. However, the more he thought about it, the more he knew that he would nonetheless suffer from this catastrophe in the decades to come, if he did not jump out a window before then. How would anyone ever hire him if he had a criminal history? In the age of the Internet, all these records would stay forever. Would he have to resign himself to never having a job?

As an architect and cardiologist, his mother and father were certainly not in desperate need of money, but living as an adult on someone else's income was unacceptable to Jason. His entire life, he had always pushed himself to do better rather than waiting for someone else to do everything for him. He needed to make a life for himself without ever having to rely on others, but was that possible now?

Of course, even that required that no one pursue him for his alleged crime, whatever it was. Jason doubted that Northport's president had been bluffing when he had mentioned the federal authorities' investigation and warned him not to set foot in the United States for the time being. Jason had no idea what the extradition accords between Australia and the United States were, but he feared the worst. What if an agent from the Federal Bureau of Investigation, or some other security agency, showed up at his door and arrested him right there, right in front of his parents?

Oh, no! His parents! How would he explain this to them? What would they do if they knew the truth? They could not know! He had to think of an explanation for his sudden return home right away.

Soon, the taxi turned onto Prince Street in the Mosman neighborhood, then parked in front of the orange-roofed house where Jason instructed him. Jason paid the driver, then hauled his bags to the front door and rang the doorbell.

Earlier today, he still felt like the proud son of his parents, not a shamed exile. He could only hope that he could hide the truth of what had transpired and feel secure in the only place where he knew he truly belonged.

Elektra Kananaskis Curran opened the door and stared at him in surprise. "Jason! What are you doing here? Is everything all right?"

Jason faced his mother. "Mami, I'm taking some time off from college to work on my project. I just had a brilliant idea, and it could not wait."

She seemed flabbergasted. "B-b-but, Jason, you just left this morning! Why come back right now?"

"See, Mami, I had a eureka moment while I was waiting for my flight, so I needed to focus on it right away." He had often acted impulsively on his urges as a child, so he hoped his mother would not sense anything unusual.

"Wow, that's, um, great, Jason! Your father needs to hear about this!" She walked a few steps up the staircase and shouted, "Liam! Look who came back!"

"Where's Chloë, by the way?" Jason asked he waited for his father to come down.

"Oh, your sister went to her friend's house, remember?"

"Right, Mami. Sorry, it's been very confusing, deciding this at the last minute."

"Well, I certainly understand!"

They were joined by an equally shocked Liam Curran. "Jason! Why are you back so soon?" he asked. "If your flight was cancelled, we didn't get any notifications on our phones."

Elektra answered first. "Liam, Jason came back to work on his business project!"

Liam Curran smiled at his son. "Well, that's great! Have you told Northport's administration that you were doing this?"

Jason frowned for a second. "They've been in touch with me about not coming back to campus immediately." Jason hated lying, but technically, this was not a lie.

"I'm very happy that you chose to do this! All of these breaks are too short. I've always wanted to see more of you since you went to live on the other side of the world," he said.

Jason's mother placed her arm around him in a typically Greek gesture. "Now, you must be tired and hungry! Are you ready for lunch?"

"Just give me a second, Mami. I need to go check on something. I'll be right back." As Jason walked into his room, he stared straight at the turquoise Northport banner on his wall. He yanked it down, then reached for the donut-shaped roll of Scotch tape on his desk and hung it back up. It would be painful to constantly have to see it, but it his parents could not notice anything suspicious.

Jason drew out his cellphone. Aurélia had to know about this—well, the official story. If rumors explaining his sudden disappearance spread around campus, she and Derek Park were the only ones he expected to dispel them, though Jason very seriously doubted that the ever-popular Student Council President would accept to associate with him once rumors of his alleged crimes started to spread.

"Hi Aurélia," he wrote, *"I'll actually be staying in Sydney for a bit longer and use the time to work on the project I've been telling you about. I hope you had a good break. Well, I'll talk to you soon!"*

He stared at the message for a few seconds, then pressed the "Send" button and wrote a similar message to Derek. Once again, he had not actually lied a single time.

✈ ✈ ✈

MONDAY, APRIL 1, 2013

CURRAN RESIDENCE, SYDNEY

Jason Curran finished the last spoonful of Thai red curry. Thankfully, in the past few years, his mother had no longer hollered when he requested vegan dishes in accordance with his moral principles. The last thing he wanted right now was for another battle to rage.

That being said, Jason would later have to find an excuse for his mother not to make him curry for the time being. Four years ago, he had eaten curry at a local Thai restaurant when he had learned of his admission to Northport. While he did not make that connection every time he ate the dish, the memories were coming back to him now.

As Elektra Kananaskis Curran brought a bowl of sliced passion fruits from her garden to the dinner table,

Jason asked her in an almost childish voice, "Mami, can we play a game?"

"Yes, Jason, of course!" Elektra replied in a tender voice. She would rather have asked him to tell them the stories of his life at Northport that he had missed telling them over Spring Break, but she knew better than to go against his will when he had an idea. "Do you want to play that game where you say the letter of a person's name and—"

"Botticelli?" Jason interrupted. "I was thinking more along the lines of Psychiatrist."

"Sure, Jason, whatever you want!"

Chloë Curran asked in a cute little eleven-year-old voice, "Mami, I forgot the rules! Can you remind me?"

Elektra could use a refresher as well. "Jason," she asked him, "How about you explain?"

"Sure. One of the players, let's say I'll play that role, pretends to be a psychiatrist asking questions to patients. All three of you think of someone, either real or fictional, that the other players all know and then answer my questions as your character would. Then, I try to figure out who you are. They can't be simple yes-or-no questions, and if one of you says something wrong, one of the others has to shout—"

Elektra did not want to confuse her daughter too much. "I think we understand, Jason. Thank you!"

"Can I be the psychiatrist, Mami?" Jason asked.

"Sure, go ahead!"

Jason smiled. It annoyed him when others played the psychiatrist because he was always unable to control the questions they asked him, even when they broke the rules egregiously.

"Dad, are you playing?" Jason asked.

Liam Curran shrugged. "Why not?"

"All right, Jason," Elektra told him, "Close your ears so we can decide!"

Chloë whispered something into her father's ear, but he answered, "No, I'd rather think of my own." He stared to the side for a few seconds, then turned back to her. "I'll be Rodrigo Oliveira."

Chloë looked puzzled. "Who?"

"The Portuguese opera singer Jason likes to listen to," he whispered.

"Oh, him." She turned to her mother. "Mami, I want to be one of Jason's good friends from Northport, but I can't remember their names!"

Elektra frowned for a second. "That's because he doesn't have any good friends."

"Oh." Chloë paused for a few moments, then gleefully said, "How about that guy who jumped up on Jason from behind when he wasn't looking?"

"Which one? Jason often doesn't pay attention to his surroundings when he's thinking about something else, so there are lots of people like that."

"No, that drunk man, remember? The guy who jumped out of nowhere, then laughed and gave Jason a high-five? Where was he? I can't remember, Mami!"

Liam Curran chuckled. "Oh, right, in Finland. It was that year all of you went with me to the cardiologists' congress in Helsinki."

Chloë smiled, clearly content with her choice. "How about you, Mami?"

"Well, I won't think of someone too hard for him. He looks exhausted." Elektra pondered whom to choose. "I'll be Northport's president, Tony DiTancini," she whispered to Chloë.

Turning to face her son, she loudly declared, "All right, Jason, we're ready!"

Jason breathed a sigh of relief. While his parents and sister had debated whom to choose as their characters, he had been unable to focus on anything but the fact that he was still waiting for Northport's Dean of Students to contact him. Now, this game provided a welcome distraction.

"First question: what would you do if you came to Sydney? Let's start with you, Mami, and then go clockwise."

Elektra thought for a second. "In Sydney? Well, probably go visit the universities."

"Okay. And you, Dad?"

"Perform at the Opera House."

Jason looked at his sister next. "Chloë?"

"Walk behind tourists and jump on them!"

Jason processed the clues for a few moments before beginning the next question round. "What kinds of food do you like?"

Elektra hesitated. The point of Psychiatrist was that one could never know more than a modicum of information about the person in question but should make an educated guess. "Pizza, pasta, I think."

"Dad?"

"Just the traditional food in—"

Jason did not want his father to waste the challenge. "No, Dad, don't tell me where you're from! I want to guess myself." He turned his gaze to the right. "Chloë?"

"I don't eat! I only drink beer!"

Jason did not have to dig too deeply into his memory before he smiled. "I know! You're that funny Finnish drunk!"

"How did you find me so quickly?"

"You made it too easy! You talk about him all the time, and you just gave yourself away." Chloë did not argue, so he picked out another classic Psychiatrist question.

"What is your greatest fear?"

Elektra wondered how to phrase her answer without making it a dead giveaway. "Having the company I run lose money or get involved in a public scandal. Liam?"

"Singing out of tune in front a whole audience or having all my albums pirated. Chloë?"

"I'm out of the game since Jason found who I was, remember?"

"Oh, right. Okay, next question, Jason. I need to go sleep very soon."

"Where do you like to go on vacation?" Jason asked his mother.

"The Caribbean, but I don't have a lot of vacation time. Liam?"

"The Azores Islands."

"What kind of music do you like?" Jason asked. He had a few suspicions about his father, though his mother had to answer the question first, according to the rules of the game.

"Frank Sinatra, probably."

Now was the time to see if he could expose his father's character. "Dad?"

"All the classic Italian operas, especially when I'm singing the songs."

Jason smiled. His hunch had been right. "Are you Rodrigo Oliveira?"

"Yes, good job! Now, I really need to go upstairs. I've had a very tiring day."

Jason could not imagine his father's day being as tiring as his own excruciating wait. It was already over sixty hours since he had received that devastating letter, and there was still no vital sign from Northport's Dean of Students. Of course, Jason could not indicate his endless torment to his family in the slightest. "Good night, Dad. Two down, one to go." Jason faced his mother, able to focus exclusively on finding her now. "What's your favorite movie?"

"The Godfather."

"Which languages do you speak?"

"English and probably some Italian."

"What do you like to do in your spare time?"

"Well, I have a rather busy job, but I like to spend time with my family."

"Do you have any children?"

"Grandchildren, probably, but Jason, I have no idea."

"The game's more fun when you have to make up the answers," Jason said, then continued, "If you had a hundred million dollars, what would you do with it?"

"Give my name to a building, probably."

Jason Curran reviewed the facts in his head for a moment. He only knew that his mother's character was Italian. Well, that and that she had mentioned something about universities and leadership—oh, wait. No, that was bad. Very, very bad. If his mother had chosen whom he thought she had, he was very unhappy.

"Have you ever heard of Northport University? What do you think of it?"

Elektra smiled, glad that her son had found her. "*Heard* of it? Certainly more than that. My life revolves around Northport."

Jason's fears had been more than mere suspicion. "Are you...Tony DiTancini?"

Elektra smiled, hoping she had made Jason happy by reminding him of his life at Northport. "Yes, great job!"

Jason had thought that a round of Psychiatrist would make him forget the entire Northport debacle, not rub it in his face. Why did everyone and everything around him constantly have to remind him of Northport? Jason yelled, "You can't be Tony DiTancini! It's not fair!"

Elektra frowned strangely, and soon Jason realized his mistake. According to the official story he was telling his parents, a mention of Northport should not do anything to upset him, but he realized that he had nearly blown his cover. He had to find an excuse for his behavior.

"Mami, you're not allowed to be him! The rules say that you need to pick a character everyone knows, and Chloë doesn't know who he is! You're cheating!"

Elektra shook her head. This again, she thought. She had assumed that Jason was past his phase of puerile tantrums over such idiotic technicalities, but clearly she had overestimated her son. "Okay, I'm sorry, Jason. I promise not to cheat again next time, okay? Well, I need to go sleep, Jason. Good night."

"Good night, Mami. Good night, Chloë," he answered before storming out.

Jason walked out of the dining room and breathed a sigh of relief. He hated fabricating excuses, but this time he had had no choice. He retired to his bedroom and checked the drawer under his desk. The empty envelope from Northport and its former contents, the printed version of the email he had received two days ago, still lay under a pile of elementary school assignments he had kept for their sentimental value. The envelope had arrived in the afternoon, so he had had to hide it very quickly before his mother brought Chloë back from school.

Jason checked his email. His mouth widened when he noticed the response from Aurélia.

Scrolling down, he read, *"Hey Jason, that's great! I'm really happy for you! Good luck on your project, and I'll talk to you soon, hopefully before you get back to campus!"* Clearly, the rumors of his suspension had not started spreading yet, and since no one ever paid attention to him, he doubted that they would anytime soon.

Before he could reply to Aurélia, however, Jason received a notification of a new message from Nathalie Washington. Jason had reread President DiTancini's letter more than enough times to recognize the name of Northport's Dean of Students.

"Dear Jason," the message read, *"I would like to speak with you at 7 P.M. New York time tonight, if you are around. If so, please call me at the number on my webpage. This is a very important conversation, so please be there on time, no excuses."*

Though he was shocked by the curtness of the message, Jason did as he was told. After replying with an innocuous, *"Thank you for reaching out to me, Dean Washington. I will call you then,"* he searched for Nathalie Washington's webpage and jotted down her phone number. While he was at it, he also glanced for a few seconds at her photograph and credentials.

Jason tucked away his cellphone. He had no reason to waste time. He was going to face a trial tomorrow. If he wanted to get through it, he needed a good night's sleep.

9. ALL I ASK OF YOU

TUESDAY, APRIL 2, 2013

MANLY BEACH MARINE PARADE, SYDNEY

It was particularly difficult at times, but Jason Curran had vowed to himself not to let the Northport fiasco consume him entirely. He truly hoped that his first outing since Saturday morning could help him change the ideas on his mind, if that was even humanely possible. His parents and sister showed tremendous affection for him, and the multiple messages he had exchanged with Aurélia since yesterday night had at least convinced him that he still had something real waiting for him for when he returned to the other side of the Pacific, whenever that was.

Besides, he was always one to enjoy the scenery, especially in Sydney. Surfers of all ages brought their boards to Manly beach to ride the waves. On the Marine Parade path lounging the shore, visitors browsed the earth-colored dotted landscape paintings in Aboriginal art galleries, while Sydneysiders looking out at the Tasman Sea sipped espressos and berry smoothies on the terraces of the many Art Deco coffeehouses. In Sydney, one could leave the city center in a ferry and fifteen minutes later be in the wilderness, with the spires of the central business district sticking out from the woods.

The oceanfront property of Manly Beach was very far out of the Currans' budget, but walking down the promenade had rivaled marveling at the animals in Taronga Zoo as their favorite weekend activity. Prior to this morning, Jason had not ridden the ferry to Manly since his high school days, but he had decided to come here to find a suitable jogging path.

Besides martial arts, Jason had never enjoyed any sports, but this school year, Aurélia had gotten him into jogging during a few of their runs together on a trail in Fort Salonga, to the north of Elton Hall. Jason had discovered how much he enjoyed the activity, especially the times he had gone and run alone, in peace. Not only was it a liberating experience for the lungs and the mind, he did not have to deal with the pressure to conform to the will of others, arbitrary definitions of success, and empty praise that accompanied team sports.

Advancing briskly on the Marine Parade, Jason accelerated, hoping that the exercise would become sufficiently strenuous to distract him. As he looped around the jagged cliffside near Shelly Beach, the strategy seemed to work rather well. Focused only on the fact that he was out of breath and beginning to feel hot under the Australian autumn sun, he forgot about anything having to do with Northport.

Jason Curran checked his watch. It was ten-fifty-five, only five minutes before he was supposed to call Dean Washington. With no time to hesitate, he scanned the periphery as he walked on the sandy rocks and very quickly found an appropriate spot. A narrow green bench perched on top of the low cliff overlooked the Tasman Sea. Perfect. If he had to undergo the most testing trial of his life, he would at least do it somewhere he liked.

Not wanting the exorbitant bill that accompanied a normal international call in addition to the rest of his troubles, Jason opened the Skype application on his cellphone. He copied Nathalie Washington's office phone number, then stared at the view of Manly Beach for a few minutes.

Finally, Jason's watch read 11 A.M., or 7 P.M. in New York time. It was time to get this over with, he thought. He pressed the "call" button on his Skype and waited for what were perhaps the ten hardest seconds of his life. Finally, a deep female voice answered. "Hello, this is Nathalie Washington speaking. Is this Jason Curran?"

Jason breathed, drawing on his decade of martial arts training. He had built up the emotional strength for this over the past three days. Now was not the time to show any sign of fear or weakness. "Yes!" he answered with all the confidence he still had. "Good evening, Dean Washington. How are you?"

"I'm doing fine, thank you. And you?"

"You know, I'd be lying if I said everything was okay, wouldn't I?" Jason chuckled nervously.

"I guess something would be wrong if you got that letter and didn't react, no?" Nathalie Washington laughed lightly. At least she had a decent sense of humor, Jason thought.

"Good point."

"All right, Jason. Let me tell you a bit about myself before we start. My name is Nathalie Washington, and I'm the Dean of Students at Northport University. I grew up in the South Side of Chicago, then I studied at Northport as an undergrad before getting a doctorate from Northport's Wagner School of Education. As they say, I'm 'Northport through-and-through'. I've stayed with this job seventeen years, because I believe that what makes a university like ours great isn't its financial endowment but the spirit of its students."

"Nice to meet you, Dean Washington."

"You too, Jason, even under these circumstances. By the way, I'm sorry we had to contact you on Friday afternoon right before closing the office and couldn't have a conversation before Monday."

"It's fine. It wasn't too bad. I had enough work to keep me more than busy," Jason responded, clenching his teeth as he lied so egregiously. The few times he had tried to think about his project, he had been utterly unable to concentrate.

"However, with all due respect, he added, "I believe you have the wrong man."

"Really? You *are* Jason Curran, are you not?"

"Yes," Jason said. Even if his name was rather common, he very strongly doubted that there was another student on campus sharing his email and home address as well.

"Jason Curran from Sydney, Australia? Senior, currently living in Lauderdale College and double major in Neuroscience and Engineering?"

"Yeah, that's me. But there must be some sort of misunderstanding."

"Oh, no, unfortunately. We received a serious complaint about you from several students, which is why I absolutely needed to speak with you."

Jason hissed softly. He had dreaded the moment when she might say this. Well, he had only one option left.

"It doesn't have to do with the fact that it's April Fools' Day in the States, does it?"

"No, Jason, though you raise a good point with that. We'll have to be careful when we talk to students on that date in the future!"

"Sounds good, but that'll be past my time!" Jason had only recently learned the use of banter to defuse a tense situation, so he drew on whatever he remembered.

Nathalie Washington chuckled again, then turned to a more serious tone. "Hopefully, Jason, we can resolve this misunderstanding quickly. Following the traditions and precedents of the Northport system, you will be given a chance to explain yourself. I will ask you a few questions, and you will answer with 'yes' or 'no,' all right?"

Jason did as he was told. "Yes, Dean Washington. You may begin."

"First, do you know Melissa Børgensen?"

"Yes," Jason answered.

"Did you ever email Melissa Børgensen?"

"Yes."

"Did you ever text her?"

"Yes."

"Did you ever call her?"

"Yes."

"Multiple times?"

"Yes."

"Did you search for her across campus?"

"Yes."

"Did you approach her at a party in Elton Hall the week before final exams?"

"Yes."

"Was she dancing with someone when you found her?"

"Yes."

"Do you know Cayley Thompson as well?"

Jason had trouble seeing where she was going, but he continued to respond normally. "Yes."

"Did you badger her repeatedly to ask her to help you in exchange for money?"

"Yes, but I wasn't badgering her. I was constantly inquiring because she agreed to this originally."

Nathalie Washington was clearly unfazed by the fact that he had answered with something other than a simple "yes." "Did you continue to try to communicate with both women via email, text message, and cellphone, even when they did not respond?" she asked. "Did you follow them to classes and social activities?"

"Yes." Jason saw where she was going. "Dean Washington, with all due respect, this is absurd. I contacted them again exactly *because* they did not respond and I needed help for my project. Please, let me explain!"

"No, that won't be necessary," Nathalie Washington interrupted.

Confused, Jason inquired, "Why not?"

"Jason, I'm just here to check the facts, not to figure out your intentions. Melissa Børgensen and Cayley Thompson alerted the administration because they were worried that you were acting strange and creepy, from the way you approached them to ask for help on a project to how you behaved like a loner outside of class. With everything that's happened on our campus and others in the last couple years, from gunmen to bomb threats, they were afraid for themselves and the whole community," she responded.

"In order to see if their claim was justified," she continued, "I tried to document if your other interactions on campus showed a pattern of suspicious behavior. Of course, I couldn't just ask around. With close to six thousand undergraduates on campus, the chance that any one of them knows a specific other student is very small. Rather than look at random, I searched for the students in your residential college, but I saw that you'd been in a single room since sophomore year. I didn't ask the others in Lauderdale College, because I needed someone who knew you well."

"I'm guessing that was hard," Jason said, laughing nervously. "I don't exactly have a massive social network on campus."

"Well, I figured that out rather quickly, and your isolation was part of their fear. I saw that you were only registered in jeet kune do as an extracurricular, so I asked the instructor if you had any friends in the class. She referred me to the only one, Derek Park, who explained to me that according to his observations, you hadn't ever done anything bizarre but that he did not know you well enough. As Student Council President, he'd know what's going on better than anyone else. I decided there wasn't anything more to learn from your friends."

For the first time since—well, he could not remember when—Jason breathed a sigh of relief. "That's great news," he responded. "I was beginning to feel really concerned. So, I assume the letter and call were merely there because it's an official procedure in the system? I'm glad we could resolve this issue so easily. Assuming I can get a plane ticket back without too much trouble, I'll be back on campus on Wednesday night."

For a moment, the other side of the line was silent. Jason took advantage of that time to plan what he had to do. He would call Qantas Airways to reschedule the flights back, explaining that he had missed them on Saturday due to a personal emergency and wagering on the phone agent's goodwill, otherwise fighting through layers of bureaucracy for a change fee refund. If his parents and sister had not really questioned his decision to return on a whim, they would probably not object when he announced to them tonight that he had decided to return to campus to work on his project there instead. As for his professors and Aurélia, he would figure that out later.

After a few seconds, though, Nathalie Washington finally responded. "No, Jason," she said in a voice that nearly sounded sad. "I'm afraid it's not that simple."

Right as he was checking his watch to see if he could catch the upcoming ferry back to Mosman, the Dean's comment brutally interrupted his train of thought. "W-w-what?"

"Jason, I believe we have a slight misunderstanding. This conversation is far more than a formality of the Northport system. I said that I was here to check. I meant that I want to check that my information is correct. I led an investigation for over a week, and so has the FBI. Though nothing's confirmed yet, it seems likely that Melissa and Cayley have a point. The campus police searched your room for evidence over Spring Break, since it *is* university property. Now, I want to know whether you actually did what my findings suggest."

Jason Curran could not believe his ears, but he made a conscious effort to not display aggressiveness. "Dean Washington, what have I done? I don't understand."

"Jason, please stop pretending to be unaware. You know exactly what you are responsible for. Now, I'll ask you some questions, and you'll answer them as you did for my previous ones. Are you ready?"

Still flabbergasted, Jason answered, "Yes, please begin."

"Have you ever spoken to Lars Børgensen?"

"Once, when he came—"

"Jason, just tell me 'yes' or 'no,' all right?"

"Yes."

"Was this when he came to give a talk at Northport?"

"Yes."

"Was this talk on the subject of nanotechnology, specifically implantable devices?"

"Yes."

"Did you attempt to contact him multiple times, including by using his daughter, Melissa, as an intermediary?"

"Yes."

"Were you so persistent about getting in touch with him because you needed help for a project on which you've been working for the past few years?"

"Yes."

"Is this the same project for which you proposed to pay Cayley Thompson for research work?"

"Yes."

Jason had noticed that his project figured prominently in her questions. Perhaps this was related to a certain policy on intellectual property, and he would have to convince a committee that he had never engaged in plagiarism, he thought. Yes, his ideas were original, but they probably wanted to make sure that that was the case. Maybe that was what they had meant when they had mentioned Northport's "precautionary policy." Maybe Lars Børgensen's work was indeed top secret, and Jason had inadvertently stumbled upon classified information. That would explain the involvement of the FBI, he thought.

"Do you stay up late in the neuroscience laboratory, especially on Thursday and Saturday nights, when most students are at social outings?"

"Yes."

"Do you often meet Chinese visitors next to the Sondheim Center for Medical Research?"

"Yes."

"Do you often exchange papers and electronic items with them?"

"Yes."

"Do you take a class in Mancini Hall on Monday, Wednesday, and Friday mornings?"

"Yes." Even more than before, Jason was unsure if there was anything unifying all of her questions, or whether she just took pleasure in asking him about every detail of his weekly routine.

"Do you often use the restroom in the basement?"

"*What?*"

"Jason Curran, do you often use the restroom in the basement of Mancini Hall?"

"Yes...but how is that relevant to anything?"

"Please, Jason, let's not get sidetracked. I have many more questions for you."

As if it had not been the case before, Nathalie Washington really sounded serious this time. "Go ahead," Jason said.

"Do you hide in one of the stalls and speak to your cellphone in various foreign languages, including Arabic and Korean?"

Jason sighed. Recently, he had made many exceptions to his reluctance to tell lies. However, this was certainly not the time. With someone—a janitor, perhaps, though

Jason had no idea why a mere custodian would even have the idea to do such a thing—feeding the administration all this information, they clearly had their facts straight. "Yes," he answered meekly.

"Do you regularly send flash drives to China from the post office on the Northport campus?"

"Yes."

"Do you receive payments from China as compensation?"

"Yes."

"Do you have a particular interest in computer coding, as evidenced by a seminar on the subject in which you took in freshman year?"

"Yes."

"Do you regularly let others into your room?"

"No."

"Do you keep an extensive collection of watches, some of them broken, there?"

"Yes."

"Have you written strange-sounding names with weird accents on a blank world map?"

"Yes." This was becoming more ridiculous by the minute, Jason thought. She was forcing him to admit random truths as part of an accusation of some crime, which was what, living his daily life?

"Have you called the Chinese-owned section of the Port of Piraeus?"

Finally, Jason broke. "Dean Washington, this is ridiculous! You can't expect me to convey the truth with a simple 'yes!' It's so much more complex! Please, just let me explain!"

"No," Nathalie Washington replied in an authoritative voice. "The way the Northport system works, you can only answer with 'yes' or 'no.'"

"Yes, Dean Washington, but right now, maybe the system needs—"

"Jason," she interrupted, "Were it not for our traditions, what would we do in situations like these?"

It was very fortunate that he was not calling Nathalie Washington through a video call, Jason thought, because she would not have liked to see the face he made. Northport's administration turned a blind eye to federal crimes like underage drinking on campus, yet they accused him of being a criminal for not spending his free time like the typical Northport undergraduate? What was the point of having such a rigid system if anyone who wanted to, like Melissa Børgensen or Cayley Thompson, could abuse it at will simply by filing a complaint whenever they felt uncomfortable around someone who did not conform to their narrow ideal of socially acceptable behavior?

However, Jason kept his thoughts to himself, not wanting to make a fatal blunder in his last chance to save himself. "Look, I understand that Northport has its protocols for most cases, and so far, I've done my best to abide by them." He inhaled and exhaled the breeze for a few seconds. "But, with all due respect, Dean Washington, this isn't like most cases. You're treating me like I'm some sort of criminal. Look, we're in total agreement on all the facts, but they mean nothing out of context. I beg you, Dean Washington, please let me explain!"

As if she had not before, this time Nathalie Washington really sounded like she meant business. "You are overstepping your boundaries, young man. If you refuse to answer 'yes' or 'no' as established in the Northport system, you will be expelled immediately, and this investigation will be turned entirely over to the federal government authorities instead of Northport's own administration. The FBI has allowed us to ask most of the questions, but I'm sure they'd be more than glad to talk to you directly. Now tell me, Jason Curran, have you called the Chinese-owned section of the Port of Piraeus?"

"Yes," he replied in a resigned tone.

"I knew you could come to your senses. Thank you, Jason. That concludes my interview. I will let you know when the administration has made its final decision. At Northport, review processes generally take a few days. Please don't contact me before then. Now, if you'll excuse me—"

"Wait!" Jason blurted out. Jason had learned many years ago not to talk out of turn, especially with a figure of authority, but this time he had no choice. At the end of the torture session, he still had no idea what he was being accused of.

"Yes, Jason? Quickly, I have other matters to attend to."

"Dean Washington, all I ask of you is that you tell me what these allegations concern."

"All right, I suppose, I will, seeing as you've been so cooperative and confirmed everything during my investigation. After all, according to the Northport system, I may mention this now that the interview is concluded. I don't remember exactly why it works that way, but I've heard that it has to do with the fact that you won't be as motivated to lie about the facts if you don't know in which direction they'll incriminate you."

Nathalie Washington stopped for a moment, probably finding a way to phrase his alleged crime, looking up the legal definition, or making him wait just to see how he would react. To pass ten seconds that were even more painful than the last, Jason stared at the majestic expanse of bays and beaches, wondering if in his pitiful state he even deserved to live among them.

Finally, the other side of the line became active again. "Jason, Northport University suspects you of acting as a spy for foreign entities, thereby potentially placing the national security of the United States of America in danger."

"*What?*" Jason asked, failing to entirely process what he had just heard.

"You heard me, Jason. Please stop playing innocent. You might hide behind the persona of a loner and creep, but it's obvious that you only do it to advance your dangerous agenda. Don't try to deny anything. We have all the evidence now. According to our obligations, we have to turn it over to the FBI as soon as we conclude our investigation. Now, I *really* have other things to deal with. Goodbye, Jason," she told him, then hung up abruptly.

Jason Curran checked his pulse frantically, making sure not to collapse from shock or exhaustion on the rocks. He then limped back to Manly Wharf to board the ferry and listened to samba on his cellphone, trying to think about something other than the fact that he had been accused of *international espionage*. It was so preposterous that he would have laughed, were it not jeopardizing his whole personal and professional future. He knew he was not dreaming either. While asleep, his mind would never have been able to piece together such a tragically complex scenario.

At last, Jason removed his headphones. The ferry had reached Mosman. He rode the bus up to his street, pulled out his key, and opened the door to his thankfully vacant house. At least there would be no one to see him in his state.

Now, the question remained what Jason would do for the next few days, or weeks, or years. He did not have the strength to advance on his project, especially considering the setback he had suffered when Lars Børgensen had still not responded, and he took little pleasure in reading or watching movies to pass the time. He walked into the kitchen to grab a bottle of pink guava juice, then took it with him into the attic.

The wonder on the dusty wooden floor shocked Jason's eyes as if he was seeing his own marvel for the first time. An endless network of wires and switches looped around the entire area. Secret to all but Jason himself and his family members dwelling under the attic, Jason's electronic circuitry laboratory was the child of countless sleepless nights from elementary to high school. He had not added anything to the model since then; most likely, the snapped wires sat on accumulating piles of dust. Well, not anymore.

If Jason Curran could not bring order to his life, at least he would bring it to his lab.

10. HONESTY

RODGERS COLLEGE, NORTHPORT UNIVERSITY

Aurélia Chitour had found it difficult to concentrate on folding her laundry today, so she wondered how she was supposed to write her latest dissertation of *Jane Eyre* for the next afternoon. For once, it was not the posters advertising outings to view the musical *The Lion King* on Broadway for twenty dollars all-inclusive or the invitations for free food at the Mexican Students' Association that distracted her. Neither was she bothered by the recurring traces of Rodgers College's two most infamous residents: the scattered pieces of hair removed by David McCosh, whose insistence on snipping his hallmates' hair with craft scissors earned him the sobriquet "The Barber of Hicksville," and the moldy socks belonging to Josh Grossmann, whose "environmentally conscious" habit of showering only once a week rendered his real last name quite appropriate.

The rumors lurking around campus had reached her since the beginning of the week, but she had at first dismissed them as mere speculation and annoying distractions. However, after overhearing a conversation by the washing machines today as she waited to check that no one accidentally poured beer on her clothing, she had begun to feel not bothered, but betrayed.

The funny thing was, Aurélia could not remember a time before this week when the Northport community had even acknowledged Jason Curran's existence. Jason's social awkwardness caused him to lay low, but someone, or several people, perspicacious enough had clearly noticed his disappearance from campus after two days. Perhaps he had more friends than he admitted to her.

Aurélia had certainly been surprised by Jason's announcement right after Spring Break that he would be taking time off from campus to work on his mysterious business project three months before graduation, but then again, it had not been out-of-character for him to obsess on one particular idea and prioritize it over everything else.

These new rumors, however, were causing Aurélia to wonder whether she had been a gullible fool. The chatter at the beginning of the week had been nonsense—in all honesty, she heavily doubted that Jason had been suspended from Northport for jewelry theft and vulgar vandalism in professors' offices. An international spy, though? That was more likely. Yes, the rumors had probably been inflated—somehow, she dismissed one student's report that Jason had been assembling bombs in his room and had now been expelled and sent to prison— but the general idea might very well be correct.

For much of his life at Northport, Jason had resided monastically in his room and never let anyone in. Whenever she went to Lauderdale College to visit him, he insisted on meeting her in the hallway, so Aurélia could only speculate on what he had been doing in his room.

What she actually knew about his life, however, could perhaps offer some clues.

Jason sometimes mentioned using money he received from a software company in China to invite her to dinner. Now that she thought about it, that was not all. Nearly every week, he acknowledged running into Chinese visitors on campus, far too often for it to be purely coincidental. She also knew that he often disappeared to drop objects off at the post office. Had his social awkwardness merely been a cover for espionage, allowing him to pursue his shady goals away from the public eye? And as for his mysterious project, had the potential name and few innocuous-sounding generalities he had mentioned when she had questioned him about it masked his real project, stealing research secrets and helping foreign entities?

Despite the rest, Aurélia had always appreciated Jason for one thing: his honesty. It was not just because he was probably the only student who would recite the Northport Honesty Code outside an examination setting. He genuinely seemed like a good person. Aurélia had naïvely assumed that he would never manipulate or deceive anyone. Now, however, she felt like she had been betrayed. She sensed a knot forming in her stomach. Time was money, and Aurélia could barely begin to count how many hours, days, months, and years she had invested into that delusion, the idea that she somehow understood Jason when no one else on campus did. What a childish fool she had been!

Just that morning, Aurélia had received a message from Jason Curran asking what was new at Northport. It was very clever, she thought, how he had tried to hide the reason for his absence and manage to deceive her. Now, however, that traitor could wait for a lifetime for her to ever respond.

That still left one crucial question unanswered: who had first heard and spread the rumor? Someone else who knew Jason well, if there even existed such a person, or a member of the administration? What was the motivation? Aurélia shook her head as she walked back to her room in Rodgers College. She was not feeling analytical at all today.

✈ ✈ ✈

WEDNESDAY, APRIL 3, 2012

CURRAN RESIDENCE, SYDNEY

"Hi Aurélia, how's your week going? Any fun plans for the weekend? Make sure to tell me if you try any new restaurants while I'm away!" Jason Curran wrote, then shot off the email.

Jason thought for a second. It was not like Aurélia to be unresponsive, even after only a day or so. He could no longer see her in his Skype contacts, which eliminated the possibility of communicating with her there. Had she deliberately excommunicated him, or was this just another frequent glitch? Jason had torn himself apart in order to force himself not to contact Nathalie Washington and request to explain himself, not wanting to disobey her command against doing so, but he had nothing to fear when he wrote to Aurélia. If she did not respond before then, he would reattempt in a day or so.

Suddenly, the shrill sound of Jason's Skype ringing pierced the air. He pulled his earbuds and pressed the "Answer" button.

"Jason! It's good to hear from you," Ares Dimitropoulos said in his deep voice.

"Yes, equally!" he responded in Greek. "How's life in Vouliagmeni?"

"Same as always, Jason! Sunny and slow, though I'm sure Sydney isn't too shabby either!"

"Well, you're certainly right about that. I miss Greece, though. I was too busy to go there the past two summers, but I really hope I have the time soon."

At night, sometimes Jason imagined that he was still a child in Pylos. In his dreams, the seaside Peloponnesian town was even more postcard-perfect than he remembered it, perhaps due to the tendency among children to embellish anything they saw in the memories they carried to adulthood. Houses with red tiled roofs, interspersed among towering cypress trees, jutted down from the cliff into a marina filled with pinewood boats and the occasional Russian oligarch's yacht. Honeymooners clasped their hands together on the white and blue-checkered tablecloths of tavernas as the sun set. Souvenir shops selling replica Cycladic statues and amphorae with designs of enchanting nymphs and dolphins lined the cobblestone streets. Back then, most of the shops had not read *"Enoikiazetai,"* or *"For Rent,"* as had occurred after the devastating debt crisis that had swept through Greece around the time Jason had entered Northport.

Every July, Liam and Elektra Curran took advantage of New South Wales's school winter holidays to visit Elektra's side of the family in Greece. While Liam Curran's ancestors had left Ireland for Australia two centuries ago, Dionysos Kananaskis had moved to Sydney as a teenager in the years following the Second World War. There, he had met another recent Greek immigrant, Valeria Delikouras, who later became the wife and mother of his only child, Elektra.

Meanwhile, Dionysos's sister, Apollonia, had remained in Greece. One of her sons, Ares Dimitropoulos, had moved to Cyprus to run transportation logistics in Limassol. Two years ago, the Chinese state-owned shipping giant COSCO Pacific had purchased a section of the Port of Piraeus near Athens and offered Ares one of the highest managerial positions not reserved for Chinese expatriates.

"Well, I hope you have the chance to come back to Greece soon!" Ares said heartily. "You're welcome anytime!"

"Thanks, Ares!" In the years since he had begun at Northport, Jason had been too busy with university-organized summer programs and his project to visit his extended family in Greece, and now he longed to go back.

"My pleasure! And your mom told me you're staying in Sydney to work on your project. Good luck with that!"

"Thanks!"

"So anyway Jason, I called you today because I was hoping you had time to follow up on the chat we had a few weeks ago about my son."

Jason thought back, digging through a memory completely clouded by the tumult of the past week until he finally remembered. "Oh, right. Has Cousin Antonis heard back from the universities he applied to?"

"Yes, and he's so happy! I thought he had decent chances, if I may say so myself. After we left Limassol, he enrolled at the International School of Athens, and he's one of the most promising International Baccalaureate students there. But now he's done better than I could ever have dreamed!"

Jason chuckled. While he certainly believed that Antonis Dimitropoulos was a very serious high school student, he still found it impossible to see his cousin as anyone but the pesky three-year-old who picked the olives off of his great-grandfather's trees and stomped on them gleefully. A cultivator of the Kalamata region's most famous export, its olives, Giorgos Kananaskis was one of the rare terrestrials to have lived in three centuries, a fact he attributed to his adherence to the Mediterranean diet.

Fourteen years ago, the extended Kananaskis family had come to Pylos to celebrate his hundredth birthday, where Jason had discussed the evolution of Greek music with his great-grandfather, who had turned to painting to pass the time since the death of his wife. Antonis, on the other hand, knew no better than to squash olives with his toenails and then chuck them at his cousins. After Giorgos passed away in his sleep five years later, his children continued to organize family reunions, now in Athens rather than Pylos. Though Antonis tended to get along better with Chloë, Jason saw Antonis on many of those occasions, and every time, the memory of his mischievous little cousin stayed at the center of his mind.

Now, though, Jason doubted that mentioning Antonis's experiments in olive oil production would be a wise move. "Congratulations! That's really amazing! So, which ones?"

"Well, he's been accepted to Harvard, Princeton, and Northport, plus some others that he isn't seriously considering, plus he's on the waiting list at Chicago. He was rejected from Stanford and Yale, though. Personally, I want Antonis to go to Harvard, because it's the best and most famous school in the world. However, he seems to really enjoy Princeton and Northport too, so we want to know the main differences between them. It's so hard to know just by reading online articles and looking at their glossy brochures."

Right now, the last thing Jason wanted to think about was Northport . It was for moments like these that he usually kept a squishy globe as a stress ball. However, he had lost it, probably while frantically moving all the meticulously organized junk on his desk around to find a place to hide his suspension letter. Desperately needing to release his tension, he grabbed a passion fruit laying on the side of his desk and crushed it, letting the yellow liquid ooze out. Well, so much for being a fartwharf, or pathetic weakling, as his elementary school peers used to call him during sports.

A few seconds later, though, Jason noticed the juice dripping onto his fingers. *"Čĕpêč,"* he muttered as he began to lift his body from the chair.

"Hey, Jason, are you all right?" Ares asked.

"Yeah, sorry," Jason apologized. "I was going to go wash my hands, but I guess I'll go later," he explained as he grabbed a tissue to wipe off as much juice as he could off his hands.

Ares, having known Jason and his childhood quirks, did not inquire into what had just happened. "So, about Northport and the other Ivy Leagues—"

"Right," Jason said. While the passion fruit incident was occurring, he had completely forgotten what had launched him into that fury. Now, though, the only thing he could do was answer Ares's question honestly. The last thing he wanted was for anyone to suspect why he was suddenly on the edge.

"So yeah, um, I think they're all similar and great all around, but they have their little differences too. Does he know what kind of environment he wants to live in?"

"Well, Antonis definitely wants to be in a very challenging and competitive environment. Don't all three universities fit that label?"

"Actually, I meant more along the lines of a big city, a suburb, a farm, you know."

"Oh, okay. Well, we haven't visited the campuses yet, so we're not exactly sure."

"Don't worry, Ares, I hadn't been able to visit them by the time I applied either, living so far. By the time of the Admitted Students' Weekend, I was done with school and building electrical circuits for a nonprofit in Cambodia, so I wasn't able to go. During my first quarter at Northport, though, I went to most of the other Ivy League campuses with an engineering club I was a member of back then. Anyway," Jason continued, making sure his habit of expounding on one personal topic forever did not come through, "Harvard is just across the river from Boston, so it's definitely more urban, but Princeton and Northport are suburban. They still have lots of shops, restaurants, and cultural opportunities."

"To be honest, Antonis has lived in Limassol and Vouliagmeni, a small city and a suburb, and I don't think he liked one more than the other. For university, it shouldn't make a difference."

"That makes sense, Ares."

"But even if you're on campus, is it also possible to leave the university and go into a big city sometimes?"

"Definitely! Anyone who wants to can spend the evening in Boston or New York City to go to the museum, opera, or the like. Most students don't, though."

"Oh, why not? Is it too expensive?"

"Not at all. It's a cheap and easy ride, and there's a lot of public transportation. It's just that most students have enough stuff to do on campus and don't see the point of going out. They're in so many clubs and activities here, and then they try to fit their classes into their very busy schedules."

"Oh, so classes aren't their main activity? It's certainly different from Europe then. Here it's common for students to still live at home or in their own apartments during their university years, but even for those in dormitories, when they go out to party, it's usually to nightclubs in the city."

"Yes, it certainly makes the American college experience unique. A common term that floats around Northport's newspaper, *The Daily Deer*, is the 'Northport Bubble.' Well, I'm sure you can also talk about the 'Harvard Bubble' or the 'Princeton Bubble' or the 'Stanford Bubble' or any of those."

"A *bubble*? I'm sorry, Jason, but I'm not following too well."

"Well, a bubble is enclosed, so it's like a campus closed off from the outside world. Students don't have to deal with the problems of the real world or of adult life, since the university takes care of cooking meals and providing housing. And not only basic needs, I should add. They bring in guest speakers, organize social events, and find internships!"

"Oh, I understand. Is that one of the reasons you wanted to go to university in the U.S.?"

"I was attracted to the great professors and research opportunities. I couldn't care less about going to all the social events on campus."

"Then are you the atypical student who always leaves campus?"

"Not really. In my case, even if I barely spend any time in clubs, my classes aren't my main activity. I've been working really hard on this project for the past few years. However, every now and then I go on a free dorm trip to the Metropolitan Opera in New York City or go by myself to the Metropolitan Museum of Art. I'm always inspired when I visit their collection of Polynesian art, especially the Tongan wooden statues."

"Oh, I see. Well, I guess my main question now is, are there any real differences between Northport, Harvard, and Princeton? From what you've said, it sounds like they're all clones of each other."

Did Ares really have to continue pressing these questions? "To be honest, Ares, they're all pretty much the same, but many people say that Princeton is more geared toward the undergraduate experience. Since they don't have any graduate professional schools, they focus more on undergrads. From what I hear, Princeton treats their undergrads very well, almost babying them. Northport and Harvard, on the other hand, are supposed to be more graduate-focused."

"Do you think undergraduate-focused is much better then?"

"Not really. Professional schools let you take courses in new areas. As for the lack of undergraduate attention, I don't think that's a real thing. Speaking from personal experience, any student at Northport who's confident enough to approach a professor and then follow up will get noticed. I guess it's the same at Harvard."

"Oh, I see. So Princeton is a bit special, but is there any difference at all in the academic experiences at Harvard and Northport?"

"In my opinion, Northport is just a lesser Harvard."

For a few seconds, Ares Dimitropoulos remained silent. "Wait, but I thought you loved Northport, Jason!"

The pure coincidence was very ironic, because Ares clearly had no idea how hard he was pressing Jason's sensitive buttons. "Not particularly," Jason replied, doing his best show no trace of the stiffening of his entire body in his voice. Apart from its hidden social curriculum, Jason loved Northport, which made him feel even more distraught to have this part of his life robbed from him.

"Oh, but then why didn't you choose Harvard?"

"In all honesty," Jason said bluntly, "I didn't get in. I was admitted to Northport, Princeton, and Stanford, and Northport was the strongest in neuroscience."

"Is there any point in going to Northport over Harvard, then?"

"Honestly, I don't see one."

"Oh, wow, all right. Thanks for your great advice, Jason! Now, if you'll please excuse me, I need to go talk to some clients. There's a shipper from Liberia who wants to bring way more cargo into Europe because he really likes the changes we've made since COSCO bought the port. I'm sorry I have to go, but I'll be sure to tell Antonis everything that you explained to me. Thank you, Jason, for being so helpful and candid!"

"You're welcome!"

"Bye! It's been nice talking to you."

As Jason closed his Skype, wrapping a tissue around his index finger to make sure he did not rub what remained of the crushed passion fruit on his keyboard, he hoped Ares would not have too many questions on the benefits of a Northport education next time. If he called again, however, Jason would make sure he had some paper to crumple up into a ball to alleviate his stress.

"Jason, time for dinner!" Elektra Kananaskis Curran called out.

"I'm coming, Mami!"

Jason walked over and breathed deeply. No, this was not as horrid as he had thought. At least his family was still there.

11. LET IT BE

WEBBER HALL, NORTHPORT UNIVERSITY

He stood at the front desk of Northport University's Office of Undergraduate Admissions. To the world, the young man with shoulder-length light blond hair and an Australian rugby shirt was a prospective Northport undergraduate, a rugby player exploiting Northport's preferential treatment for athletes to obtain a private tour of campus. However, Jason Curran knew very well that he was none of these things. He was merely a broken man, an exile using an idiotic disguise in the hope of rejoining the world he knew.

Jason stared at the jutting roof of the ultramodern admissions building, the work of a Pritzker Prize-winning architect, for a few minutes, and then his heart sank. He immediately recognized the figure walking towards him. He had seen her picture on her official webpage after inquiring into who would decide his fate the week before. He had thought the Office of Undergraduate Admissions would refer him to the next large group campus tour, but instead the Dean of Students was here to speak to him personally.

"Good morning!" the woman called out cheerfully. "Thank you for coming to Northport! Where are you visiting us from today?"

Jason pondered what to answer for a few moments. Mentioning Australia would raise too many red flags, seeing as she had recently had a not-too-pleasant phone call with one of the rare Australians studying at Northport. Unfortunately, during his studies of fifteen languages, Jason had never mastered the art of faking accents, so there were not many nationalities he could reasonably pass for.

Finally, he thought of an idea that could save him for the moment. "Cape Town, South Africa."

Jason stared at the Australian shirt he was wearing, then cursed silently at himself. On most days, that would have been a stupid move. Any true South African would pick up on his Australian accent and know the difference between a gazelle-like springbok found on their team's rugby shirts and the kangaroo-like wallaby on Jason's. Sure, he could always explain his Australian accent by passing off as one of the many South Africans who had settled in Australia, but he would be more discreet without having to go into any details. Instead, Jason just wagered that he was safe. The African-American woman in front of his was most likely not a recent immigrant from South Africa.

His gamble had worked. "What is your name?" she asked him.

"Ja...uh, um, Jacob." Lying was foreign to him; it took effort to suppress the urge to be honest. Jason paused for a few seconds, trying to think of a typically South African last name. "Jacob...Kruger."

The woman did not seem amused by his long hesitation, if Jason understood her emotions correctly, but her face quickly turned back to a smile. "Welcome to Northport, Jacob. I'm Nathalie Washington, Dean of Students."

"Nice to meet you, Dean Washington."

"So what can I do for you today, Jacob?"

"Well, first of all, I'm hoping I can audit a class."

"Yes, definitely. It's very simple—just contact the professors of the ones that interest you, and I'm sure they'd be very open to you auditing their classes."

"Thanks! Now," he asked, remembering who he allegedly was, "Could you please tell me more about the rugby team here at Northport? I practice rugby every day in South Africa. It's such a big part of my life," wondering if his voice was gruff enough for the tough athlete stereotype he was aiming to imitate.

"Actually, we have a rugby club at Northport. I take it you've already been in touch with the coach, right?"

"Of course," Jason replied, making a mental note to kick himself later for the lie. He had not even googled the coach's name.

Thankfully, Nathalie Washington skipped straight to her next question. "Do you need a map to Williams Gym?"

"No thanks, I know how to get there," Jason replied instinctively before hissing softly. Mentioning that had been a very bad move.

"Oh, have you visited us before?"

"No, I just...um...well...oh, well, I've studied the online campus map extensively!"

She did not seem to buy it. "Really? You've never been here at all?"

Jason did his best to hide his fear. "No, why would you think that?"

Nathalie Washington stood still for a few seconds, then grabbed his hair and yanked off his light blond wig. "Nice try, *Jason*."

✈✈✈

THURSDAY, APRIL 4, 2013

POTTS POINT PROFESSIONAL PARK, SYDNEY

"So, Jason, please tell me more about this dream you keep having," Orosz Sólyom asked Jason as he lay, tense yet composed, on the couch.

"Well," Jason began, "As I told you, since I got that letter from Northport, part of me has wanted to forget I ever went there, yet I've still really wanted to go back. I did spend the last four years of my life there, you know. Northport's really a part of me now. Why do they want me out like this, less than three months before graduation? I just don't get it."

Orosz nodded with a slight frown. "So your dream was about being readmitted?"

"Not really. Over the past few days, I've dreamed pretty much every night that I sneak back in. Every time, I find some other trick, usually by going to the admissions office and asking for a tour. This morning, I woke up from a dream where I was disguised as a South African rugby player. I got further this time—it took almost ten exchanges in the conversation for the Dean to notice me—but I don't know if she kicked me back out after that, since I woke up."

"Well, be very glad you were not living in Communist Hungary. They would have done far worse than throw you off campus if you had tried to go in undercover!" Sólyom replied, chuckling. "But, jokes aside, is this why you came to my office this morning?"

"Yes, it was, Doctor Orosz. When people see therapists, it's generally not to talk about what good movies they just saw." Right up until he had left for college, his parents had forced him to attend weekly therapy sessions, which were certainly not his fondest childhood memory. However, there had been one therapist, Orosz Sólyom, whom he had genuinely enjoyed talking to. Unfortunately, after only about six months of seeing Jason, Orosz had moved his office across the country to Perth.

This very morning, following the dream where he had failed to pass off as Jacob Kruger, Jason had finally overcome his reluctance to mention the letter from President DiTancini to anyone at all. After searching online, he discovered that Orosz was back in Sydney. He had come to Orosz's office in Potts Point Professional Park and reintroduced himself to a therapist he had not seen in nearly a decade, then told him the story of his dismissal and acknowledged his intermittent luck when Orosz had accepted to talk to him as a friend, not a paying patient. Thankfully, his parents had no reason to learn of the encounter—as far as they were concerned, Jason was merely taking some time off from college to work on his business project.

"This dream was just stupid, but I'm getting more stressed about the whole Northport thing every day. This morning, I was wondering whether I could ever get a job now that anyone with the right tools can probably dig up a record of what happened to me. And what if the FBI comes over to arrest me at home or next time I try to cross a border? I don't feel safe anymore!"

Catching his breath, Jason added, "Oh, and then there's the question of Aurélia. She's one of my only friends—one of two, pretty much—and the only one with whom I've kept in contact since the end of Spring Break. We've exchanged a decent number of messages since then, just so I can have at least someone outside my family to talk to and stay sane. In the past few days, though, she hasn't answered any of my messages. She's also blocked me on Skype, which can't be a coincidence. The isolation is really painful, so I've looked back at my past messages with her. Look, you know my social skills aren't too sharp, but I really can't find what I did that could have offended her. Did she not believe me when I said I was working on my project and somehow figure out that I'd been suspended? Is someone on campus spreading rumors about what I did, and Aurélia heard them? I thought about it, but then I told myself I was becoming paranoid."

Jason caught his breath. "As I've said, Doctor, I still don't understand how I've done anything wrong, so the incident with Northport has been really stressful for me. What doesn't kill you makes you stronger, as long as it doesn't kill you. As I'm surviving these very difficult days, I've really changed as a person. I feel like I've aged five years in the five days since it happened. It's as if I'm past college, past graduate school, past my unsuccessful first job, and just trying to figure out whether I actually belong in this world. "

Jason stared for a second at the hundred toy cars aligned on the floor. They were probably the work of one of Orosz's younger patients, Jason thought, judging by the fact that he had been the one making those rows in the past.

"Jason, I'll be honest with you," Orosz began. "My domain is cognitive behavioral therapy. I help children whose social skills need practice, not patients who seek relief from traumatic life events, especially situations as bizarre as this one. So, just keep in mind that anything I tell you now comes from my own intuition and not from any medical training. "

"Thank you, Doctor. Right now, I honestly think I'll take any help I can get. "

"That's what I'm here for, Jason. Okay, so I think Northport's administration has acted like a bunch of—ah, how do you say someone who's very mean and takes pleasure in it?"

"A *jerk*?"

"Hmm, I don't think I've heard that word before."

"Well, it's not very Australian. I've been called a jerk at Northport more than a few times. And a creep, too, but that's different."

"Oh. Well, like I was saying, Northport's administration have really been jerks in this situation. Absurdly paranoid jerks. How they've treated you and how you've suffered directly and indirectly as a result. I mean, the fact that your girlfriend—"

"Well, she's not my girlfriend." Jason clarified.

"The fact that your *female friend* would ignore you when you were always nice to her is so ridiculous, but what's so painful is that if she really heard and believed that you were a spy, there wasn't much else she could do. Maybe Northport explicitly told her not to stay in contact with you. And you still haven't gotten seen their formal complaint with the exact accusations against you?"

"No, not yet, Doctor. I don't see why they would ever give it to me. It's almost like they're taking pleasure in this."

"Well, let's not speculate, Jason. It's not wise to make unverified assumptions."

"True, Doctor, but I don't care about their motivations. It's their actions that are the issue for me at the moment."

"How can they accuse you with no proof at all? It's almost criminal!"

Jason's blood began to boil. "Yes! It is! I need to call the law down on them! I'm innocent, and I *will* have justice!"

"How so? Will you bring them to court?"

"Of course! America is the land of lawsuits. I'll sue them for what they did to me! I'm entitled to my side. I'm entitled to a lawyer. I'm entitled to my fair—"

"And then, Jason?" Doctor Orosz interrupted. "Will you settle out of court for money?"

"That's never a bad idea, is it, Doctor? I'll become rich and use the money to fund my project!"

"What if they don't? It's not a fair situation. They have the greatest resource, Jason. Not money, though that's certainly not a bad thing to have in the case of a lawsuit, and they have plenty of that. No, power. The ability to torture you, when you're unable to do anything more than—please excuse the metaphor—tickle them and make them giggle."

"But I have proof of what they did to me, Doctor Orosz! I'll show it to the court!"

"Jason, do you realize that if you do that, the authorities will be alerted even more and your case will become public? When people search for Jason Curran on Google, the first thing they'll find is "*Curran v. Northport.*" What will a potential employer think? The only thing saving you right now is that the procedure is still internal to the university."

"But what about the FBI? The administration mentioned something about that in their letter, and Dean Washington told he she'd report her findings to the FBI as soon as she was done."

"Look, Jason, the FBI has other things to take care of. Even if they sent an investigator or two to Northport, they'll go back to tracking down Public Enemy Number One, and Northport's administration will take care of you. Sorry to break it to you, but you're not that important," he explained, chuckling.

"If they've been alerted to me, it doesn't matter if I'm not their priority. They can still catch me at any moment!"

"It really hurts me to say it, Jason, but there's nothing you can do about it. Just hope it doesn't happen. As I said, it's unlikely."

With the facts so bluntly in front of him, Jason did not need an eternity to concur with Orosz. "I'm sorry, Doctor. I'm usually far more logical than this. I just got carried away really badly, that's all."

"I don't blame you. Now, Jason, here's what I think you should do. Let it be."

"I'm sorry?"

"Let it be. Leave things as they are, because you can't change them, and you'll suffer if you try to."

"But how can I? It's so unfair! I still don't know what I did wrong, and they can throw out my four years at Northport, just like that?"

"Look, if you're innocent, and I'm sure you are, at some point they'll realize their mistake and invite you back."

"But what'll I do in the meantime? And what if they don't?"

"Let it be. Work on yourself, think about not behaving in a way that others find annoying in the future, but as for the rest, let it be."

"Well, it's easier said than done, but I guess you're right, Doctor. Thanks, then."

"Always glad to be of help, Jason. Remember, you can come back anytime if you need counseling."

"Thank you. Oh, and thanks for not mentioning any of this to my parents."

"No problem. Goodbye, now."

Jason Curran walked out of Orosz's office and left Potts Point Professional Park—a misnomer, really, for a reconverted apartment building, then returned to find the ferry back to Mosman. Orosz Sólyom was right, after all.

Jason would hope for more mercy when he next talked to Nathalie Washington, but there was really nothing he could do at all to force Northport to give him his life back. Every day, he felt more powerless to change his own destiny. Why him? Why this? Why now? Would things have happened differently if he, like Derek, had a web of friends who would have mobilized themselves to rescue him?

After half an hour or so, Jason arrived at Circular Quay, the main ferry terminal for the Sydney central business district. As he advanced on the pathway to the five wharves, he saw an Australian Aborigine with shoulder-length scruffy white hair and red markings on his dark skin clapping two painted boomerangs together for percussion as his less conspicuous assistant blew into a brown didgeridoo, a noisy woodwind instrument from the Australian desert. While the yellow circle and red and black stripes of the Aboriginal Flag on their headbands suggested that they organized a zealous political demonstration, Jason had passed by them enough times to know that they merely ran a business of taking pictures with visitors playing their instruments.

As he stared at the musicians, Jason clumsily tripped on a didgeridoo and began rolling to the ground, thankfully minimizing the pain as he fell by employing a technique from his martial arts training.

"*Čêpêč!*" he shouted.

In order to not appear rude, Jason generally avoided cursing, but experience had taught him that sometimes the urge was irresistible. For situations like these, he had lately added a repertory of expletives such as *"čêpêč"*, *"ğön,"* and *"kàmiŷà"* to the Nå-Ïtïčïht language he had begun creating as a child.

Even when he used it to vulgarly express his discontent, Jason kept a particular fondness in his heart for his imaginary language and culture. He was especially proud to have recently found space on the map for his nation in the frigid steppes of Russia and Mongolia. In his room, he still kept colored pencil sketches of the massive domes stretching across the skyline of Nå-Ïtïčïht's capital city, Dnålkčïrb, a testament to the creative folly of his youth, a time when he could build upon an idea without having to wait for years and arrive nowhere.

Jason really wished that new project could be exactly like Dnålkčïrb. When he designed Nå-Ïtïčïht, at least, he had to rely on no one but himself. No one would ever judge him for what he created.

Oh, of course. He had forgotten that. According to Nathalie Washington, drawing maps of Nå-Ïtïčïht was grounds for a crime. Right...

12. CANDLE IN THE WIND

FRIDAY, APRIL 5, 2013

TARONGA ZOO, SYDNEY

Jason Curran walked through the copper-domed archway into Taronga Zoo. Normally, he regretted having to come by bus from Mosman rather than being able to ride the cable car catering to those who arrived from the other bays, but today he appreciated the lack of distractions in the monotonous bus ride. He had watched a podcast of *The Linda Weinstein Show*, a San Francisco-based political commentary television program he had discovered in his freshman year "POL 201: Introduction to American Politics" class.

For Jason, the real benefit of learning about terrorist insurgency on the Afghanistan-Pakistan border and Libya's struggle to form a functional government was not connecting him with the outside world, a goal he already accomplished unconsciously. Learning about the horrid disasters across the world allowed him to focus on something else than the mess inside his head.

By coming to Taronga Zoo, Jason was hoping to forget the fact that his status at Northport and in life was still uncertain and instead focus on the tremendous diversity of local fauna. Soot-colored koalas cuddled trees as they slept, and protective kangaroo mothers with baby joeys in their pockets hopped across the woodchips, relieving those ill-informed tourists who were disappointed after not seeing any kangaroos roaming the streets of Sydney. Slurping giraffes and spotted zebras that would have fit better in the Serengeti plains of Kenya and Tanzania focused on the zookeeper feeding them carrots rather than on the skyline panorama, the reason the zoo had been named for an Aboriginal word meaning "beautiful view."

While every animal in the zoo had a story to tell, Jason had come to Taronga for one in particular. He entered the somber enclosure whose most famous animal, the platypus, swam in the murky water behind a blurry panel of glass. Jason still could not intellectualize why as a child, he had acquired such a fascination for the furry, duck-billed critter. Perhaps it was just the originality of an egg-laying mammal.

Suddenly, Jason's cellphone buzzed, pulling his eyes off the glass case enclosing the waddling platypus. Jason quickly read the sender's name in order to gauge the urgency of his response, and oh, was he ready to reply to this one. After his agonizing three-day wait, Nathalie Washington had returned. With a response from her finally bursting from his screen, Jason laughed at the irony that he was nearly overjoyed to have received an email from the enforcer of Northport's disciplinary procedures.

"Dear Jason," the email read, *"Unfortunately, the investigation is taking longer than we expected, so we have not yet been able to accurately assess the validity of the allegations against you in light of the surprise that you expressed during our conversation on*

the telephone. As a result, we believe that you are not ready to be readmitted to Northport at this moment."

This time, Jason did not reread her email. If he planned to receive an answer within the next week, he was probably best off replying right away, while Dean Washington might still be near her computer. Night had long ago fallen on New York, so Jason did not have much time before she presumably went to sleep.

"Dear Dean Washington," he wrote, *"I am glad to finally hear some news from Northport's administration. With regards to your last comment, I can promise that I was utterly surprised by every element of the accusation of international espionage, which seems so absurd and misguided, even if I do not dispute any of the actual facts. As a result, I respectfully request to view the word-for-word complaint from all the plaintiffs in order to comprehend the connection between my actions and the allegations. I hope that you can then transmit a message to at least Lars and Melissa Børgensen, Cayley Thompson, and the others involved, since they will most likely not respond to me personally, explaining my understanding of the situation."*

Before Jason could once again concentrate on the platypus's pudgy hooves, he heard another buzz from his cellphone and checked the reply.

"Under the Northport system, the administration may not recontact any of the plaintiffs in the case of a complaint, since receiving a message from a person in a position of authority would likely intimidate them into mitigating or outright removing their allegations. In addition, in this case, you may not view the original complaint or know the exact string of evidence we have accumulated against you."

Before replying, Jason opened Northport's website, quickly turning his eyes away from the prominent banner image of the iconic Memorial Chapel among the fall foliage, then scrolled down to the *"Administrative Guide"* page. It seemed that Nathalie Washington did not know the Northport system as well as the omniscient Internet.

"Dear Dean Washington, under Section II.B.iii.d.(2) of Northport's Administrative Guide, I am entitled to view the allegations brought forth against me. Thank you. Sincerely, Jason," he typed.

Jason stared back at the platypus, intermittently checking his phone for a new reply, but after ten minutes or so, he concluded that in the time it had taken him to find the exact policy, Nathalie Washington had finally gone to sleep. As he left the concrete-walled enclosure, he noticed a dark blue candle placed on a wooden table to its side, probably an Easter decoration that the platypus caretaker kept lighting a few days later for its aesthetic value. The flame burned brightly in until a gust of wind from the breeze abruptly cut it out.

Jason Curran fixed his eyes on the blue stick of paraffin wax for a few seconds. He was not the most empathetic of individuals, but he could feel the pain of others when he saw himself in them. Like him, the candle in front of him had, while in its prime, lost everything in a split second. After receiving a single email six days ago, he was no longer the heir to a bright future. His flame had vanished. He was merely a candle in the wind.

✦✦✦

SATURDAY, APRIL 6, 2013

CURRAN RESIDENCE, SYDNEY

For once, Jason Curran was glad not to have a room with a view. When he traveled with his family, he was always ecstatic if his hotel room window opened on a gorgeous view. At home in Sydney, however, that was not the case, even though Jason admitted, pride aside, that his hometown was the most beautiful city in the world. The reason here was that tall eucalyptus trees blocked the second-floor vantage point on the other side of Prince Street. The Currans could not afford a house with a view on serene Sydney Harbour in a city whose cost of living exceeded that of Luxembourg.

As he rose from bed, Jason took a quick look out the window, checking the weather. It was usually warm and sunny during the fall in Sydney, though he could actually see some raindrops sticking to the window today. Well, there went his plans for a long jog from Mosman all the way to Bondi Beach. Instead of running shorts, Jason picked a pair of dark blue jeans and finally placed a sky blue t-shirt he had bought at Canada's Banff National Park on top.

Jason went downstairs and logged into his email. His cellphone was at it again, refusing to download any messages even when it claimed to have perfect reception, so he had to rely on his laptop instead. If he knew his cellphone well, it would come back to its senses and display the messages at some random point later in the day.

Well, for once, Nathalie Washington's response time was definitely not exaggerated. She had already replied to his query from the previous afternoon on whether Northport's policies allowed him to contact President DiTancini directly.

"Since you have been suspended from Northport, you no longer have the same rights and privileges as a current student."

As he read the message, Jason could not say he was surprised. He had not exactly come to expect much more compassion from her or Northport's dogmatic and byzantine procedures. Well, he was out of options for the moment. Instead, he logged out of his email, grabbed his phone, and walked over to the living room to check on his sister. Sometime in the next half hour, she would be leaving for her Cuban dance class, unless Jason was mixing up the days.

"Chloë," he greeted her, "I have lots of time today, so I'll take you up on your offer of filming a war between your stuffed animals and putting it on YouTube."

"Ooooh! Do you think the dinosaurs should attack the pigs, or the other way around?"

"Actually, I was thinking it would be funnier if the dolphins fought against everyone else."

"You're such a troll! But I like it. Do you want to set it up before I leave for my dance class? I've already had breakfast."

"Well, I'm going to wash my hands first. We can start when I come back."

"Swell."

Jason placed his phone on the table and left for the kitchen sink as Elektra Curran arrived to keep Chloë company. "Do you want yo leave for your class earlier today, since you're ready?"

"No, Mami, not yet," Chloë replied. "Jason and I want to film a war between my plush toys!"

"Aren't you *both* a little too old for that? I mean…okay, go ahead. But then we need to go."

"Well, Mami, Jason's washing his hands, so as soon as he comes back, we'll start the war."

About a minute later, Jason's cellphone buzzed in the same sound that her mother's made when she received an email message. Chloë could still hear the gushing sound of a waterfall in her kitchen. She probably had at least another minute to take a peek. Jason had never mentioned having romantic feelings for any girls to his family, but Chloë often lightheartedly annoyed him by checking his messages in front of him to see if he was hiding anything.

At last, Jason passed through the living room entrance, wiping his over-sanitized hands on his light blue shirt. "Hey, Jason!" his sister asked him playfully. "Who's Nathalie Washington, your secret girlfriend?"

Jason's heart nearly burst out of his chest. "Nooooo!" he screamed, horrified as he saw Chloë holding his phone, which had decided to download the email at the worst moment imaginable.

"What—oh," Chloë's mother asked in a very puzzled tone, then stared down at the email and read the first line to Chloë.

"Since you have been suspended from Northport..."

"Jason, what have you done?" she yelled.

Rather than responding, Jason dove towards the table, yanked his cellphone away from his mother's grasp, and dashed up the stairs to his room. He grabbed the navy blue backpack he had used at Northport, reached for the folded clothes on his bed, and stuffed all that could fit into his backpack. He could not face his family's utter disappointment, so fleeing was his only viable option.

Jason would spend the money he had saved on this; he had no other use for it anymore. He had yet to decide what to do after catching the bus to Sydney Airport. He wanted to go somewhere far, that was for sure, but where? Madagascar, with its white sand beaches? No, he would quickly become a lazy bum—exactly what he had *not* wanted to do after being suspended from Northport. Norway, with the sun that never set north of the Arctic Circle? No, by the time he could find the necessary extreme-weather gear, his parents would already have quarantined him inside the house. He would figure all of that out later.

Jason Curran bolted down the stairs towards the front door. In his current state, pulling the handle felt like trying to pry open a locked bank coffer. Finally, he took one last look at his living room. Chloë rose from the couch, but her mother pushed her legs back down into a sitting position and helplessly said, "It's no use."

"I'm sorry," he told them, the gaze of his almost teary eyes dropping to the wooden floor. Before closing the door behind him, he briefly fixated his eyes on a small object lying on the table next to them. Suddenly, he knew exactly where he was going.

What he would be doing there was another question.

PART III

13. THE SOUND OF SILENCE

SATURDAY, APRIL 6, 2013

LAS CONDES, SANTIAGO

Jason Curran stared out of his hotel room as the polluted sky of day turned to pink. The towers of Chile's capital nestled between the Andes made for a stunning view, and until being seated in the bus from the airport to the center of Santiago, Jason had not been sure that he would ever see it. It had not been until the prying Australian Customs and Border Protection agent had begun asking Jason about the purpose of his visit to Chile that Jason had wondered if the international authorities knew anything about him.

During the interminable and insomniac transpacific flight, those fears had really stung. When Northport's administration had mentioned contacting the federal authorities, had they been bluffing? Would Jason go from being trapped in his loving family home to being trapped in an interrogation facility? Even if he made it past the gauntlets at Sydney and Santiago, would he ever be completely safe? Yes, Doctor Orosz had said that the FBI would not waste their time on him, but a one-paragraph file on someone's suspicious behavior was bound to have an indelible digital record and might be enough to have him arrested. Jason had escaped from home so impulsively, not asking himself those questions before he bought his flight ticket, that he counted himself lucky not to have gotten into more trouble. In the future, if there ever was a future, he would need to think through these things before doing them.

Normally, when he had any amount of time in a foreign city, Jason would use the occasion to surmount his fatigue and snap a few hundred photographs of the city's architecture, museums, and local dishes. However, today he was in no mood for sightseeing. He felt a singular urge to rest after such a restless day. Before he could finally turn his exasperated shell over to sleep, though, he had a few tasks to complete.

Jason searched for the hotel's wireless internet network. He had resolved not to contact his parents or even his loving little sister, being too afraid of how they would react. However, he had one last person to write to: Dean Washington. He had never replied to her last absurd statement that having been suspended, he apparently no longer held any rights under the Northport system. He looked back at the fading colors of the skyline for a second, then pulled his eyes down to stare at his cellphone again. Could he just pretend everything was fine, wait for the next step on the administration's part, and let it be, as Doctor Orosz had suggested? No, he had to do this.

"Dear Dean Washington, I will not be able to be reached in the near future. Do not recontact me until you have readmitted me to Northport, apologized for the university's rash conduct, restored my tarnished reputation, and made up somehow for my agony. Sincerely, Jason Curran", he wrote. He thought of adding something else, but then sent the message. It was fine, after all, since she would probably not regret his disappearance from her life. Besides, there was not much else he could actually do. Whether he liked it or not, whether he understood it or not, in two months graduation would go on without him.

Before finally calling it a day, Jason pulled his cellphone out, opened his Internet browser, and checked in for his flight the next day. His impulsive escape from Sydney was draining the money he had painstakingly saved all these years from his translation work for a Chinese software company to launch his project, but it was not like he intended to burn much money anymore. Where he was going, he would not be worrying about any of that.

Jason took a last look at the Santiago sunset before closing the curtains at last. Normally, he would have appreciated the addition of an instrumental opera piece to the ambience, but just this once, he enjoyed—well, not enjoyed, but appreciated in context—the background noise as it was. This was the sound of silence.

✈✈✈

ROUTE 89, GLENDALE

It was a sleepy night in Glendale, Utah, but then again Joe McSmithson could not recall the last time anything had happened here since the Great Depression his grandfather had told him about more than enough times. Old tires sat on piles of hay to the side of the road, and cracking power lines crushed abandoned trailers. No new buildings had been erected in Joe's own lifetime, as far as he could remember. Not that he would generally care, but with only four hundred people living in Glendale, one of the largest cities in the area, whenever something actually happened he would be aware of it.

The last tourists had left Bryce Canyon National Park after catching a final glimpse of the sunset, and Joe did not doubt that they had failed to notice the sleepy small town of Glendale on their way to nearby Zion. Every now and then, a vagabond with a funny accent would park near the garage he owned and offer to buy one of the auto carcasses rotting in the nearby grass for a very hefty price. He had no idea why anyone would want one of those, but there were many things he did not understand about today's world.

Parking his derelict pickup truck, Joe walked back into the trailer home he, his wife Jane, and their son Bob had been forced to move into when they had finally given up on trying to pay the mortgage on their old house. He grabbed a beer can from the six-pack—now a five-pack, so he made a mental note to go back to the store soon—lying on his dusty kitchen counter. He looked for the remote buried in the old sofa and turned on the television he had bought thanks to the windfall from a traveler from one of those big, fancy cities on the coast who had purchased a decrepit Ford Forty-Nine. He did regret having to drive his own pickup truck two hundred miles to find a store selling televisions, especially since it was only the second time in his life he had left Kane County. It was daunting world out there. Hopefully, his favorite television show would help him make more sense of it.

A flow of stars and stripes covered Joe's cracked television screen. "Now, live from Atlanta, Georgia, this is Luke Gregor!" A middle-aged man with a chubby face and graying brown hair removed his fiery eyes from the script he held in his hands to stare at the screen instead.

"Good evening, people of America! You're listening to *The Dolphin Conspiracy Show*! Tonight, I have new evidence for you that the dolphins are poisoning our minds in their plan for world domination!" Joe stared at the screen, rapt with attention towards the apparent genius he had begun following—no, worshipping—since the day he had bought his television.

Luke Gregor pointed at what looked like a child's doodle of a dolphin, but edited with the insertion of bloodshot red eyes and an angry-looking squiggle for its mouth. "As a nation, we're still bitter about losing the Iraq War, which we know was sabotaged by the federal government. However, the government was as manipulated as we were, citizens of America—manipulated by dolphins! Look at this picture," Gregor said, showing an image of a dolphin with a sensor probe attached to one of its fins jumping out of the water in front of a U.S. soldier. "The U.S. Army used *military dolphins* in Iraq, and look what happened!"

It did not matter to Luke Gregor that the dolphins had been used by the U.S. Military during the First Gulf War, a lightning-fast American victory. His audience did not exactly consist of historical experts. "I tell you, people of America! The war effort was sabotaged by dolphins! They are responsible for Korea and Vietnam as well!"

Luke pulled out a map of the Florida coast. "Global warming is a myth!" he continued. "Rising sea levels are not the result of our factories and cars, as those so-called elite scientists say; they are the result of the dolphins' conspiracy for world domination! Look at Miami! Sea levels are rising and will wipe out the entire city soon! The dolphins have started by taking over the city's most famous football team—the Miami Dolphins—and soon they'll conquer the entire city, and the country, and the world!"

Long ago, Luke would have found it almost impossible not to crack up at his own wild conspiracy theory, but the more he propagated it to a captive audience every night, the more he became convinced that it might be correct. As a child, he had enjoyed vacationing in Florida with his parents and had taken particular pleasure in watching dolphin shows—until he became old enough to realize how much money the show's coordinators were able to snatch from visiting families and wonder whether he could not find a grand moneymaking scheme involving dolphins. Thus *The Dolphin Conspiracy Show* had been born. Now, however, he avoided traveling to Florida at all costs, out of fear that the dolphins who had taken over the state might capture and torture him.

"Also, look at this country called Greece. The world financial crisis began in Greece, not here in America as the dolphin propaganda agents want you to believe. The country has been ruined by corporate failures and political turmoil, and why? Well, look at their ancient art—it has dolphins *everywhere*!"

Joe McSmithson had not felt such an epiphany since that one time he had heard an Evangelical sermon. Of course! He had known that the financial crisis that had sent his wife to the unemployment office and himself to the liquor store more often than ever had to be the work of conspirators, and now he finally knew who was behind it. Oh, those dolphins. All the pieces of the puzzle finally fit together.

"But the worst, my fellow American citizens, is not this." Luke Gregor held up a laptop-sized photo of Russia's leader being kissed on both cheeks by dolphins. "Do you see this? The Russian leader is captive to the dolphins!" He beat his hands on his chest like a gorilla in a kids' cartoon. "I used to think Russia was our main enemy, then I thought it was the terrorists, and then I thought it was the federal government. However, now I know that they're all pawns of the dolphins! The dolphins have infiltrated all the world's governments! We have all the proof!"

Now, Luke thought, it was time for the showstopper—the ultimate moneymaker. He waved his finger in between his captive audience and the photo, then bellowed, "Do you see this, people of America? It's a conspiracy! Tyranny, terrorism, taxes, healthcare, gays— they're all the work of the evil dolphins! The dolphins are trying to disappear us into underwater forced labor camps and imprison us in coral reefs! They must be stopped! We will have justice, people of America!"

"Now," Gregor continued in an only slightly less psychotic voice, "many of you here'll just try to lock your doors or run away, just as you have done when the government's tax collectors threatened you with force in the past. However, those of you who are truly concerned citizens help me build a militia to defend us patriotic, righteous Americans from the dolphin menace and continue to make the truth of the dolphins' conspiracy known to all of America."

Joe reached into his cupboard, where he and his wife kept some savings from the previous year's auto repairs. They had originally intended on using it for their son to attend community college if he graduated high school, but now he would be mailing a check to Luke Gregor as early as possible. "Good night, good citizens of America," Gregor concluded. "I pray that no dolphins will threaten you tonight."

Joe McSmithson switched off his television. He had never seen any dolphins in Utah, but if any ever came knocking at his door, they would be talking to his shotgun first.

✈✈✈

NATHALIE WASHINGTON'S HOUSE, ASHAROKEN

Nathalie Washington had tried to go to sleep, so far without success. She would have thought that something as tiring as dealing with Jason Curran would provide her with the necessary exhaustion to collapse in bed when she wanted to, but sleep was a funny and sadistic thing. She just needed to keep herself occupied in the meantime.

Nathalie looked at the unfinished thousand-piece puzzle of Saint Lucia's volcanic Pitons on the wooden table next to her bed. She pondered trying to fit together the remaining pieces, but she was too exasperated from her busy day. She instead reached for her television remote, turned on the screen, and scrolled down to the most recently recorded program: *The Linda Weinstein Show*. With the screen on, she could mentally get away from the whole affair with Jason—with the FBI's decision to delegate the case to Northport's administration, the chance that it would somehow appear on national television was close to nonexistent. It was a good thing that he had not been raised in the United States, with its pervasive legalist culture. A lawsuit by the Currans would only bring more unnecessary exhaustion for her and unwanted publicity for Northport.

The screen showed an intellectual-looking woman with twilight falling on San Francisco's Golden Gate Bridge in the backdrop. "Welcome," Linda Weinstein began, "To *The Linda Weinstein Show*, restoring sanity to America. As the nation dives deeper into debt, investors and analysts fear the possibility of a federal government shutdown and default later in the year if Congress cannot get its act together. Congressional approval ratings are diving even deeper, especially with their inability to pass stricter gun control laws in response to continued massacres since Newtown. Sometimes, I wonder what's happening to this country."

Linda Weinstein frowned for a second. "Now, for tonight's special, I will be showing you just how far we have fallen." The photo of a middle-aged man clenching his teeth in an almost reptilian face now occupied about a third of the screen. "Luke Gregor has a neat little theory on how the world's governments and corporations are being manipulated behind the scenes by—hear this, now—*dolphins*."

Nathalie could not repress a chuckle as Linda Weinstein showed clips of this conspiracy theorist ranting wildly on how dolphins were somehow behind the outcome of the Iraq War, the financial crisis, and some even wilder theory about Russia's president. On the other hand, some of her beliefs—wait, Linda Weinstein was about to finish her exact thought for her.

"Now, I can't stop laughing, but how am I supposed to believe that humans are good, intelligent people when I see all these demagogues who feed on bigotry," Linda said, barely catching her breath as she became almost as animated and angry as Luke Gregor himself, "when I see millions of poor saps out there who actually gave their life savings to fuel these demagogues' war machines of idiocy?"

Rehydrating after her impassioned rant, Linda sipped her cappuccino, then resumed in a calmer tone of voice. "Now, in other news—and particularly heartwarming for me and my partner, I must add—the State of California has just passed a law that would make it significantly easier for gay and lesb—"

Nathalie Washington looked over at her watch. Eleven already! She switched off the television, still laughing out loud at the dolphin conspiracy theory. Luke Gregor might be a deranged man, but he certainly had his value as a humorist. She wished she could have shown this to her husband, had he not left her after twenty years of marriage for a thirty-something woman. How absurd and sad it was that some people found it reasonable to take completely random and unrelated facts, arbitrarily spin them into a wild conspiracy theory, and call it analysis. The most ironic part, however, was that all the individual pieces of the puzzle were indisputably true. Only the final conclusion was paranoid.

Before reattempting to sleep, Nathalie rose slightly to pick up her cellphone. She combed through emails from the usual suspects: Northport's President, Provost, Dean of Admissions, Head of Disability Services, and General Counsel, as well as her sons and Jason Curran...*Jason Curran...*

Nathalie's head fell on her pillow, and she froze as if she had just been stabbed in her own bed. What if she had treated Jason like Luke Gregor had done with the dolphins, just assuming the worst without any concrete proof? What if she had helped President DiTancini, like Luke Gregor, invent malicious motivations as part of the subject in question's so-called grand plan, when all the factual pieces of the puzzle were completely unrelated? What if Jason had done nothing but live a nonconformist and lonely life? Had she been as gullible as those who believed the dolphin conspiracy theory?

No, she would certainly not be getting any sleep tonight.

14. SOMEWHERE

SUNDAY, APRIL 7, 2013

KAIRAKU INN, HANGA ROA

Tahaine Kapuo sat at her desk, watching the same view she had seen every day since she started her work here as an innkeeper. It was said that those who spent every hour of the day looking at the same image would soon come to passionately love or hate it, but Tahaine firmly considered herself to be the exception to that rule. She had never left Rapa Nui, and the prices she charged for rooms in her inn would not enable her to anytime soon, so she had learned over the years to just accept the view as something that would never change.

There were things to like about the vista, she had to admit. The grass in between the inn's lobby and the rooms was littered with mango trees and hibiscus flowers, and on it lay a slab of rock supporting five small wooden replicas of her lifeblood—moai, the statues that brought international tourists to Rapa Nui, or Easter Island as they called it. In less than a hundred square miles, Rapa Nui held nearly a thousand moai, not all of them erect. If one counted all the replicas, from the wood carvings being made in locals' backyards to the plush toys sold in souvenir shops, that figure was sure to increase. As long as there were still moai on Rapa Nui, there would be tourists, the Kairaku Inn would still stand in the provincial capital of Hanga Roa, and she would be able to feed herself and her seven sisters.

Sure, some moai had left Rapa Nui. Many islanders still talked with remorse of Hoa Hakananai'a, the Master Wave-Breaker and stolen friend, who since 1869 lived in London's British Museum, and there were a few others isolated in museums around the world. However, even putting aside the political impossibility of stealing a national treasure from a country in the twenty-first as opposed to the nineteenth century, the cost of uprooting a moai from the ground and transporting it on the two-thousand-mile-long journey to the South American mainland was far too extreme. For the visible future, it seemed that all the moai would stay, and life would go on as it always had.

Or so she had thought. In recent years, political extremists on Rapa Nui had pushed for complete independence from the Chile, which they claimed had, since annexing Rapa Nui in 1888, repeatedly attempted to repress the island's native Polynesian culture. A part of Tahaine could not do anything but agree with the radical demands of the Rapa Nui Parliament. She was a proud Polynesian, and she did feel uncomfortable that the continentals, or Chilean mainlanders, now outnumbered the Polynesians on Rapa Nui. She had not and certainly would never empathize with the diseases and slave raids brought by the Europeans who had claimed Rapa Nui as their own Easter Island.

However, she understood very well that for all its exploitation of *"La Isla de Pascua,"* as they called Rapa Nui, the national government in Santiago brought cash, infrastructure, and most importantly, tourists to her exiguous island. With no human life at all between here and an island a thousand miles away with less than fifty inhabitants, there were not countless other places on which Rapa Nui could rely, Tahaine thought. Articles discussing the often-violent independence movement in *The New York Times* had scared off many tourists, who now chose safer end-of-the-world locales such as the Maldives for their exotic vacations, and the outside world's most precious resource was shrinking day by day.

Then there was her husband. An Australian cameraman, Bill Morris had been very eager for an exotic escapade after a difficult divorce. He had come to Rapa Nui to shoot scenes in front of moai for the globally renowned, and decried, film *Rapa Nui* in 1994. He had expected to return to his native Adelaide by the time of the film's release, but then he had fallen in love with the mysticism surrounding the origins of the moai—and with her.

Viewing himself as a man without a past, Bill had opened the Kairaku Inn with her to cater to all the tourists drawn to the intriguing island by the film. However, over the years he had grown tired with the moai and frustrated with the island's extreme remoteness. Last year, he had finally left her and moved back to Adelaide, claiming that he needed to escape before Rapa Nui's isolation drove him completely insane.

Well, Tahaine could not afford to speculate or mourn. A customer was coming towards her desk, and with tourist numbers dwindling, she would not pass up on the occasion. "*Iorana!*" she called out to the dapper tourist. "Welcome to Easter Island!"

The man pulled the straps on his backpack, the only item he had brought with him. "Thank you."

"How many nights are you staying, sir?" Tahaine asked him.

"None."

Tahaine looked puzzled. "Are you coming her for lunch then? Our restaurant is to the left. If you're interested, our daily special is—"

"Actually, no," he cut her off curtly. "I just need to leave my bag here. I'm going on an adventure. I don't know how long I'll be gone. It could be until tomorrow, or it could be forever."

Nearly two decades in the tourist industry had taught Tahaine that unless a visitor seemed to be a clear and present danger to her safety, she should not ask questions. "Very well, sir," she replied. "There's a locker in the cabin to my right," she told him as she passed a small wooden key attached to the same ring a small coconut-wood dolphin. "It'll be five thousand pesos."

"I only have Australian dollars on me at the moment, is that fine?" he asked before catching himself. "Or, I can just find a nearby bank—"

"No, I have quite a large collection of Australian dollars," she replied, recalling all the money Bill had brought along with him. "That'll be ten."

"Great."

"I didn't get your name, sir," Tahaine added. "Could I please add it to the inn's list of customers?"

"Jason," he said as he left for the cabin with the locker.

"Last name?"

"Doesn't matter," he replied, a tone of sadness evident in his voice. "I feel like I don't have a family anymore."

"Oh. Sorry, sir." Those who ventured to Rapa Nui were often unconventional types, but she had no time to wonder. She had a business to run.

✈✈✈

MONDAY, APRIL 8, 2013

CURRAN RESIDENCE, SYDNEY

Chloë Curran had not been able to do any of her algebra homework this week. Her parents generally insisted that when she missed school, she catch up as quickly as possible, but given the circumstances, they had not had the energy to enforce that rule. Instead of lying on the couch by the television, her spot for working—with surprising accuracy, despite the distractions—she had retreated to her bedroom.

She had probably cried enough tears to wet all of her mother's passion fruit plants many times over. Everything had changed when her brother had left impulsively and without any clue as to his destination sometime earlier. She thought it had been two days ago, but since she had taken sick days from school and had been too distraught with nightmares to sleep since, her count of days was sure to be off.

The worst, Chloë thought, was the slight feeling that she might be responsible for what had happened to Jason. Why did she have to pick up that cellphone when it buzzed? If she had just left it there and not made it a recurring point to see if he had a secret girlfriend, maybe he would have been able to be readmitted to Northport, no one would have known what had happened, and everything would be all right.

Chloë buried herself in a mound of plush toys. At first, she felt very calm as she stroked her purple lamb and spun her sock monkey by the arms. She then reached for a pink-cheeked frog, Zunini, stared at it, and burst into tears on her covers. Jason had bought her Zunini four years ago, when he had spent the summer in Okinawa for a Japanese language immersion program. Ever since then, she had dreamed of going to Japan, the land of cuteness, as she called it. She was sure that it would make Jason proud. Oh, Jason, Jason! Anywhere she went, she only thought of him. She kissed Zunini on the cheeks, then grabbed a princess doll and started weeping on it. It did not matter; she had never liked it too much anyway.

"Chloë!" her mother called out. "Time for breakfast!"

This time, Chloë made a real effort to hold back her tears. "Yes, Mami. I'm coming." She walked down the stairs as slowly as her grandfather Dionysos would. She did not want to break her leg—the last thing her parents wanted would be to have to deal with that in addition to the rest.

"What are we having this morning, Mami?"

"I don't know, Chloë," she replied in an exhausted voice. "I just put something together. I haven't been able to eat anything for the past couple days." She subsequently burst into a tidal wave of tears, and Chloë hugged her like a stuffed animal.

Chloë's father then limped across the dining room to take his seat. His mouth was still shut tight, as it had been since Jason's sudden flight. When she saw him closed off like this, Chloë could not help but recall the worst, when her grandmother had passed away two years before. As she had heard the story, her father had been at his mother's deathbed, and Jason had skipped his midyear exams to attend her funeral in Brisbane. Chloë was just old enough to realize that Jason did not show much care for his family members' feelings in everyday situations but took death more seriously than anyone else. As for her father, he had come back barely speaking to anyone at all or going to work for two weeks. Before that, she had not known that doctors could be sick.

Chloë could catch him staring at the chair at the head of the table. As far back as she could remember, Jason had felt better when he sat there. Her brother had always shown interest in the weirdest little details.

Finally, though, her father broke his own silence. "He's a good boy," he told his wife and daughter, holding back the tears that were clearly trying to force their way out of his eyes. "Let's just hope he didn't do anything stupid. He's somewhere, and I hope we'll hear from him sometime soon."

Her father threw his body from his chair, gliding over the table to grab her in his arms. And then, for the first time since—well, since the beginning of her life, because she had not been there when her grandmother died, Chloë thought—he wept. Her mother cried almost every day, often for the most ridiculous things, like for a character on a televised comedy. She even cried of joy when she was happy about a Greek athlete winning an international sports competition. But to see her father crying was even worse, because he had forty-something years of unused tears behind those sad green eyes.

No, it wasn't fair for an eleven-year-old girl to go through this. Everyone, from her parents to her teachers to her pediatrician, had told her that she was soon going to go through a period of very quick change in life. Perhaps that was what they had meant. She just hoped that they had been making it up to scare her.

15. SACRIFICE

SUNDAY, APRIL 7, 2013

AHU TONGARIKI, EASTER ISLAND

The trek had led the fifteen tourists through an expanse of grassy cliffs. An hour after leaving the provincial capital of Hanga Roa in their bus, the visitors had finally arrived at their destination. Before hopping on the sunset tour of Easter Island's south side, Jason Curran had stopped at a Fijian restaurant in Hanga Roa and then deposited all of his belongings except for the clothes on his body and his worst memories at a backpackers' inn.

Though he had wanted to separate himself from everything and everyone as much as was humanly possible, Jason had finally resolved to write to his parents and sister. Using an old coding trick to mask his IP address, he had sent a message from an Internet café in Hanga Roa reassuring them that he was fine and would contact them again sometime in the next month, even telling Chloë to say hello to her plush frog Zunini in order to prove that the message truly came from him.

Knowing his affectionate yet overprotective parents, they would probably trigger an international police investigation if he stayed invisible for more than two days. When they received the message, however, they were likely to trust him and leave him in peace.

The sun was about to set on Easter Island. The final stop, the ceremonial platform of Ahu Tongariki on the island's southeastern shore, was an ethereal sight, with the sky painted orange and pink. A row of fifteen moai, Easter Island's fabled stone giants, stood on the plate of rock. Their backs, carved with drawings of birds, faced the rough waves of the Pacific Ocean, while the gray crevasses where their white coral and red scoria stone eyes had once stood still kept a watchful gaze over their domain.

Jason had wanted to lay eyes on this for so long. As a child, he had been fascinated by the mystery of Easter Island, but his family had never had the opportunity to visit the remote Polynesian destination. While fleeing Sydney, Jason had quickly settled on coming to Easter Island to find himself…and lose himself.

Unfortunately, he could not remain at the ahu for long. Mustering up the courage to utter a complete lie, he told the tour operator, "I'm actually going to head out now, since I'm meeting a friend from another tour nearby. Goodbye!" It did not matter much what excuse he found; the guide would not focus just on one nondescript tourist rather than on the fourteen others shooting twenty identical pictures of the same moai from the same angle.

Jason walked through the seemingly endless grass under the celeste, then orange, then cerulean sky. Night had not fully enveloped the island yet, so he could still make out the burnt brown color of ground on his path. Horses ran on the distant meadows, but this portion of the island was, for the moment, devoid of any visible sentient life.

Soon, he reached the top of a small hill and rooted his hands on the earth immediately when he noticed the opening. This was probably one of the numerous caves Wikitravel had mentioned.

A seeming lifetime ago, Cayley Thompson had told him to go back to his cave. Now, that was exactly what Jason intended to do.

He slowly descended on the slope, then noticed a small pool of water and some bananas, taro, and plants he could not recognize growing in the area exposed to the sunlight during the day. He paced through the total darkness, using his sense of touch to guide him. Finally, he stumbled on a rock and caught himself by pressing both hands on the walls. He had discovered a tunnel.

Jason Curran stood still for a second and took one last look at the bright stars overhead, then walked through the passageway into the gates of hell.

✦✦✦

MONDAY, APRIL 8, 2013

RAPA NUI NATIONAL PARK, EASTER ISLAND

Jason Curran squatted on the rocky floor and drew out an oblong green taro leaf he had detached from its stem, then pulled a familiar banana from nearby and began gnawing on it instead. That might be a safer move for someone with no botanical experience whatsoever. Well, at least he could retain his vegan diet in here, Jason thought. Besides, it was not like he would survive very long in the hunting business, and discovering all the new plants would offer him a welcome pastime while in the belly of Easter Island.

Earlier in the day—or the day before, if it was already past midnight—Jason had promised to his parents and Chloë that he would write to them in the next month. Despite his general tendency towards honesty, he was not sure he could keep this vow. He had settled in a cave deep inside Rapa Nui National Park with nothing but the clothes on his back. He had sacrificed everything and everyone he knew to reflect on the meaning of his life, not his cellphone. Until he found what he had come for, he would not return to civilization.

Yet, understanding how to live his life was certainly not a lesson that would take three months to learn. Most would consider the reduction of their lives to pacing around a cave an unfathomable punishment, but Jason viewed it as the greatest reward possible. A few hours away from all distractions had led him to learn the truth. The reason for every single one of his problems in life: the ostracizing by his popular elementary school classmates, his inability to advance his project, his disastrous suspension from Northport, was evident.

Jason slapped himself across the cheek. He had been an ignorant fool for taking so long to realize it. All his life, he had suffered whenever he forced himself to interact with others.

The plague had begun spreading early. In kindergarten, he made the unfortunate mistake of volunteering for show-and-tell, an American export in which students brought objects of sentimental value from home and presented them to their peers. While most gleefully displayed their plush echidna toys or jumbo crayons, Jason brought in an electronic abacus and demonstrated its ability to perform calculations in front of a half-asleep classroom. As he was about to leave school that day, his teacher had held him back and scolded his helpless self for his bizarre choice, warning him never to redo anything so inappropriate.

While in middle and high school, Jason's lack of invitations to any exclusive social events had made him hate them, yet he had never been able to shake off a fascination for the occasionally glamorous and usually not-so-glamorous parties, leading him to experiment with one during his first quarter at Northport. At least that mistake and his brief foray into Facebook had taught him a valuable lesson: attempting to conform to the hidden social curriculum was a recipe for disaster and he should back off immediately, lest he not finish the year with stellar grades.

Jason had instead attempted to integrate himself into the intangible social network of specialized online forums. At first, he had enjoyed sharing his many ethical frustrations with fellow vegans and responding to in-depth analyses of Jacen Solo's controversial character development in the *Star Wars* Expanded Universe novels. Joining discussions of Kuwait Airways's economic outlook for the future on airline forums offered him a welcome break of fun from his project research and classwork.

However, once he began to assert the future dominance of Boeing's 777-9X project against a crowd that predominantly supported the Boeing 787-10, he realized that this form of social interaction was prone to the same fundamental issues as any other. Most people followed the loudest voices that emerged, stealing Jason's precious work time for useless debates. He was mad whenever other participants belittled him for his unconventional opinions, and when they agreed to his claims, Jason wondered why he could not rely on himself exclusively for validation.

Perhaps nothing convinced Jason of the perils of companionship more than his experience with Fatma Karabakhova. In the last two years, Jason had been too consumed by the development of his project to obsess about his ex-girlfriend, but when he began thinking about her, he could play a movie of every second he had spent with her in his mind. A Turkmen student at Scotland's University of St. Andrews, Fatma Karabakhova had come to Northport as a foreign exchange student during the Winter Quarter of their sophomore year.

When he had met Fatma in one of his computer engineering classes and asked her where she was visiting from, she had replied Turkmenistan, to which he had inquired whether she hailed from the capital of Ashgabat. She had been superbly impressed that he had acquired such a vast array of knowledge in geography not through the Model United Nations conferences where students role-played international delegates in policy conferences, but rather an ambitious plan back in sixth grade to learn every world capital. After he had repented the fact that Turkmen was not one of the fifteen languages in which he could comfortably converse, he had sowed the seeds of a fulfilling friendship.

Jason had always enjoyed the company of foreign exchange students at Northport, from the Cameroonian neuroscientist to the Croatian aficionado of modern architecture. As much as he enjoyed discussing international affairs and learning phrases in new foreign languages, what really drew him to them was their isolation from the aspect of the undergraduate experience Jason most deplored. By only coming for three months, they did not feel the magnetic pull of the conformist bubble that inevitably absorbed most of those who stayed on campus long enough.

Fatma Karabakhova's brief sojourn on campus discouraged her from overcommitting herself to long-term extracurricular activities, while her aversion to the widespread drinking culture caused her to spend most of her evenings in the libraries that Jason frequented when he left the sanctity of his room or the vacant neuroscience laboratory. Jason had introduced her to many ethnic cuisines in downtown Northport, inspiring his later dinners with Aurélia. With most students other than Jason too integrated in their social circles to care about a transient member of the community, Jason and Fatma had remained entirely out of the public eye as they had begun a casual romantic relationship and gone as far as to kiss a few times.

After Fatma had said farewell to Northport at end of the Winter Quarter, he had initially exchanged hundreds of messages a day over the week of Spring Break. He had promised her that he would apply for the Gibb Study Abroad Program's Summer Seminar in Anthropology, "ANT 96B: Samarkand: Crossroads of Fire and Faith," in Uzbekistan for the following summer and visit her in her neighboring home country on the occasion. Upon reintegrating herself into St. Andrews, she had responded less frequently to his emails until finally, he had not heard from her in about a year and a half. She had never even bothered to send him a formal breakup message.

Often times, Jason wondered if there had been any point to his relationship with Fatma Karabakhova. He had invested a significant amount of useful time, and where had he landed? Exactly where he had started, but with the momentum of his project development lost and his heart damaged in the process. Recently, Jason had frequently considered the possibility that he might be diving blindly into the same mistake with Aurélia Chitour. For some reason, whenever he attempted to focus exclusively on himself, love reared its ugly head in the way.

But Aurélia was not the same. If the dragon of conformity had not had the time to grab Fatma, Aurélia had not consciously resisted it. While she was a very extroverted person, she was not a slave to popularity. Because of that, Jason did not only tolerate Aurélia's company; he enjoyed it. He always felt a childlike rush of excitement in his blood on the mornings of their weekly dinners. No matter what he had told Doctor Orosz, he saw her as more than just a friend.

When he thought about it, Jason did not particularly know Aurélia as a person. They only talked about international affairs, travel, music, movies…just not their feelings. Maybe he only liked her because she liked him. Why was she doing that, however? She had said that she put up with him because she found him brilliant, but was that really enough to like, no, to *love* someone?

Suddenly, Jason pulled the hair on his leg. He was such an idiot. As much as he wanted to, he could not escape the evil, rotten facts. He refused to accept it, but who else knew and could have told Northport's administration the secrets he admitted to her? Who could have told them to look for printed bank statements in his room? Had she planned to gain his trust all along in order to search for the secrets to his project once he had gone? He had never disclosed anything beyond the basics, after all, so maybe she had wished to find them. If he did not let her into his room, she might have a better chance with the campus police.

No, that was ridiculous. It did not add up at all. He could not allow himself to become as paranoid as Northport's administration.

Aurélia might have deserted Jason, but his closest friend had not turned overnight into an invisible enemy. She was not the instigator of the whole crisis, but rather collateral damage. Yes, she had disappeared to the netherworld of his life and leaving him to speculate for eternity, but most of the blame lay not with her. What was she supposed to do in the face of rumors that he was in fact an international spy, or worse? No, he had no reason to detest her.

As much as Jason wanted to hate Melissa Børgensen and Cayley Thompson, he almost pitied them more. They might subscribe to a dogmatic and absurd definition of what was right and wrong, or rather cool and uncool, but they were only adherents to the system, soldiers taking orders blindly from a deranged despot. No, Northport was the true villain, sacrificing Jason's humanity to protect its own reputation and promote its hidden social curriculum.

Was that really the case, though? No, *he* was the villain, the traitor. *He* was the one who had promised Aurélia that for all the time she had invested into understanding him when the others had given up, he would stick up for her as a loyal friend, only to disappear without forewarning. *He* was the one who had lied to his parents about his fate. *He* was the one who had deluded himself into thinking that he could find a happy place for himself in a game where he failed to grasp the rules. *He* was the one who had pulled others into the convoluted mess that was his life. Why should he be surprised that they had messed it up even more?

The painful sensation felt like a brutal murder that not only killed, but also lingered. Instead of decapitating him with a swift stroke at the neck, so to speak, the whole crisis was like a venomous parasite that would feed on his organs and conscience for a lifetime of deafening screams, always leaving him with the infinitesimal figment of hope that one day, he would win the battle. Only here, now that he was in the pits of hell, could he understand himself and escape the suffering he had brought upon himself.

Jason had not sacrificed his family for eternity, at least not yet. He still had the option of running out of the cave, pulling his cellphone out of the Kairaku Inn's locker, and calling them today if he wanted to. But not with Aurélia, whose loss tore so much at his veins, now more than his more consequential but impersonal separation from Northport. Whatever he tried to think about, Aurélia jumped to the forefront of his thoughts, drowning out all others.

All his life, even when he had been far less bearable than his Northport-era new-and-improved self, Jason had known in his brain and heart that short of murder, whatever he did would not preclude his parents and Chloë from seeing him as their son and brother. Aurélia, however, had always made the conscious choice to follow him even when she could very well have abandoned him for his annoying antics and found a best friend in a more conventional Northport student. She had only put up with him because she genuinely liked—perhaps loved—him. Now, though, he had to shove all these memories into the past. They fell like mounds of dirt, disintegrating into dust through the crevasse in between his cupped hands.

Jason Curran yawned, then finally lay on the rocky floor. If he wanted to fall asleep after the second of two very long days, he could not obsess about the past.

No, he had to forget Aurélia now. She would be his sacrifice.

16. MUSIC OF THE NIGHT

FRIDAY, APRIL 19, 2013

STRAUSS LIBRARY FOR THE HUMANITIES, NORTHPORT UNIVERSITY

Nathalie Washington walked past the hallway of dusty crates, unlocked the door, and switched the lights on. She had asked the librarian at the door for a very quiet room that no students would ever try to enter. After a journey into the macabre basement of Strauss, she reached the place where she could conduct her interview in secret. She rearranged the furniture, using her burly arms to move a cracking desk into the center and four chairs, three on one side of it and one on the other.

Nathalie's eyes scanned the periphery. Yellow-paged manuscripts covered in arcane lettering stood on the decrepit bookshelves. With two of the three lights broken, it was still rather dim, and she was not a very young woman, so it took her a while to find the label identifying them as ancient Syriac and Tibetan books. After a few moments, she finally understood. She had always believed this room to be an urban legend among Northport's leadership, but now she recognized that the fabled one was the one right before her eyes. She doubted that even President DiTancini knew of its existence.

The number of Northport undergraduates majoring in Computer Science and Financial Engineering rose relentlessly every year, and she could recount the creation of several new majors during her tenure, such as

Neuroscience. However, no one ever talked about the dark side of these trends. Every few years, some departments collapsed once no student declared interest in taking the classes. Now, once all the professors had moved to other departments if they were lucky and otherwise had been laid off, their materials were buried in an old dungeon. There, they waited to be sold to the universities where these disciplines were moribund but still alive, and otherwise they slowly gave themselves over to the elements. This was where knowledge went to die.

Quickly, though, Nathalie remembered that her objective today was not archaeology. The past two weeks, she had been too swamped organizing the hectic Admitted Students' Weekend. The Regular Decision admission results at the end of March had turned the tables in favor of the students who now had to choose between Northport and other universities of the same caliber, and she had been in charge of wooing them and their parents with sample classes, club fairs, and parties. As a result, it had taken her nearly two weeks before she could reopen her investigation of Jason Curran's alleged crimes, something she had been longing to do so since the fateful night she had watched an excerpt of *The Dolphin Conspiracy Show*.

She called out softly to the three trembling students waiting in the hallway, then gestured for them to come in and locked the door behind them. "Gentlemen," she addressed them, "Thank you for joining me today on such short notice. I must apologize dearly for calling you here without an explanation. I will say this ahead of time: you are not in any trouble."

Immediately, the three students' shoulders sank in relief. "While I do feel very bad about bothering all of you," she admitted, "The circumstances demand that the four of us go through this right now."

She wondered how she would explain her unprecedented behavior to the three of them, but she interrupted her own train of thought. "Before I explain why you are all here, though, I believe it's not polite to start without an introduction. I'm Nathalie Washington, Dean of Students at Northport University. After growing up in Chicago, I was at Northport as an undergrad and grad student at the Wagner School of Education. The spirit of Northport's students has kept me loving my job, despite the less glamorous aspects, for the past seventeen years."

"Now," she added, "I know you'd rather be interrogating the next Nobel Prize laureate or hanging out with your friends at the Marley Student Center, so I'll be fair and make this as short as possible. If my understanding is correct, the three of you were in Simon College as freshmen. Were you all in Room 421 with Jason Curran?"

Immediately, the student in the middle opened his mouth and blurted out, "Is it true that—"

Nathalie placed her index finger in front of her mouth, feeling like a kindergarten teacher reprimanding a pupil for talking without raising his hand. "At this point, I can't say anything. And, I must add," she said, checking that the door was shut tight and no one was lurking next to it, "This meeting is off the record. As far as everyone is concerned, you just ran into your freshman year roommates at the library, which isn't a lie."

Nathalie Washington pointed to the student in front of her and the one slightly to the right. "Leave us for a minute, please." They did as instructed, and Nathalie looked at her interviewee. He was dressed in a Bermuda of a unique color nicknamed Nantucket red, a dark pink endemic to the prep schools and elite universities of the Northeast. His light yellow crewneck sweater did everything but conceal his muscular shoulders, toned from over a decade of nonstop exercise. "Now, are you John Wolforth III from Gold Coast, Connecticut, Political Science major?"

"Call me Jack," he replied in a clipped New England accent. "My father went by John Junior when he was at Northport. My grandfather John also majored in Political Science here, so you get why it's confusing."

"I understand, Jack. It's wonderful that you're keeping on the family tradition." Not wanting to comment on the pervasive sense of entitlement among his type, she continued, "Now, tell me, did Jason Curran ever work on strange projects at night? Muttering foreign things on the telephone, perhaps, either in or out of the room?"

"To be honest, Dean Washington, I have no idea. See, I went to sleep at eight almost every night so I could wake up at four for crew. Sports make you a deep sleeper."

"I see. Did you request not to room with him in sophomore year?"

"No, as I said, Dean Washington, I never knew him and had no reason to complain. We were always on a different schedule, so we really didn't know each other."

Well, she would certainly not be getting anything useful out of him. "Great. Thank you very much for your trouble. You're free to go back."

"Good day, Madam."

Nathalie opened the door for Jack, then pointed to the shorter student and led him to come in. He wore a slightly faded black *Halo* t-shirt and had an ovoid face, dark eyes and hair, and brownish-black rectangular glasses. "You are Nick Rubenfeld from Princeton, New Jersey, Computer Science major, correct?"

"Not bad," he replied, chuckling. "What do you want to know?"

"When he was in your quad, did Jason Curran ever bring in any friends? If so, did the same ones seem to come back?"

Nick laughed, seeming as if he thought this interview was some kind of joke. "I'll be perfectly honest with you, I wouldn't know. All I know is I never saw him on the leaderboards for *Call of Duty*, which is pretty much the only place I saw anyone after classes my freshman year. And it hasn't changed today," he added, still amused.

"Did Jason ever play games with you guys?"

"Not really. He joined us once or twice during Orientation, but he said these games were a waste of time and he'd rather just chill by himself."

"So did you specifically request not to be in his room in sophomore year?"

"No, why? As far as I'm concerned, I didn't know him. It was nothing personal against Jason—I barely recognized my two other roommates when they walked in today. I asked to be placed in a room with my gaming bros."

Nathalie shook her head in disappointment. She did not know whether she should pity the students who wasted their nonstop opportunities for personal enrichment to spend countless hours playing violent videogames. But, to each his own, she thought. "Well, thank you for your time." She led him out, then called in the last student.

By process of elimination, she already knew that he was Chris Garvey, a Visual Arts major from Kingston, Jamaica. His skin was slightly lighter than her own, and he wore his black hair in long, unkempt deadlocks under a green, red, and gold bonnet. He reeked of cannabis, which the university administration only disallowed on paper. He held some arcane doodles in his hand, and his ripped-up Bob Marley t-shirt partly covered a camouflage-print cargo short. His bare feet had not likely seen a shower for longer than Nathalie wanted to know. She could not figure out if the pencil sketches he carried to his side carried a symbolic message about society or were just the effects of recreational drug abuse.

While reading Chris's file, she had learned that his father was a high-ranking government employee in Jamaica, but the elder Garvey's money was invisible in his son. If Jack Wolforth III spent a hundred dollars a week on clothes and Nick Rubenfeld did not care much about the way he dressed, Chris Garvey seemed to waging a guerilla war on fashion.

And then, Nathalie realized that it did not matter. The three young men sitting on the chairs in the back might have once shared the same quad, but they could not look more alien next to each other. They were a true testament to the soul of Northport. In the twenty-first century world-class American university, diversity in all respects was not merely a goal to strive for. It was a way of life so ingrained in the mentality of the students and staff that they did not even notice it.

Nathalie reprimanded herself for her haphazard thoughts. "Now, I take it you're Chris Garvey," she resumed. "Tell me, Chris, do you know if during freshman year, Jason Curran did anything that you considered weird or suspicious? Did any ever complain about his behavior?"

Chris looked up at the roof, obviously not registering her question, so she asked him again, this time louder and enunciating each word more slowly and clearly.

"Oh, right, um, no, mon," Chris replied. "Well, I don't know. I don't remember much of that year. I experimented with new things with my bredren, and I know I came closer to Jah in Zion, but that's all I know. Sorry, mon."

"It's fine."

"Ya, don't worry, mon. Apprecilove it."

Nathalie left her desk and opened the door. Chris did not seem to react, so she snapped her fingers and guided him out. All three students were gone now, so she could finally return to her official duties. She walked up the stairs and through the ground floor of Strauss Library, turning her head the other way when she spotted two students laying on top of each other and kissing fondly between the bookshelves.

As she walked back through the flower-strewn path to Lloyd Hall, Nathalie reflected on the very strange results of her illicit interview. At first, it had seemed as if her mission had been a complete waste of time. She had hoped that Jason's freshman year roommates would have revealed the details of his personality in exhaustive detail, but the early sleeper, the gaming addict, and the stoner had nothing useful to say about Jason Curran.

However, her clandestine investigation had proved the cliché that minimal knowledge was often the most instructive. For a while, she had believed President DiTancini's theory that none of Jason's roommates had requested to live with him again during sophomore year because he had made them feel uncomfortable, even worried. In fact, she had been the one to propose the idea that he had been the one to exile himself in order to pursue his suspicious activities in private. Now, the administration's first claim against Jason had vaporized into thin air. With just one of the thousand pieces lost, the puzzle formed a far less coherent image.

Nathalie Washington smacked herself on the cheek. Seventeen years of this job, and she was still more naïve than a freshman.

✈ ✈ ✈

SUNDAY, APRIL 21, 2013

RAPA NUI NATIONAL PARK, EASTER ISLAND

The continentals had told him that change was coming to Rapa Nui. For years, I'Kiti Vapui had dismissed their claims as superstition, an ironic comment for the very man mocked by the Chilean mainlanders for spreading his shamanic beliefs in a futile defiance of the grasp the Vatican now held on Easter Island. And yet, his most recent walks had suggested that the continentals might be telling the truth.

Every morning, I'Kiti made the long but physically and spiritually rewarding trek from his hut at Ovahe to the slopes of Rano Raraku. He always returned after sunset, when the noisy tour buses no longer raged across the sole route traversing the center of the island and when he could reflect on the Mana more clearly. His northward path back to Ovahe led him past a small-mouthed cave which his exploration of Rapa Nui as a child had taught him held a larger subterranean ecosystem of plants and animals. About a week ago, he had begun to hear some strange sounds emanating from it. Was this somehow related to the change the continentals had mentioned?

At first, he had attributed the noise to a feral dog who had probably been chased away from Hanga Roa after stalking one too many customers in the capital's souvenir shops. However, every day he ventured slightly closer to the cave itself, and he was definitely convinced that the sound was too complex to be of animal origin. This time, I'Kiti decided, the period for speculation had passed. If the Mana had been knocked out of balance, it was his responsibility to set it back. It was time to learn about the music of the night.

I'Kiti held his torch upright walked across the expanse of brown earth, probably scorched by a tourist who had carelessly thrown a still-lit cigarette. The dark path led to a small aperture in the hill, which I'Kiti was glad to have known of from all his previous visits to the area, or else he would have fallen straight through. In the very limited light, he tried his best to detect the solid branches and rocks on the steep slope and grabbed a hold of them. If he tumbled down, he strongly doubted that whoever stood inside the cave would rescue him.

Finally, I'Kiti blessed the flat ground under his feet and slowly advanced, using his torch to detect any potential threats. The part of the cave with an outlet on the sky and a small source of water running through it was a greenhouse of bananas, taro, and other edible plants.

However, as he walked, I'Kiti only found eternal night. Narrow passageways swiveled interminably through an expanse of rock walls too somber for cave drawings, probably even during the day. Oh, and then there was the smell. I'Kiti had tried to ignore it at first, but every time he calmed his fear slightly, the putrid stench bothered him instead. In the cave, his troubles piled up, but now that he had resolved to come down here, he would set the Mana back into balance, no matter the cost.

After having mostly died down for the past few minutes, the sound intensified. I'Kiti could not identify it specifically, but it sounded like one word being shouted over and over again. Finally, the tunnels widened, and the sound was beginning to appear much clearer.

"Aurélia! Aurélia! Aurélia!"

I'Kiti Vapui raised his eyebrows. It sounded like a woman's name. Very strange indeed. He walked through to the end of the cavern, then finally saw where the sound had been coming from. "Excuse me, can I come in?" he asked in the native Rapa Nui tongue. The figure did not seem to react and continued to raise his arms up, so I'Kiti reattempted, this time in Spanish.

Finally, the shadowy figure turned around and began to limp towards I'Kiti, who stepped back slightly, holding his torch in front of him to get a good look. The young man seemed to be about a third of I'Kiti's age. His dirty blond hair was short on the sides but very unruly, and somber circles surrounded his mad eyes. His dark pants and light-colored shirt were drenched in a fetid pool of mud.

Finally, the haggard figure faced I'Kiti. "They robbed me!" he shouted, pulling his arms up and clenching his fists.

I'Kiti paused for a second. "Who?" he asked.

"E-e-e-everyone! Everyone! Everyone!"

"They robbed you...of what?"

"E-e-everything! Everything! Do you understand me? Everything!"

I'Kiti began, "What—" but stopped himself. It was no use.

The cave dweller placed his hands on his face and began pacing frantically in circles. For some reason, maybe because he was merely speaking to himself this whole time, he switched to English, and with the eloquence more of a rehearsed speech than incoherent rambling. "Do you understand what it is like to be betrayed by the few people you thought you could trust? To be accused of something you never did and be deprived of any chance to defend yourself? To come to exile yet be unable to find peace, because at night you're too tormented by the sound of your own madness?"

He now began to scratch his hair madly. "To detest yourself so much that you no longer know who you are and would prefer to kill this madman who has replaced you, yet find no easy escape from agony, even death? To stop eating, yet throw yourself on whatever piece of food you can find after a few days because you cannot endure the horrible toll it takes on you? To finally learn life's most agonizing lesson: that the only way to escape pain is through more pain, so you'll suffer for eternity?" He grabbed a rock, extended his arm, and rammed his own forehead with it a few times. "You have no idea!"

I'Kiti stared around for a few moments, wondering what to tell the man. Clearly, judging by his coherent tirade, he was clearly someone who had fallen from grace, possibly an exile who had lost his way, yet maybe he was not beyond repair.

"Look," I'Kiti said slowly, "I don't know who you are, but I know for sure that you were once someone. Someone other than...this. To set the Mana back in place, you must come with me and rejoin your former self."

The lost exile yanked wildly on his own ripped-up shirt. "Mana? No Mana!"

I'Kiti Vapui sighed. This was going to be more difficult than he had thought. He watched as the lost exile paced aimlessly around the cave and muttered words in a foreign language, then finally collapsed from exhaustion.

Now was his only chance. I'Kiti carried the unconscious body back through the seemingly interminable tunnels, until the two men finally reached the soothing breeze of the night sky.

17. MANUREVA

MONDAY, APRIL 22, 2013

CURRAN RESIDENCE, SYDNEY

"Come on, Ellie," Liam Curran pleaded with his over-energetic wife. "It's eleven, and I have a really important procedure to perform at nine in the morning. No one likes a sloppy cardiologist."

"I'm sorry, Liam, but we need to do this!" she responded, waving her arms almost hopelessly in the air. "We still have no idea what happened to Jason, and no one'll tell us!"

"I know, I know! But if we haven't been able to reach the Dean of Students the ten times we called, do you really think we have a shot of talking to the *President*?" Liam looked at the floor and shook his head slowly. It was a lost cause.

"Well, it's worth a shot, isn't it?"

"All right. One extra call won't make a difference. We're past that point now."

"You know, Liam, I like the way you think," she replied, kissing him on the cheek with the affection he so badly needed these days.

Liam Curran pulled the telephone off the kitchen counter and passed it to his wife. In twenty-plus years of marriage, they had developed a division of labor that caused Elektra to handle such stressful communications.

"I'll put in on speaker phone so you can hear the conversation," she told him.

"I don't think that'll be necessary. I told you, I can't deal with this any longer. I don't like these people, Ellie. They take our money, yet they won't take our call!"

"But maybe you'll have something to say! You never know, Liam!"

In twenty-plus years, Liam had also learned when not to argue with her. "Okay, why not?"

Liam waited as the phone rang. For about ten seconds, it seemed like a repeat of all of the times when they had not been lucky enough to hear a secretary apologize for the Dean of Students being out of her office after they had introduced themselves.

Fortunately, today was their lucky day. "Good morning, this is Tony DiTancini, President of Northport University," a voice answered. "How may I help you today?"

Elektra smiled. They had done the impossible, directly reaching a man who had a higher statistical chance of being on a fundraising tour to Angola than of being alone in his office. What were the odds that they would be calling right when the President's assistant was in the kitchen fetching him some coffee?

"This is Elektra Kananaskis Curran, mother of Jason Curran."

"Hello, nice to hear from you, Mrs. Curran. How are you?" he replied.

"I can't say I'm in great shape, unfortunately. With all due respect, President DiTancini, you've punished Jason way beyond suspending him from Northport. It seems like he's shattered beyond repair. We still have no idea what the allegations are, but I'm sure if you tell us, we can explain. This has to be a misunderstanding."

"Mrs. Curran, let me begin by saying that I'm deeply sorry for what happened to your son and we've given him a completely fair process under the traditions and precedents of the Northport system. Unfortunately, under the Family Educational Rights and Privacy Act of 1974, also known as FERPA, we are unable to release any confidential academic or disciplinary information to the parents of a legal adult who has not given us the explicit permission to do so."

Liam Curran clenched his fist. Why did so many of the Americans he knew obsess about every single legal detail? He remembered once performing a positive diagnosis of coronary artery disease on an American expatriate who had spent nearly the whole session worrying about whether once he returned to the United States, his new health service provider would classify his malady as a "preeminent condition," or a term of that sort.

Elektra responded with zeal that Liam himself would never have been able to force through the telephone in such a distraught state. "President DiTancini, we understand your procedures, but in this case, it's not exactly simple to receive our son's permission. He left home two weeks ago, completely agitated, without telling us where he was going. I don't even think *he* knew where he was going! Do you realize how worried we are?"

"I genuinely empathize with your pain, Mrs. Curran. However, there is nothing we can do. FERPA's a federal law, and I cannot allow the university to place itself in a position that might endanger its standing."

"Can't you at least *show* some compassion? We're telling you that we have no idea where our son is!"

Liam pulled his wife's shoulder towards him. "It's no use, Ellie," he said.

She placed the phone to her side and responded, "You're right, Liam."

"Oh, and by the way, Mrs. Curran, the tuition reimbursement for this quarter is on its way to your bank account."

On a better day, Liam would have laughed. Tony DiTancini had said those words on a tone that almost begged them to respond with gratitude, as if they should somehow be very thankful that in addition to what he had put the Currans through, DiTancini was not also trying to rob them of nearly twenty thousand dollars! Having a taxi driver in Bangkok swindle *ten* dollars from them last month had been stressful enough.

Elektra replied with a simple, "Thank you."

"Is there anything else I can do for you today, Mrs. Curran?"

"No, that'll be all. Thank you for your time." She promptly hung up.

Suddenly, Liam hatched a brilliant plan. "What if we dig into all of Jason's emails from when he was still at Northport? We might find some new information there."

Elektra sighed. "We've been through this already, haven't we, Liam? It would take a professional hacker to get through all the security layers on his account."

Liam nearly kicked himself. "Of course, you're right. I'm sorry, I can't think clearly."

She patted him gently on the shoulder. "You should go sleep, Liam. You have a long day ahead of you."

"You're right, Ellie. I need it."

Elektra frowned at him. "We *all* need it."

✈✈✈

RANO RARAKU QUARRY, EASTER ISLAND

"Was it a woman?" the tall man asked him.

It had been several days since the figure facing him had rescued him from, literally, the darkest phase of his life, and now, Jason could finally see everything clearly. He stared down at the shorts and moai-motif t-shirt I'Kiti had bought for him at a souvenir shop, essentially the only clothing stores on Easter Island, to replace the ragged remains of the jeans and polo shirt he had worn for two weeks in the cave.

"W-what?" Jason Curran responded, still in English. While he would generally take advantage of a trip to Chile to practice his Spanish, he knew that some of Easter

Island's Polynesian natives vehemently opposed the use of the colonial Iberian language, and the figure in front of him was the poster child of a Polynesian travel brochure. Dried plant fibers enveloped most of his body, and white tattoos swirled around his copper body and face. He wore a necklace of coconut wood in the design of a dolphin around his neck and wedge-shaped earrings of the same material. Despite his gray beard and ponytail, he was in flawless physical shape, clearly able to turn the long wooden staff to his side into a weapon at lightning speed if anyone ever threatened him.

The native was not postcard-perfect without the surrounding landscape, however. From his vantage point at the top of the hill, Jason observed hundreds of moai, all volcanic gray apart from the patches of white moss growing on some of their heads. Unlike the ones at Ahu Tongariki, these moai were not just standing in the Rano Raraku Quarry. They were *growing*. Heads of moai sprouted haphazardly from the patches of grass, some upright, some tilted down and to the side, some buried to their noses.

Soon, the tattooed man interrupted. "It looks like you dozed off for a while. I'll repeat my question. Was it a woman who brought you here?"

Jason wondered how to answer correctly, yet without revealing too much about himself. He had no idea who the figure in front of him was or whether his motives for rescuing him from the hellish cave were altruistic. "No. Well, yes. Sort of. Several women. Well, not really."

The tattooed man shook his head. "How about we try something different? After almost a week of this, you have yet to tell me your name."

For the moment, at least, the tattooed man was the only thing between him and a slow, agonizing death in the cave, so Jason had no reason to play hardball. "It's Jason," he replied. "Jason Curran. And you?"

"My name is I'Kiti Vapui. Nice to meet you, Jason. But I will call you Irirangi. It means 'Spirit Voice,' because the voice with which you yelled in pain—to your lost woman, perhaps—had an ethereal quality to it."

"'Irirangi'. I like the sound of that. Please teach me more of your language."

"I will, Irirangi. But not right now. First, we need to fix the damage that has been done."

"To me? No thank you, I mean, thanks for taking the time to ask, but—"

"Not just to you, Irirangi. To the Mana."

"The Mana?" Jason dug past the dust clouding his memory. It was still taking him time to regain the sanity he had lost in the cave, but as a child he had read so much about Easter Island's history. "Oh, isn't that in Polynesian mythology? A metaphysical life energy or something?"

I'Kiti nearly fell back, then thrust his arms forward to keep his balance in a gesture that might very well be another one of his eccentric teaching methods. "Oh, no, Irirangi. Not *metaphysical*. Very physical."

While Jason would never be one to accuse others of being bizarre, every minute I'Kiti seemed more mystical with his replies.

"Let me explain, Irirangi. How did you come to Rapa Nui?"

"What do you mean?" Jason asked quizzically.

"Well, you were not born on Rapa Nui, I assume, so you must have come here one way or another. Even my ancestors did not swim across the Pacific Ocean, and I don't know—somehow, you don't look like you constructed a catamaran. This makes me believe that like everyone else coming to Rapa Nui today, you flew on an airplane. Is that correct?"

"Yes," Jason replied, wondering even more fervently where I'Kiti was going now that not only his answers, but also his questions were also inscrutable.

"Take an airplane, Irirangi. *Manureva*, we call it in Rapa Nui. What is a *manureva*?"

Jason thought for a few seconds, wondering how to respond. Clearly, I'Kiti was not asking him because he was unaware of the answer. He recognized the classic Socratic technique employed by some of his professors at Northport. While Jason rarely knew where to turn when he did not have concrete, indisputable facts in front of him, his intellectually curiosity had long made him more patient than those who desired only the straightforward pedagogy that would make them exit the classroom the soonest.

"An airplane? Well, it's a large flying vehicle."

"Made of what?"

"Aluminum, generally, though some are made of composite plastics. But I mean, they're collections of materials pieced together. So this relates how to the Mana?"

"Patience, Irirangi. Stop being so impulsive. Don't always seek the quickest answer to every question."

"All right. You know," he said, staring at his uncovered left wrist, "I have all the time in the world."

"What powers a *manureva*?"

"Kerosene being burned. Kerosene is a hydrocarbon with energy stored in its bonds, so the heat releases the energy."

"But what keeps a *manureva* up in the air? A car burns gasoline too, but I have yet to see one fly."

"Well, there's something called Bernoulli's principle. The air pressure under the wings is stronger, which pushes them up."

"The lift component of the force, no?"

"Exactly." Jason wondered how a hermit in the middle of nowhere had come to learn physics, but he listened. This approach to science was a lesson he had never learned, and would certainly never learn, at Northport.

"So how exactly do you explain the movement of a *manureva*?"

"Well, I just told you, didn't I? Fuel being burned and air pressure."

"No, you did not tell me, Irirangi. You only mentioned some vague terms such as 'burning' and 'pressure.' You did quite a poor job, I must add, because you didn't even bother to distinguish between fluid pressure, or vapor pressure, or kinematic pressure, or any other type of pressure. What you entirely failed to do was explain *why* this happens."

"I thought I did! The kerosene is burned, so the energy is released."

"Energy! Oh, energy! What is energy, Irirangi?"

"*Energy?*" Jason tried without success to figure out whether I'Kiti's question was supposed to be rhetorical. "Well, it's impossible to explain it in one word. The definition I've generally seen is 'the ability to do work,' but otherwise, I guess I can just say that it's a constant in a moving system."

"There's one simple word to describe what you just told me, Irirangi. One very simple word."

"Work? But energy isn't exactly work. It's the ability to do work."

"You think too specifically. Try looking at a wider scope. Here, maybe this will help." I'Kiti knelt down on the grass, then began waving his hands up in the air and performing a very loud, almost caricatured tribal chant.

Suddenly, Jason saw where he was going. "Mana! Energy is Mana!"

I'Kiti smiled. "I knew there was potential in you, Irirangi. Yet why did it take a falsified ritual for you to make the connection?"

"Well, when you asked me physics questions, I was thinking in scientific terms, but when you knelt down and chanted, I was thinking in religious terms."

"What is the difference between the two?"

It took a few seconds for Jason to think of a vaguely decent way of explaining the distinction between science and religion. A secular family and technical education had inevitably made him see one as an insider and the other as an outsider, so he made an effort to provide an answer free of bias. "Religion describes the world through legends, but science describes it through experiment."

"How about this? Religion searches for ways to explain the things we cannot explain, and science explains them."

Jason nodded. He wished he had found the time to enroll in philosophy classes, or at least have enough time free from the obsession of his project to reflect on these questions. Unfortunately, while in the cave, it had not been long after he had found a peace of mind for his own insanity to fill the vacant spot. "I like it."

I'Kiti frowned. "You may like it, Jason, but it's grossly incomplete."

"How so?"

"Religion fills an evident gap in science. While science clarifies how things work, it fails to connect this to a unifying theory. Think of what you told me about how the *manureva* moves. You walked me through a detailed process, yet you utterly failed to describe the crucial element: the one fundamental entity behind the physics."

"So that's where Mana comes in?"

"Precisely. I knew you would understand quickly, Irirangi. Now, consider this: with the Mana connecting them, are science and religion completely independent of one another? Are they rival theories, or rather complements?"

"Well, with what you explained about religious theories completing scientific ones, I would say that they're complementary. That sounds reasonable."

"Just complements? Are they not more?"

"How so?"

"Think of how they operate. Both teach their members from birth that theirs is the only way. Both cite indisputable texts. Both claim to be for everyone, yet fall into the hands of dominant leaders and exclusive councils. Both are in large part controlled by massive corporations, selling products for profit. Yet not all the similarities are bad. People are passionate about both and work together to advance them. Most importantly, both give us a refuge from what I call the 'abyss of ignorance.'"

"That's brilliant," Jason responded. "It makes things so much clearer than what I learned in school. In the West, too often we're taught that science and religion are incompatible."

"Well, that is correct."

Jason wondered if the cave had stolen his ability to hear correctly. Was I'Kiti actually telling him that one of the ideas he had brought with him to Easter Island was right?

"Science and religion are incompatible because the concept of compatibility means nothing." Of course, Jason thought, he should have known better. How many times so far had I'Kiti begun by presuming that something was true, then dismantled the idea entirely?

"One cannot even talk of combining them because they are two opposite ideas," I'Kiti continued. "Science and religion are the same, since they are merely a reflection of the Mana. The Mana is the only certainty in the universe. Nothing else stands forever."

"I think I understand. Because everything else is a matter of subjectivity, right? Just like if you draw a picture with a pencil on paper, to some it's a fabulous work of art, and to others it's a hideous scribble."

"True, but you can go much further. Take a typical souvenir shop in Hanga Roa. They sell everything in moai form: keychains, t-shirts, stuffed toys. To some residents of Rapa Nui, these are abominations; to others, they are merely the way of putting taro on the table. But if you take a wooden dolphin and say it is a moai, that is technically correct."

Jason wondered whether he had misinterpreted the linguistics. "Does the word 'moai' mean 'relic' and not specifically 'stone statue?'"

"Not at all. Your problem is, you focus entirely on the details rather than the big picture."

That was ironic, Jason thought. If he thought Jason viewed the universe too superficially, I'Kiti would have a blast talking to most of his former Northport classmates.

"A moai and a wooden dolphin are the same in the sense that they are both incarnations of the Mana. The forms in which this matter appears to us is irrelevant, since it is different for any two individuals. I mean, a chicken can see more colors than we, the so-called 'masters of the universe!' What we see does not matter; only what is does. Why do physicists say that energy is conserved in an isolated system? Because energy is the Mana, and the whole universe is the only system that is fully isolated. The Mana is the only entity in the universe that never changes! Atoms, quarks, bosons, gluons—they are all vehicles to carry the Mana, as are our bodies. When we die, the Mana fades slowly out us, from both the sudden loss of our conscience and the gradual decomposition of our bodies, then joins a newborn or anything else—a rushing river, perhaps, or the shining of the sun."

"I've never thought about it this way, but suddenly everything makes more sense! Where did you learn all this?"

"I guess I should tell you a bit about my background, shouldn't I? About forty years ago, I started working at the Hivamotu Inn in Hanga Roa, taking orders and washing dishes in the restaurant. One day, I stumbled upon a physics textbook left by a tourist. I gave it to my boss so she could return it to its rightful owner, but she told me not to bother with it and throw it away. However, I was curious, so I glanced inside. I was fascinated by the information, but the language barrier was too strong, so I spent ten years learning English, mostly from the Australian tourists here. "

That would explain his startling proficiency in English, Jason thought.

"When my English was good enough," I'Kiti resumed, "I spent hours and hours a day reading the book I had found nearly ten years earlier, leaving my job and disapproving wife to live on Ovahe and have more time and space to reflect. Why did I do all this? Because the cover of the book had a simple word on it: 'energy.' I had been raised Catholic, but I was still in touch with my Polynesian roots, so I knew all about the Mana. I understood the parallel between my ancestors' religious traditions and the next big scientific discovery."

"Well, that's impressive!"

"Indeed, it's been more rewarding than waiting tables at the Hivamotu Inn." I'Kiti paused, then resumed. "Why did you ask me, Irirangi? Oh, I already know. Your thoughts are very clear. How can a mere shaman dealing in superstition, a man without any store-bought clothing, be a particle physicist? I don't fit the stereotype at all, do I?"

"To be honest, I'Kiti, I don't have lots of respect for those who try to conform to some image."

"Good, you should not. The Mana within us takes a specific form when we are born. We have no reason to expend more Mana to change this. It seems you already knew part of this philosophy unconsciously."

"What do you mean by 'expending' Mana?"

"Using the Mana to change the Mana."

"But is that always wrong, I'Kiti? If we never use energy—well, Mana—how can we ever create anything at all?" Jason had seen many inefficient uses of energy in his time—for example, the treadmills in Williams Gymnasium. It had always seemed bizarre that someone would see the need to use an energy-consuming machine to consume more energy. When he practiced martial arts, he did not need an artificial motor to activate the motor inside his body. Perhaps the treadmill runners were too busy trying to refine their appearance in their nearly nonexistent free time to ever wonder that.

"Here is what you should remember. Nothing is ever created without destruction somewhere else in the universe. Build a *manureva*, and you've destroyed mountains to find the aluminum. Pick bananas off a tree for food, and you've disrupted the ecosystem. This isn't to say that progress is anything but desirable, not at all. It just goes to show that since more Mana cannot be created, everything has a consequence. When the result is unstable, the Mana will revert the situation back to its original state. Conservation of energy, as Mayer and Joule explained it. Come, I'll show you a simple example," I'Kiti told Jason.

I'Kiti grabbed a small black lava rock off the ground and threw it up lightly. "Look at this. When I throw this rock up, it must come down. Why? Because gravity acts as a vector on the rock, pulling it back down. I have changed the Mana through my action, and the Mana, though it has no conscience, still wishes one thing—to return to its fundamental state. Now, look at this. If I throw the rock higher up, it's because I have used more Mana, which means that more Mana, and therefore more time, is required to bring it back to the ground. However, at some point, it'll fall."

Before Jason could respond, I'Kiti kicked the rock and continued. "Here, I can use an analogy to illustrate this. If someone commits a crime, the Mana has been thrown out of balance. Even if it seems that this will never be the case, at some point the right will be wronged, and the Mana will return to balance.

"Well, maybe I should tell you a bit more about my life, then. Where I come from, often we feel like we don't have enough criminals, so we invent new ones, and the real criminals are never caught."

I'Kiti Vapui stared incredulously at Jason. "Do you really think that, Irirangi?"

18. AMAZING GRACE

SUNDAY, APRIL 28, 2013

PALAIS OMNISPORTS DE PARIS-BERCY, PARIS

The crowds were cheering like wild animals. Rodrigo Oliveira took a moment to breathe after he and Sarah Brightman finished their duo of "Phantom of the Opera." Everything was coming so quickly to him. He had risen to fame so rapidly in the last decade that he was often invited to replace the recently deceased Luciano Pavarotti alongside the two surviving members of the Three Tenors, the Spanish Plácido Domingo and José Carreras.

Now, it was time for Rodrigo to conclude his and Sarah Brightman's UNICEF benefit concert with a solo performance from his most popular album, *Affettuoso*. Seventeen thousand faces of all ages and trades watched as the conductor waved his wand to the side. So many souls to please, Rodrigo mused, and hopefully not disappoint. Sometimes, Rodrigo wondered whether he had truly deserved the honor—and the burden—placed on his shoulders.

Well, it was time to begin. *"Amazing grace, how sweet the sound, that saved a wretch like me..."* Rodrigo looked around as he sang. There was perhaps one empty seat here and there, but otherwise the arena was an agoraphobic's worst nightmare. With the glaring stage lights, it was hard for

Rodrigo to see further than the conductor, but he could guess that all seventeen thousand occupants of the red seats had their eyes and ears fixated on him.

He continued through the verses. It was almost the end... *"And we've been here ten thousand years, bright shining as the sun..."* Rodrigo lifted his left arm, extending it up in a breathing technique he had learned early after beginning his training in Lisbon. *"We've no less days to sing God's praise than when we first—"* Rodrigo Oliveira felt a hiccup coming in his throat, then quickly suppressed it—*"Be-unh-guuun!"*

Rodrigo thought he heard a gasp coming from Sarah Brightman. He turned to her, hoping that she had been the only one to hear his mistake. He thought she would be. After all, only a professional would notice the difference when he had sung only slightly out of tune.

Then, Rodrigo realized how wrong he had been. Not too long ago, he had still been singing only in the shower, but in such a gargantuan arena, things were different. His off-key phrase had reverberated ten thousand times worse through the microphone and acoustic amplification systems.

Seventeen thousand voices turned to shock, then silence, then laughter. Rodrigo Oliveira had failed them.

✈✈✈

RODGERS COLLEGE, NORTHPORT UNIVERSITY

Some students at Northport hated being sexiled by their roommates, but Aurélia Chitour never minded being sent to Rodgers College's common room by Leila

Bouazzaoui and her new boyfriend. Before starting her paper due the next day, she scrolled down her Facebook news feed. Though she did not care much about learning the insignificant tidbits of so-called "news" that her Facebook friends posted, she briefly checked her news feed every day, just enough to stay in tune with the general flow of what was going on around her.

According to Aurélia's news feed, one of her Facebook friends—though really a vague acquaintance—from freshman year had changed her relationship status from "in a relationship" to "single." Funny, Aurélia thought. She was almost sure that the girl had posted that change the other way around two weeks ago. There were photos of "Gitmo-style" hazing leaked by a disgruntled shadow brother of Pi Omicron Omega, congratulatory messages to Northport's basketball team, the Deer, for their last-minute victory against their Ivy League rival Columbia, and links to extremely biased blog posts calling for various solutions to the Syrian Civil War.

Otherwise, there was not much to see, until she noticed a YouTube video that had become completely viral in the last hour. Fifty of her several hundred Facebook friends, most of them from her choir group, had shared it, so it was probably worth checking out.

Aurélia opened the link to *"Rodrigo Oliveira Amazing Grace FAIL."* The low-quality recording picked up in the middle of a song by a Portuguese tenor during a concert in Paris. Aurélia rarely listened to any music besides contemporary pop, Brazilian bossa nova, and jazz, but she vaguely remembered hearing Rodrigo's name in the past, from Jason Curran, of all people. She watched as the opera singer veered slightly out of tune, then culminated in an off-key note that reverberated very badly through the arena.

Was it really *that* funny, so much that her constantly busy Facebook friends wasted so much time writing an endless string of "LOL" and "LMAO" comments? Sure, Rodrigo Oliveira had made a fool of himself to some, but Aurélia knew of celebrities who had done far worse and been the subject of admiration rather than ridicule. This was an awkward moment, but awkwardness was no crime. That was why Aurélia had put up with Jason Curran all those years—well, at least when she thought herself sure that he had no malicious intentions.

She had heard nothing of Jason recently. Perhaps her friends had just found new people to obsess about. Oh, why did it matter? That was all behind her.

Aurélia hummed some bossa nova as she opened her Dropbox folder. Sunday or not, she had more than enough work to do.

✈✈✈

MONDAY, APRIL 30, 2013

LLOYD HALL, NORTHPORT UNIVERSITY

Tony DiTancini crouched forward on the mahogany desk and read the papers. The recent report from the Office of Undergraduate Admissions was not as positive as he hoped. Northport had aggressively expanded the use of affirmative action policies over the past few years, applying them more generously to multiracial applicants, but it still trailed behind some of its Ivy League competitors by a percentage point or two in the statistics on the number of minorities represented.

Keeping up with the Yalies was not Tony's greatest fear, though. Neither were the growing accusations of anti-Asian discrimination on the part of Northport and its peer institutions in the admissions process. Handling those was up to the Dean of Admissions, but Tony had faith in his colleague's ability to avoid a scandal. Proving the existence of a quota for or against a particular race was impossible in the holistic admissions process, where the individual coefficients given to grades, standardized test scores, leadership, sports, music, charity work, demographics, and life experiences were never formally laid out.

The most pressing issue, however, was repairing Northport's public relations in response to a viral editorial on affirmative action written by an irritated alumnus in *The New Yorker*. The most damaging element of the article was no secret to Tony: contemporary affirmative action policies cut corners for good publicity. The columnist, a refugee from El Salvador who had grown up in a disadvantaged neighborhood of central Baltimore and benefited from Northport's affirmative action policies, decried the university's almost nonexistent efforts to draw more students from his socioeconomic background.

In his scathing claims of Northport's hypocrisy, he had cited Argentines of fully Polish ancestry being admitted as "Hispanic" and the children of Nigerian oil barons falling into the same "African-American" category as the natives of Detroit's gunshot-laden inner city. In his conclusion, he asserted that focusing only on arbitrary racial markers scandalously avoided the real issue of economic inequality in higher education and that the latter should be the target of new affirmative action policies.

Unfortunately, Tony DiTancini knew very well that everything the article had stated was true. His native Philadelphia was still very segregated, with Caucasians and Asians overwhelmingly residing in far higher-rent districts than African-Americans and Hispanics. While the details of undergraduate admissions were not directly his responsibility, the negative publicity affecting the university the week that a lucky group of high school seniors decided between Northport and other colleges was. What could he do? Reaching out to underprivileged students was not as easy as it sounded, even for a corporation with bottomless coffers. Could he find one current student from a disadvantaged background and have someone interview him or her to post a counter to the editorial on Northport's webpage?

Maybe that would not be enough. Most readers were probably unaware that Northport spent the same exorbitant amount of money subsidizing the education of those who could not afford it as they gained from tuition fees. Their profits, after all, came from successful alumni who donated a percentage of their earnings to their alma mater and the recruited athletes who drew the alumni to basketball games, and fundraisers while they were at it. Posting a factoid about earnings, though, would not repair the damage.

Suddenly, Tony heard a knock. "Come in," he instructed the visitor. "I've left the door unlocked."

Tony did his best to wipe off the coffee stains he had recently made on his jacket, then turned his head to stare at the new arrival as she opened the door. "Ah, Nathalie. Good to see you. What brings you here today?"

Nathalie Washington paused, thinking of how to explain her request. She was still not sure if her doubts regarding the affair with Jason Curran were justified or not, so she did not want to try to convince her boss of anything when her own opinions were still so nebulous.

"It's about Jason Curran. I've been thinking a lot about the issue recently."

Tony shrugged. He thought he had buried that issue in the pit of university history after the phone call with the elder Currans a week before. "What's there to say? You've done a great job of handling the issue. After all, I hired you for your expediency, not your amazing grace."

"About that, Tony. I think I acted too rashly. We *all* acted too rashly. I'm sure there's more to this than we thought, or rather, that there's *less* to this than we thought."

"Nathalie, I thought you agreed with the committee when we went over this. Sure, the FBI told us that Jason didn't present a clear and present danger to our national security, but *national* security isn't what we're focused on. We need to focus all our attention on *Northport's* security. Think globally, act locally, Nathalie. If someone on campus is a potential gunman, or worse, we need to remove him as a threat. We've been through Columbine; we've been through Virginia Tech. We had a frustrated student call in a bomb threat two years ago. We can't afford to take any chances."

Though Nathalie certainly agreed with Tony's logic— she had been the first to suggest most of it to him—she was no longer convinced of its appropriateness in context. Sure, all the elements added up, but they could also add up to a million alternative stories.

Before she could voice that concern, however, Tony continued, "You know, I haven't written off the gunman idea entirely, despite what we concluded about Jason probably being a spy. If Jason ever does anything really bad that makes it into the news, we certainly don't want anyone to be able to cite him as a Northport alumnus. That would be a public relations apocalypse! And in case another government employee ever finds it funny to release a bunch of confidential government documents, including our communications with the FBI, we want only one message to come out of that: we acted swiftly, strongly, and preemptively."

Of course. Tony DiTancini always insisted on the university's reputation—it was his job, after all, and as the architect of Northport's recent rise from fourth to third in US News & World Report's Best College rankings, he was excellent at it. That being said, Nathalie had not focused on that argument when she had been convinced that Jason was a criminal. "What if we were being paranoid and all the pieces of the puzzle were completely independent of one another? What if he was completely innocent? Would we have to worry about our reputation then?"

Tony's eyes rose in surprise. "You think he's *innocent?* How?"

"I don't know. I've been thinking about it for a while now, but until today I was overwhelmed. I had to deal with the Admitted Students' Weekend, and then I had to rescind the offer of the Slovak student who was found guilty of drug dealing. Spring Quarter's really the worst. So now my main question is, how can we conclude anything about Jason's various activities if we know nothing about his personality? Practically no one on campus knows him!"

"Which suggests that he's a loner, and loners are dangerous. Don't you remember what the FBI profiler said when he came over a few weeks ago?"

"That's exactly the point, Tony. It *suggests* that. We don't know. Our whole case against him rests on the fact that he's a criminal, but we're only speculating. That's why I have a request for you: the permission to reopen the investigation. Maybe all the claims will make more sense if I know something substantial about Jason's personality. The only problem is, he told me he wanted no further contact until we fully readmitted him."

"Actually, Nathalie, his parents called me about a week ago and told me that Jason had run away from home. It's rather convenient for us, actually."

Nathalie could not believe her ears. "*Convenient?*"

"Obviously, if he's gone and his parents don't know anything besides the fact that he was suspended, they can't prove we did anything bad. That way, we won't have to worry about a lawsuit. We can just let it go, and at some point his parents will give up. And come on, they're not American! I doubt they'll even think of suing us. As I said, Nathalie, I don't think we have to worry about our national security. The FBI told us that this wasn't a top priority for them, which is why they let us take care of all this garbage ourselves. He seems like a pretty inept spy, with all the evidence he left laying around his room. If we're able to avoid being sued, we're completely fine."

"So you think he's bound to do bad things?"

"I don't know, Nathalie. But if there's one thing we learned about Jason, it's that he's withdrawn. Even if he isn't actually a danger to others, I know he might be a danger to himself. I definitely don't want that to happen on my watch. I've seen my share of tragic student suicide stories on campus. Now, if you'll excuse me," he said, rising and pulling his white Panama hat off his desk, "I have to go home and pack before my flight to Doha."

"What are you doing in Doha? Another alumni event?"

"Yes, I'm appearing at a fundraising dinner on Sunday." He was not looking forward to the trip much himself, especially seeing as his wife and daughter always complained that he did not spend enough time with his grandchildren. "You wouldn't believe how many alumni we have living in Qatar!"

"Oh, I didn't know the Qatari Royal Family sent its children to Northport," Nathalie replied. "I've met a few members of the Omani Royal Family, though."

"The Qataris prefer Princeton, actually, just like the Saudis prefer Harvard. But there are tons of American expats working in big oil in Qatar, some of which are our own," Tony replied. "Okay, I need to go, Nathalie. And really, don't worry about Jason Curran. Everything's fine. You've taken great care of the whole situation."

"Thanks. I guess I stress about too many things."

"Why, are only students allowed to get stressed?" Both chuckled.

"Have a safe flight, Tony."

Nathalie Washington walked out through Lloyd Hall's creaking wooden doors, then stared back at the domed Neoclassical edifice of Lloyd Hall. She had reached an impasse. As long as she knew nothing substantial of Jason Curran's personality, she would be unable to decide whether the allegations of espionage were an accurate portrayal or a gross misunderstanding.

However, Nathalie had no need to find new questions to ask for the moment. If seventeen years of this job had taught her anything, the questions would find *her*.

19. CIRCLE OF LIFE

WEDNESDAY, MAY 1, 2013

AHU KO TE RIKU, EASTER ISLAND

The lone moai stood on the bed of rock, staring out at the vast expanse of land outside Hanga Roa. It was a very special moai indeed, as it was the only one of a thousand that could actually stare. At the end of the twentieth century, French archaeologists had restored the eyes on just this moai. The oblong white plates of coral and the red scoria stone dots in the middle complemented the cylindrical red pukao hat on the moai that the tourists to the Tahai Ceremonial Complex photographed incessantly. It was now, as far as Jason Curran was concerned, the perfect moai.

Jason could vividly remember his first encounter with the mystery of the moai. When he was five, he had intruded on his parents one day as they watched an investigative television report on the mystery of Easter Island and the various theories concerning how the moai had come to stand on their ceremonial platforms. Archeological records pointed to an absence of wheels, and horses did not roam the island before the nineteenth century. Theories about how the Rapa Nui people had transported the massive statues from the quarries to the ahu ran from the recently suggested pulling of moai with strings from both sides to the resource-draining rolling of them on logs to the far-fetched transportation by extraterrestrials.

Fascinated, Jason had begged his parents to buy him all the books and cassette tapes they could find on Easter Island and had devoured them for a year. At one point, he had pulled about a hundred gray, brown, black, and white pieces from his collection of toy LEGO bricks and built a replica of the fully restored moai at Ahu Ko Te Riku. He had loved his LEGO creation so much that when his parents had invited two guests from Singapore, or maybe it was Hong Kong, to their home, he had been extremely excited to show them his LEGO moai. While the man had been busy talking to the adult Currans, the woman had begun asking Jason what toys he liked to play with, in response to his creation, and then some other typical questions to ask to a six-year-old boy.

Instead of answering them, however, Jason had begun to recount the various theories on how the Rapa Nui people had constructed and transported the moai to the ceremonial platforms such as Ahu Ko Te Riku. After Jason had spent the guests' whole visit explaining the intricacies of Easter Island and his LEGO moai to the woman, she had told his parents in words that he still remembered exactly, "He'll do great things in life. I hope I'll see him again one day."

When he had been at home in Sydney, it had not been uncommon for him to think back to the encounter. Every time he saw the LEGO moai still standing as an artwork display on his living room table, he recalled of his intense childhood passion for Easter Island. When the circumstances had forced him to run away from home, a quick look at the LEGO model on the way to the front door had convinced him to choose Easter Island as his place of exile. It bothered Jason that he was unable to recall more details of that encounter with the Asian woman fifteen years ago, not so much because it had been prophetic but more because he so needed his memories of the facts he knew to be so precise.

Suddenly, I'Kiti Vapui walked to Jason's side and asked, "Tell me, Irirangi, have you ever heard of the *Tangata manu*? It's a famous legend on Rapa Nui, and I heard it even made its way into a Japanese videogame."

"I was never into gaming, but the name sounds familiar. Why?"

"Because, when I found you, you reminded me of him in many ways. See, the *Tangata manu* was a cross between a bird and a human in our legends. Back when we still believed in supernatural beings, we worshipped the *Tangata manu* as one of the servants of the supreme god, Makemake. To honor him, we organized a yearly competition in which a few nobles chose young men to swim over to Motu Nui, one of the rocks to the side of Rapa Nui. The first to bring back the egg of the Manutara—the Sooty Tern, as you say in English— became *Tangata manu*. He won the contest and would spend a month in a cave, giving him a sacred status."

"So when you found me in the cave, you thought I was like the *Tangata manu*? I mean, not literally, but in the sense that I lived in a cave and grew as a person?"

"Yes, though I would have saved anyone from that horrible fate. Now, though, with what you've revealed to me about your past, you remind me of far more than just the *Tangata manu.*"

A few days ago, Jason had finally conceded to himself that it would be best to reveal his uncensored past to the man who had rescued him from peril. I'Kiti seemed interested in proselytizing the religious and scientific beliefs for which others shunned him, not bringing undue pain to anyone.

"What do I remind you of, then?" Jason inquired.

"Look around you, Irirangi. What do you see to your right?" he asked. It was a typical I'Kiti Vapui question, a seeming *non sequitur* that would turn into a general lesson on life.

Jason took a quick look, then picked the most obvious answer. "A moai?"

"Only one moai?"

"I can see a few more moai over there," said Jason, pointing to a distant ahu.

"Only a *few?*"

"Well, the island has almost a thousand, no? But I can't see them all from here."

"A thousand moai. Do you, realize, Irirangi, that in complete isolation from the rest of the world, my ancestors built a thousand moai?"

"It's impressive, certainly."

I'Kiti frowned slightly. "Do you really think that, or are you merely trying to be culturally sensitive?"

Jason hoped his comment had not come down as offensive. "No, I definitely think it's great. If I didn't appreciate the moai, I wouldn't have decided to come to Rapa Nui when I fled my home."

"All right, so what do you admire so much about the moai?"

I'Kiti might very well be going for a trick question, but Jason still picked the most truthful and straightforward answer. "Well, I guess their design, or maybe something about their form that's, I don't know, almost ethereal."

"Perhaps you do, but do you really find them as marvelous as the Great Pyramid of Giza, the Great Wall of China, or Greek and Roman sculptures from hundreds, no, thousands of years before?

"I mean, can you really compare the two?" Jason asked, making sure he avoided what he viewed as a Western condescension of so-called "less civilized" peoples. "The Rapa Nui built something unique. I've even seen a replica of a moai in the most random place, by the side of the road in Connecticut! They need to have a really noticeable design to make it all the way there."

"Yes, Irirangi. We did something great by ourselves, without copying anyone else. But it only took us so far."

"What do you mean?"

"Well, you know what happened to Rapa Nui a few hundred years ago, no?"

"To be honest, I don't remember all the details. I read so much about the moai themselves, but I didn't learn as much as I should have about Rapa Nui history. All I know is you were conquered, then raided, then decimated."

"Yes, we were," I'Kiti responded.

"By raiders from Europe, right? Or South America?"

"Not really. By the time they came here, we were already dead."

"Why? I don't know that story."

I'Kiti exhaled for a few seconds, then admitted, "We destroyed ourselves."

Jason jumped back at the revelation. "Wait, how?"

"Partly because our luck was terrible, and partly because we were fools."

"What happened?"

"We focused entirely on ourselves and not on the outside world. It was inevitable, really—we're the most remote inhabited place in the world. Yes, we built something that no other civilization did, but there was a natural limit to how far we could go. We had no metal in our earth, and with no neighbors, we were limited to the basic tools Hotu Matu'a and his really small crew brought across Polynesia. So we couldn't borrow technology from anyone else, and since we had no one to compete with, we stayed with what we had. For hundreds of years, we didn't innovate; we only kept what we had. Every time, we made the moai slightly bigger, until we built Paro, the tallest of them all."

I'Kiti looked down and frowned. "But our fate was not purely the result of geographical determinism. We also made terrible decisions. We didn't care at all about our environment, so we cut down all our trees. As you can guess, it was very hard to kindle fires, so we couldn't develop anything new. Irirangi, do you know why so many moai are on the ground?"

"Because they were never brought to the ahu?" Jason guessed. "I read that the people here rolling the moai on logs, so with no trees and no wood, they were stuck."

"Well, that was part of it. But more importantly, we cannibalized our homeland. Since the Mana is always in motion, conflict is inevitable. We had no one around ourselves, so we turned on each other. We toppled each other's moai like little children, jealous and desperate."

I'Kiti paused, then spoke more softly. "Do you know why I am telling this story to you, Irirangi? Because when you brag about being isolated—"

"I don't *brag* about it," Jason clarified. "I just admit it as a fact of my life."

"You try to draw attention to yourself. That's definitely bragging."

"Fine, but what does this have to do with the wars here?"

"Because you remind me of Rapa Nui as a whole. Think back to when you were in the cave. What did you eat? Did you hunt? Did you fish?"

"No, I don't eat any animal products."

"Neither do I, Irirangi. Then from personal experience, I assume you ate taro, bananas, and whatever else grew near you."

"Yes, so I was self-sufficient."

"You weren't, Irirangi. You might not have bought your bananas from a supermarket, but someone had to plant them there in the first place, seeing as they're not native to Rapa Nui."

"That doesn't count, does it?"

"Really, Irirangi? Try it as an experiment, then. See where you get the Mana you need to survive if you don't eat anyone else's plants."

"I'll find a way," Jason replied with fierce determination. "I'll forage—"

"To what avail? Do you really think if you're living in a cave, you're protected from all of life's problems?"

"Yes, and I actually think I would have lost my insanity had I stayed there for more than two weeks. After a while, I would have forgotten all about Aurélia, Dean

Washington, and the rest of them. Northport might have a network in every little corner of the world, but I still think a cave on Rapa Nui is beyond their reach."

"You may run away from problems, Irirangi, but you can't shield yourself from them. What would you have done if a band of feral dogs had attacked you?"

"Come on, that's unlikely, isn't it?"

"Perhaps, but so were so many things in history, like the discovery of Rapa Nui. If my ancestors found this minuscule speck of land with so little technology, wasn't it obvious that at some point, the European explorers with all their fancy cargo would find it too? They came and conquered us, decimating us with a silent weapon. Do you know what this was?"

"Rifles?"

"No, not at all. It was a killer none of us could actually see. I'm not even sure the Europeans knew they had brought it. Microorganisms, Irirangi. The agents of disease. Our isolation might have protected us from disease for centuries, but when the plague finally caught up with us, we couldn't resist it."

"See, Irirangi," I'Kiti explained didactically, "Living like a hermit kills you in the long run, and since you can't ever be completely isolated, you can't benefit from it. Look at me, Irirangi. I might live in my own hut in Ovahe, but every once in a while I talk to the other residents, because we share our basic resources. We can't just pretend that everything's just our own."

Jason looked up at I'Kiti. "It seems so simple this way, but real life is so much more complicated..."

"Is it really complicated, Irirangi? Or rather, are you the one manipulating the Mana inside you to make it more complicated? Remember what I told you: repainting yourself the way the world views you disturbs the Mana. Repainting the world in your own vision of it is no different. We're all made of the Mana, but it takes different forms in all of us."

"I understand, but keeping things as simple as they actually are, I was able to live most of my life without relying on others. I learned most of my fifteen languages through self-study, and I developed most of my interests by myself."

"Is that so? How did you find the time to do all that by yourself?"

"By not wasting any time focusing on being cool and popular, of course."

"Only that?"

"What do you mean?"

"While you were busy with all of this, weren't your parents cooking and shopping for you? Weren't they cleaning your clothes, providing a roof over your head, and driving you to school and activities? Didn't you rely on their money for your education and visits to the doctor?"

Jason thought back to his childhood, wondering how he had created the illusion of complete self-sufficiency.

Perhaps he had not seen the value of the time that freed up when he did not have to deal with all the day-to-day tasks I'Kiti had mentioned.

"I guess I should have been more thankful," Jason admitted, "Especially now that I can't go home and face my parents' wrath."

"What you still don't understand, Irirangi, is how interactions with others work."

"No, I've heard the story," Jason said with a scoff. His parents and therapists had driven more than enough lessons on that through him. "Reciprocity, tit-for-tat, ping-pong."

"Then you heard wrong. Whoever explained that to you has a terrible understanding of how the universe works. I saved you from your doom in the cave, but that does not mean that you have to pay me back in return. Rather, at some point you'll help someone else, who'll help or have helped someone else, who'll then help or have helped someone else, until it comes back to me in a cycle. I call it the Circle of Life."

"I think I understand. The Mana flows from individual to individual—"

"From transient entity to transient entity," I'Kiti corrected.

"The Mana flows from transient entity to transient entity, and since it occupies the entire universe, it has no reason to return where it was right before."

"Exactly. I knew you were a quick learner." I'Kiti paused, then continued, "Here, I can give you another example. Think about money. Economists understood the Circle of Life before anyone else. Why was barter an inefficient system?"

"Because tastes were not always compatible," Jason replied, regurgitating what he recalled from his sophomore year economics class.

"Oh, they could be completely compatible, but not always at the same time and place. If I bring you a bunch of sweet potatoes and you offer me a spear in exchange, I will not be ready to make the trade because I have no intention of going to war. However, bring me in cowry shells that I can trade for firewood from another merchant, and I will sell you my sweet potatoes. What is currency, Irirangi? Merely the economic equivalent of Mana in the Circle of Life."

Jason processed I'Kiti's clever explanation for a few seconds, then replied, "That's brilliant! Did you find an abandoned economics textbook along with the physics one? Why don't you go work at the International Monetary Fund?" Seeing I'Kiti's frown, he clarified, "Really, I'm serious."

"Regardless of what my economic theories are, what do you think they'll say when I introduce myself as a shaman? They'll laugh at me, call me superstitious, and throw me out the door!"

"You can never get past the stereotypes, can you?"

"Unfortunately not. You, on the other hand, will be a different story when it comes to success."

"Working for the IMF? No, I doubt it."

"No, Irirangi, with your project. You have yet to tell me the details."

Not too long ago, Jason had been paranoid about revealing more than the bare minimum of details about his project to anyone, even Aurélia and Derek, but now he no longer worried. The chance that I'Kiti Vapui would copy it was even slimmer than the chance that Jason would ever return to Northport.

"All right, so it's called Intuner. It's an implantable device that connects directly to the brain so that when you sing, the pitch that comes out of your mouth is always the same as the one stored in your memory. If you have a musical ear, it prevents you from singing off-key."

I'Kiti tilted his head at an angle and nodded. "Impressive."

"I hope the market agrees with me! Unfortunately, I've been at a roadblock for a while now."

"Because you were suspended?"

"That certainly didn't help, since I can't concentrate on it. But even before that, I haven't been able to figure out how to relay the signal directly from the place in the brain where the memory is stored to the mouth. A direct flow is impossible."

"Oh, I see. Well, you have something to think about when you're back at the hut in Ovahe, no?"

"Indeed. I have all the time in the world."

20. DESAFINADO

FRIDAY, MAY 3, 2013

GARVARENTZ BOULEVARD,
NORTHPORT UNIVERSITY

Nathalie Washington walked on the wide passageway down from her office to the location where she was set to meet her guests. On Friday mornings, Garvarentz Boulevard—or simply "The Boulevard", as most of its nocturnal visitors referred to it—was not a happy sight. Many students raved about the raucous parties thrown on the lawn right between the Boulevard and May House on Thursday nights, but most were too busy rushing to classes the morning after to notice what followed.

In recent years, the bastion of Iota Nu Alpha had surpassed the nearby fraternity houses Newton, Lauper, and Rota as the hottest party venue. There were even rumors that the Morricone School of Public Policy had moved across campus last year because of the rap music emanating from May House had been unbearable. Natalie understood that May House deserved its reputation as she stared at the bits of vodka bottles, used condoms, and shattered cellphones spread across the beer-inundated grass. The putrid stench of vomit filled the air as a hungover student who had clearly just woken up on the steps of May House rather than in his dorm room yelled incomprehensibly, possibly trying to attract the attention of the female students rushing frantically to class.

Despite the unwelcome distractions, Nathalie Washington tried to stay focused on her objective for the day. The Office of Undergraduate Admissions had requested her presence at the Jobim Sculpture Garden to greet the family of a student admitted in December under Northport's Early Action program. She had not heard many details about her assignment besides that, though she assumed it was relatively straightforward. After a brief conversation with the Jacots, if she recalled their last name correctly, she would turn them over for a campus tour to the very pleasant Northport senior she had met the day before.

A few minutes later, after leaving the post-apocalyptic landscape of the Boulevard, Nathalie reached the garden. While Northport's standard campus tours departed from Webber Hall to accommodate the masses of high school students and families who listened to the admissions sessions, over the years it had become standard procedure for private tours to depart from the garden, a more discreet location that, as had been discovered by experience, seemed to draw visitors back to campus time and time again.

Nathalie Washington had never paid too much attention to art, but every time she met students here, she admitted to herself that the Jobim Sculpture Garden was an impressive sight. An eclectic mix of artworks identified by labeled copper plates as Parisian bronze philosopher sculptures, Papua New Guinean wooden crocodiles, and stateless piles of plastic and steel of indeterminate significance populated the space in between the crabapple trees. It was no wonder that some Northport alumni who chose to marry at their alma mater picked this location over the Northport Memorial Chapel, Nathalie thought.

After unsuccessfully trying to decipher the meaning of a fake plastic shoe resting on a slab of marble, Nathalie looked around. Under a pink cherry blossom tree sat a family of four, with two middle-aged parents, a teenage son with oversized glasses, and a smiling toddler daughter. Nathalie spoke in a voice that was loud enough to draw the attention of the father without waking the toddler, whom her mother caressed in the stroller. "Good morning! I am Nathalie Washington, Dean of Students at Northport University. Are you Mr. Jacot?"

"Ah! Dean Washington!" he responded excitedly. "Thank you so much for taking the time to do this!"

"It's my pleasure, Mr. Jacot, and my job." She turned to face the son. "And you must be Philippe! Congratulations on your admission."

The teenager rose from his seat. "Th-thank you, Dean Washington! N-nice to meet you!" he replied nervously, picking his fingernails.

"Welcome to Northport, Philippe! Now, for the sake of introductions, could you please remind me of your names?"

"I am Yves Jacot, and this is my wife, Michèle. You already know Philippe, and our daughter, Camille, is just waking up from a nap."

"And where are you all visiting from?"

"Rennes, France," Yves Jacot replied.

"Oh, that's great! I hear it's a very beautiful country! My ex-husband always talked of taking me to Paris! So, are you here on vacation?"

"Yes, we had a week-long vacation right now. Sorry we could not make it to the Admitted Students' Weekend, but we are very happy to know that meeting us now has not been a problem for you."

"No problem at all—my pleasure! And is this your first time in the United States?"

"For me, no. I work as a computer scientist, so I have been to California, but my wife's job as a workplace doctor makes it difficult for her to travel. For the kids, it has been a wonderful experience."

"When did you come over?"

"We left France four days ago and spent a day in Iceland, since the cheapest plane ticket stopped there. We arrived in New York yesterday and toured the city, and we left it this morning to come to the campus."

"Welcome to Northport! Nathalie replied. "How's your visit been so far?"

"Wonderful! The campus is so beautiful. Also, I am amazed by how generous your financial aid is! It is so impressive that you give such discounts to families like ours who cannot pay the whole bill. Well, enough with me. You should talk to my son instead. He will have more to say."

"Welcome, Philippe! It's so great to have you on campus!"

"Thank you!" Philippe replied, much of his unease fading away.

"What do you think of our university so far?"

"It's fascinating! I'm very glad to be here. The campus architecture is so beautiful, and the opportunities are so much better than in France. I still can't believe I got in!"

"Congratulations again!"

"Thank you. But now, one thing has been bothering me. I haven't seen many trains in Northport; is there a station nearby?"

Nathalie frowned for a second as she wondered what he meant, then remembered that she was here to make the best possible impression and smiled. Philippe Jacot had just confirmed his enrollment at Northport, so the last thing she wanted to do was to chase him away now. Still, she could not ignore her curiosity over Philippe's interests. "Are you very interested in trains?"

This time, it was his mother, Michèle, who interjected. "Oh, Philippe loves ze trains! Zey are all of ouich he talks—ouell, zat and ze ouezer previsions."

Nathalie tried to pry under Michèle's strong accent for a few moments, then understood and responded, "Oh, the weather forecasts!"

"Yes, yes! Ouen he is not memorizing ze ouezer previsions for some city in ze ourld, he only tinks about trains. He has a very big collection of modele trains in his—um, ouat do yu call ze room under ze house?"

"Oh, you mean the basement!"

"Ah, yes, tank yu. Ouell, ze trains Philippe has occupy our ole basement. It can be a little problem ouen ouee ouant to put ouaine in ze cellar, but it is very impressionant. Here, I have an image on my telephone."

Nathalie looked at the picture. At first, she had instinctively assumed that Michèle had been just trying to brag about her son's greatness, as most mothers did, but now she understood that if anything, Michèle had underrated how impressive the display was. Model trains of countless shapes, sizes, and colors extended across the surface area of about five Northport dorm rooms. Endless silver rails weaved between plastic houses and trees. Nathalie did not have time to scan all the details, but she let out a chuckle when she saw a blond-haired doll probably belonging to Philippe's younger sister laying on one of the train tracks. Considering the impact that the installation had made on her, Nathalie wondered how someone who knew more than the bare minimum about model trains would react.

"I'm speechless," Nathalie told the Jacots. "How did Philippe have the time to do all this? I mean, the grades and activities students need to get into Northport are so much already. But more importantly, Mrs. Jacot, how did your son even have the idea in the first place? I don't know if collecting trains is a big thing in France, but even if it is, I don't think a normal kid would launch and pursue such a creative project. Though of course, not just anyone can get into Northport."

Michèle smiled at her. "Ouell, my husband speaks English better, so he ouill explicate."

Yves Jacot sighed, seemingly hesitating as if he were about to reveal a crucial secret. "The truth is," he began, "That our son Philippe has Asperger syndrome. I am so sorry. We should have told Northport before."

Nathalie Washington seemed taken aback. "Oh. I've heard the name before. Isn't it some type of mental illness?"

Philippe raised his eyebrows in disapproval. "Oh, it is certainly not a disease. It is what they call an autism spectrum disorder, and it has its positives and negatives. People like Philippe have trouble when it comes to social interactions, especially non-verbal communication and understanding how others feel. It certainly makes life in the school difficult, but it is wondrous as well. They are so intelligent, and they have creative ideas and focus on them like no others ever could. Remember Philippe's obsession with trains? No neurotypical—as they call those who do not have Asperger's—could ever concentrate so intensely. They would say that something like the trains is so bizarre and worry instead about the way they dress."

"Oh, I didn't know that. I thought students with autism had difficulties with speaking. For someone with autism to do something so great is just spectacular!"

"Well, autism is a spectrum. Just like any condition, there are some who display far more severe symptoms. There are people whose legs sometimes hurt a little bit when they walk, and there are others whose legs are paralyzed for life. Philippe is, as the scientists say, high-functioning."

"Oh, definitely. I would never have guessed that he had autism had you not mentioned it!" Nathalie replied.

"That is exactly the problem for Philippe now. When he was a little boy, he was very different from his classmates, but now, he has done much therapy, and the people that he does not know well do not even notice. Because they have no idea that he has Asperger's, they expect him to behave exactly as they do, but of course, since he is different, he does not, and they think he is bizarre."

"Ah, I see. So you mention that he did therapy. Is France very advanced when it comes to treating autism?"

Yves Jacot laughed, then returned to a more serious expression. "On the contraire, we are in the Middle Age. It is a horrible scandal. The autism was very much studied by an Austrian psychoanalyst named Bruno Bettelheim, whose research was discredited in most of the world but continues to be the gold standard in France. The French medical community still mostly believes that autism is caused by mothers who did not want to have children and acted very coldly towards them in the womb. The only solution, they say, is psychoanalysis."

"Wow, I'm so sorry to hear that. Do scientists in other countries know what causes it?"

"In reality, autism is still a very mysterious field, but much evidence points to the fact that it is neurological and, most importantly, genetic. I would not be surprised, since after our son was diagnosed, my wife suggested that I might have mild symptoms of it myself. Anyway, as a result of these beliefs, about a quarter of children with autism in France go to school, and the others are sent to psychiatric hospitals, whereas in the United States about nine out of ten autistic children go to school."

"That's horrible!" Nathalie interjected emotionally. "So, how were you able to avoid that?"

"Of course, there are some parents in France who are appalled by this treatment. Some move to Belgium to seek better help. Once Philippe was diagnosed with Asperger's at the age of seven, we decided to seek a specialist who practiced behavioral therapy like in the United States and other advanced countries rather than psychoanalysis in the French style. This therapy has been so helpful, which is the reason it is hard for many people to tell that Philippe is affected. We are confident that by coming to the United States for the university, he can be better treated in the land of diversity, never being discriminated against because he is socially different."

"Well, I'm very glad that you were able to find help for Philippe! Now, from what you have told me, I'm sure that Philippe will excel academically at Northport, but do you think he needs any special accommodations to help him navigate the social scene? After all, we are a 'living and learning' community. If you have some time after your campus tour, I can take you to the Albinoni Center for Disability Services."

"Thank you very much, Dean Washington," Yves Jacot responded with a combination of determination and offense, "But I do not believe that Asperger's is a disability. It is merely a difference and should not be removed, just like some people have different colors of the skin or attitudes about the life. We will continue to give him therapy once a week, but otherwise we believe as a family that it is better for Philippe to have experience interacting in a new environment rather than constantly be sheltered and protected by a social aide."

Always sure to please the visitors, Nathalie responded "That makes perfect sense, Mr. Jacot. And he needs to take advantage of his extraordinary abilities!"

"Oh, of course! Now, trains and the weather might not be the best places for Philippe to shine, but I am sure that he will develop interests that he can pursue in the university. Not to sound arrogant, but who knows," Yves said, chuckling, "He could be the planet's next genius. Da Vinci, Newton, Mozart, Einstein, and Zuckerberg—they are all speculated to have had Asperger's. Do you see a pattern, Dean Washington? They have all become world-famous people for what they have done, not who they are, unlike many celebrities and politicians. That part is certainly not something I want to change, especially if he works on the social aspects and can better understand others before coming here. Oh, and I should add, those who have Asperger's are generally very honest and genuine, so we don't want him to go from that to a liar!"

"Well, that sends like an impressive plan! I'm sure Philippe will have an amazing experience at Northport!"

"Oh, he is so excited to come, Dean Washington. American universities are definitely great places for extraordinary individuals to shine."

"I certainly agree! Have you ever heard of Avad Patel?"

"No, who is he?"

"They call him the 'Boy Genius of Edison, New Jersey.' I doubt his fame's reached France...yet. He was admitted to Harvard this year, at the age of thirteen. You know, I think Northport is falling behind." Nathalie and Yves both chuckled.

"Dean Washington?" a voice sounded from behind. "I'm ready. Sorry, I was running late—I had to rush here from Loewe Hall. My English professor seemed to be out of tune with what the phrase of 'end of class' meant."

"No problem, Aurélia."

SLIGHTLY OUT OF TUNE

Nathalie turned her head to face Aurélia Chitour and explained, "As I told you yesterday, Mr. and Mrs. Jacot are visiting campus with their son Philippe, a Northport admit. They've come from Rennes, France to tour campus during their vacation." She now faced the French visitors. "She's Aurélia Chitour, the lovely Northport senior who will be taking you around campus. Have a good time! It has been a pleasure meeting you, Mr. and Mrs. Jacot. And Philippe, I'm sure you'll do great things. I cannot wait to see you shine at Northport!"

"Ze pleasire is all ze mine, Dean Washington!" Michèle told her, smiling. "Tank yu so much ouance more!"

As the Jacots began to follow Aurélia out of the Jobim Sculpture Garden, Nathalie Washington stole a glance at the cute toddler sitting placidly in her stroller. Unable to resist, Nathalie told the child's mother, "She's adorable! Is she at all—"

"Oh, no, she is not at all like him," Michèle responded before Nathalie could finish her question, preemptively guessing what she was trying to ask. "She is already friends ouiz her ole crèche. She is pratique too, like ouen she helped us pick ze new apartement! She is so...easy!"

✈ ✈ ✈

JOBIM SCULPTURE GARDEN, NORTHPORT UNIVERSITY

Nathalie Washington continued to marvel at the works of art. She had previously never taken the time to appreciate the hidden wonders of the Northport campus, but with barely an hour to kill before the student tour guide returned from her campus visit with the Jacots, Nathalie had resolved not to make a quick stop back at Lloyd Hall, but rather to stay and learn. How many other times in her life would she have the time to compare Ancient Jordanian and Kiribatian artwork? Finally, as she moved towards the fountain in the middle of the garden, she saw the woman she was waiting for.

"Ah, Aurélia. You're back. How was the visit?"

"It was a great experience," Aurélia Chitour responded. "It's visits like these that make me proud to be a Northport tour guide."

"Because the others don't? How disappointing," Nathalie said with a chuckle.

"Good point, but this one was certainly unique—and memorable, I should add." For reasons that Nathalie could not guess, Aurélia seemed to alternate constantly between a sly smile and a slight frown.

"Oh, how so?"

"Well, Dean Washington, it's funny. Philippe Jacot reminded me a lot of a former friend of mine."

"In what sense, honey?"

"Everything, really. All the things he talked about. Well, let me rephrase that. The *way* he talked about things. When I wasn't telling him about campus life, he talked only about two things—his love for trains and his knowledge of the weather."

Nathalie Washington grinned. It was nothing personal.

"He didn't ask me much about myself," Aurélia continued, "Except for where I was from, and when I told him Rio de Janeiro, he regurgitated the day's weather forecast and average highs and lows for May in a split second. I don't think he was being arrogant. It really seemed like he was passionate about everything he talked about. Well, you know, my old friend was a milder version of Philippe. I guess people learn to blend in as they age."

"So your friend, was he from home?"

"Oh, no. See, in Rio, most young people—or most people, period—only care about getting tanned in a mini bathing suit on the beach. When I went to school there, the few others who didn't care much for that lifestyle were cooped up in their apartments, reading books. That left me pretty much friendless there, which is why I was so glad to have so many new social opportunities at Northport."

"So which year did your friend graduate from Northport?"

"Never. He disappeared from campus a few weeks ago."

Nathalie Washington felt a sudden shiver in her stomach as she guessed where Aurélia was going. "Do you know anything about the circumstances under which he left?" Then, she caught herself and added, "You know, it's not fair of me to ask. I should respect your privacy."

"No, it's perfectly fine," Aurélia responded. "There's nothing to know, really. I never learned why he left. I've heard some rumors on campus, but I'm not sure how much I believe them."

Nathalie sighed. Normally, her question would be wrong under the laws of both Northport University and common decency, but given the extenuating circumstances, things were different, and she would do what she had to. "Aurélia, was your friend...Jason Curran?"

Aurélia almost fell on the gravel, but she caught herself right in the nick of time. "W-w-what? H-how did you guess?"

"Because any rumors you've heard about Jason Curran being kicked out of Northport are true. And how do I know that? Honey, I was the one who suspended him."

Aurélia seemed horrified by the admittance, though it was difficult to tell if she was more shocked by the fact that the woman in front of her had betrayed a true friend or the fact that her worst fears were true. "W-what did he do?"

"Well, at first two students told me that they were fearful because he was behaving weirdly. They were afraid he might represent a danger to the campus community. As I looked into it, I found out other bizarre things about him. Pretty soon, I grew increasingly worried myself. When I told President DiTancini, he and the other members of the administration accepted and, I am afraid, embellished my theory: Jason Curran was an international spy."

Aurélia seemed very saddened by the revelation yet reassured by the fact that she had heard the truth from her classmates. "So, you're telling me that what I heard is true?"

"At first I would have thought so. We called in the FBI, and even though they didn't think there was an immediate danger, we continued to worry about his behavior, both for the campus and for himself. But then, I began to doubt my own conclusion. It's funny how I got to that point—it involved dolphins, go figure—but anyway, I wondered if the glue I had placed between all the pieces of the puzzle hadn't painted a completely wrong picture. Perhaps if I'd tried to tape them together instead, I would've realized that they didn't fit. And now that you mention Philippe, I think I've found my roll of tape."

Aurélia looked slightly confused. "I'm sorry, Dean Washington, but I don't see the connection."

"It's fine, honey. You weren't there, and it's so new to me as well. The truth is, Philippe has Asperger syndrome."

"Sorry, I'm an English major. I'm afraid I don't know much medicine."

"Neither did I, before I spoke to the Jacots this morning. Asperger's is an autism spectrum disorder, though Philippe is what they call high-functioning. People with Asperger's have trouble when it comes to understanding and communicating subtly with others, but on the other hand, they're extremely creative and intelligent, and they'll pursue interests and goals that others would consider weird or impossible. They might not be wired for empathy, but they tend to be honest. Now that you've made me realize that Jason must have Asperger's as well, I understand at least some bits of the enigma."

Aurélia seemed to ponder the information. "There's a word in Brazil applies very well to people like Jason. He's a *desafinado*, someone who's always very slightly out of tune."

Nathalie smiled. "'Slightly out of tune.' I like that description. Perhaps the administration would find this enlightening."

"I still don't understand what this has to do with whether or not Jason's guilty."

"Because, honey," Nathalie explained, "The reason the others and I were so suspicious is because Jason was socially awkward."

"You don't say. But how does that make him a criminal?" Aurélia asked, seemingly horrified.

"It doesn't, that's what I'm trying to say. At first, we thought he was hiding from everyone because he was some loner with a grudge against the campus community. Then we looked at all the details and wondered if he wasn't a spy? But I now realize he might be neither of those. Maybe he's just happy beating his own drum and dancing to his own tune. Like Philippe, he just does what he wants and doesn't care what society thinks of him. Oh, honey, I'm worried we made a terrible mistake."

"What should I do about this, Dean Washington? Should I talk to Jason? I really want to help."

"No, please don't. I don't think that will help. He sent me an email a few weeks ago saying he would be out of contact for a while."

"Maybe he's working on his project," Aurélia suggested. "He's been busy for so long with this idea called, um, 'Intuner.' Wow, I'm surprised I can still remember the name!"

"I'll look into it," Nathalie responded.

"Is there anything more I can do?"

"If I ever need you again, I'll tell you. For now, fly freely like a bird. Go enjoy yourself, honey. You're a college senior. Nathalie caressed her gray streaks of hair with her hands. "Enjoy it before you become an actual senior!"

21. DIE ANOTHER DAY

MATAVERI INTERNATIONAL AIRPORT, HANGA ROA

Four hours of walking from the turquoise beach at Ovahe to the verdant slopes of the Rano Kau volcano was a debilitating experience. Even with his martial arts endurance training, Jason lagged behind the man much older than his own father.

"Tell me, Irirangi," I'Kiti Vapui began didactically. "What do you think of this?"

"Of the runway?" Jason responded hesitantly. I'Kiti was at it yet again with his questions. The two of them stood close to Mataveri International Airport's exiguous brown terminal building, in the first pseudo-residential area Jason had seen in a while.

"Yes. Look at its length for an airport with less than two flights a day. It was created for the space shuttle, in case an aborted landing was necessary."

"In most cases, I'd just say that was a cool factoid. However, since it comes from you, there must be a lesson behind it."

"You know me too well by now, do you not, Irirangi? Tell me the lesson."

"I'm sorry?" Jason asked, startled by I'Kiti's request.

"No, you heard me correctly. Today, I want you to be your own teacher, Irirangi. Tell me the lesson I should be teaching you."

Jason thought for a few moments. He would never have expected an emergency landing spot for a space shuttle here, of all places, until reading about it some time ago. "Does it mean that wherever we go, there's more than meets the eye? That a seeming backwater like Hanga Roa has a bunch of hidden charms?"

"Actually, Irirangi, I was going to say that we should always prepare for unexpected situations, but it seems you outdid me with your brilliant analysis." I'Kiti removed the coconut-wood dolphin necklace from his neck, then gave it to Jason. "Take this, Irirangi, as a gift for the son I never had."

"I'Kiti, I don't know what to say," Jason replied. "This is such an honor!"

"I know it's in good hands. Come, I must show you something." I'Kiti led Jason across a patch of grass from the parking lot to the runway. In New York, this move would be a free ticket into jail, but this was Easter Island.

To the side, Jason could recognize the gray star on the blue tail of the LAN Airlines Boeing 767-300ER, a sister aircraft of the one he had flown to Easter Island. The passengers had all disembarked, and another patch waited in the distance for the return flight to Santiago. On the runway itself, a cluster of enraged locals shouted angrily at each other.

"Don't worry, Irirangi," I'Kiti reassured him. "The police will do nothing to us. They have better things to focus on."

"Good. I've dealt with enough legal procedures for a lifetime."

"Yes, I would assume so. Well, do you know what this is?"

"A protest for independence?"

"Yes, exactly. These are becoming frequent on Rapa Nui."

Not too long ago, Jason had read in the news about one where the demonstrators had occupied a resort and the local police had organized a raid to remove them. "I've heard of them," he responded. "What are their main complaints?"

"Culture and demographics, mostly. There are as many or more continentals as Rapa Nui on the island now, and it's clear that lots of them want to erase our Polynesian past."

"Language plays a crucial role, doesn't it?"

"Certainly. To many of my people, Spanish is a weapon the continentals use, and they hate it."

"I don't know if you noticed that I didn't speak Spanish to you."

"Well, except when I found you."

"I was insane. It doesn't count," Jason said, laughing.

"In this case, Irirangi," I'Kiti clarified, "I really couldn't care less about superficial details like the language you pick, as long as I can understand it. However, remember that we are responsible for how we change the Mana, so self-inflicted disabilities such as being secluded or drunk are never an excuse for the behavior that results."

Jason repressed an additional comment about teaching that lesson to the wild partiers at Northport. "I guess I'm just happy you found me and took me as your son."

"It's been my pleasure, Irirangi," I'Kiti said, then scanned the periphery. "You've learned so much."

"Speaking of which, can you show me more about these protests?"

"Yes. Do you see the police?"

"I don't, actually."

"Exactly. They don't want to get involved because whatever they do, it'll be a disaster. If they attack the Rapa Nui calling for independence, they'll create a scandal . And remember, this is a two-way protest. If the police tries to end it, they'll come under fire from both sides."

"But there has to be an alternative to standing here and watching!"

"You know very well, Irirangi, that sometimes there's nothing we can do."

"Like with Northport and its procedures? Sure, I can see that." Jason paused for a few seconds, then shook the regret out of his mind. That was behind him.

"By the way, I'Kiti, if I may ask, what's your stance on Rapa Nui independence?"

"I support it with my heart, but I disapprove of the methods they often use. They can be quite extreme."

"But does independence not lead to isolation?"

"Only if we consciously decide that it should. I would rather we decide how to run our island than be Chile's rear end and get involved with their problems."

"Wouldn't your economy collapse without Chile? Wouldn't you return to the same issues as before the European arrival?"

"No, because this is the twenty-first century. Chile's national airline won't end its service to Rapa Nui as retaliation if we gain our independence. Even if that does happen, we can always make an effort to draw flights from other Polynesian islands, like New Zealand and Hawaii. With the Internet, tourists all over the world can learn about our cultural heritage, but thankfully, the cost of coming here will keep their numbers low enough that they don't harm our environment too much."

"The world has changed so much even since *I* was born," Jason remarked.

"Generally, these changes are far slower to come to Rapa Nui than to the rest of the world, but we still see some. It might not have made news in a country like Korea with countless students at elite international universities every year, but this year, when a student from Rapa Nui was admitted to Harvard, it was the most extraordinary news for us."

"Well, Northport certainly couldn't have done that," Jason replied, wondering whether he was being more spiteful than sarcastic.

"Well, who knows. We cannot always predict how the Mana will flow. But really, Irirangi, to think that when Harvard was founded, we were busy toppling each other's moai..."

"The way I see it, even if we deal with conflicts, over time we progress. It just happens when we're careful enough to change the Mana in intelligent ways, I guess." Jason looked back to I'Kiti, who had just lifted his eyebrows in dismay. "I'Kiti, what is it?"

I'Kiti remained silent for a few seconds, then finally spoke. "Oh, no. This looks bad. Very bad."

"What is—oh, right." Jason stared in horror as a few of the protesters initiated a crossfire of sticks and stones. "An angry mob, and they're armed. Come on, we need to leave!"

"No, Irirangi." I'Kiti ran impulsively onto the runway, then began waving his arms up in the air. "*Aroha!*" he shouted. While I'Kiti had not had the time in his philosophical lectures to teach Jason more than basic Rapa Nui vocabulary, Jason recognized the word for "mercy."

Suddenly, a stone that one of the protesters had aimed at another missed and instead hit I'Kiti right on the forehead, then caused him to fall headfirst onto the pavement of the runway.

"No!" Jason screamed, then ran over to the still-conscious body, diving under all the rocks the protesters hurled at each other. Blood flowed rapidly from the back of I'Kiti's head, but he still seemed conscious.

"Someone call a doctor!" Jason yelled at the top of his lungs.

As Jason looked around, hoping that help would arrive, I'Kiti began to utter a few words with surprising eloquence. "Irirangi, when I was struck by the stone, I saw a vision of the universe. As much of my own Mana left my cracking shell, I saw it going in a loop, and then I finally understood."

"U-u-understood what?" Jason asked, weeping.

"Your project, Irirangi. It all makes sense to me now. You can't relay the proper pitch directly from your brain to your mouth. You need to send it in a circle. Send a signal somewhere from the brain, and it will relay a signal somewhere else, and somewhere else, until it finally reaches your mouth. You have to research the science behind it, but I think it'll work. I have faith in you, Irirangi."

Jason nearly jumped up from his genuflecting pose. "That's...that's the element I was missing the whole time! Thank you, I'Kiti—for everything that you've done," he said, tears pouring out.

"There is no...need to thank me. Go, now. Die another day," I'Kiti muttered, forcing through whatever sounds he could. "Forget...your...past. You, you have...a...future. Your...project...*Jason*..."

I'Kiti Vapui's body collapsed onto the dark runway. "Please, help! Someone get an ambulance!" Jason yelled.

It was no use, though. The man who had been a second father to Jason was gone. Jason poured out tears from his eyes, and he pulled up one of the arms, but the limp form would not budge.

Immediately, the pounding of lava rocks came to an abrupt halt. Rapa Nui and continentals alike dropped their projectiles on the ground and agglutinated themselves around Jason. After the deafening shriek of ambulances and police cars was over, the men who had not run off the tarmac joined to lift I'Kiti's body. Jason dropped his hands, then waited for one of the men as he ran and returned soon afterwards with a shovel, probably from one of the airport repair crews. Jason walked in front of them and led them all the way to Tahai, to a grassy patch facing Ahu Ko Te Riku. The entire procession had been conducted in utter silence, but Jason felt compelled to end with something.

"*Mauviviu. Gracias*," he thanked the initiators of the ceasefire. "In any language, thank you."

As the locals walked away, Jason grabbed the shovel off the ground and began digging. He had just happened to choose one of the rockiest locations on the whole island. Without further hesitation, however, Jason dug through the rough earth. He would have thought it to be an impossible task, though not so much due to the physical labor. A vigorous current of Mana rushed through his veins, uprooting all the lousy rocks that stood in his path. Rather, Jason had been fearful that he could not stand for two minutes without collapsing from the burden of his own exhaustion. Soon, though, that did not turn out to be an issue either. A slight detail obsessed him, endowing him with the single-minded distraction he needed to get through his task.

Had I'Kiti meant something in referring to Jason by his real name?

✦✦✦

SATURDAY, MAY 4, 2013

AHU KO TE RIKU, EASTER ISLAND

It had been a difficult night, to say the least, even more than when he had arrived in Santiago or in the cave. Then again, so was every new beginning. The loss of his mentor and second father the day before had torn him apart, yet it had also convinced him to begin his life anew. In only a few hours, he would fly on his way back to Sydney, where he would hopefully find someone to guide him through the development of Intuner from start to finish, now that I'Kiti Vapui had immortalized himself in the idea Jason had been looking for desperately for so long. Every single minute when he could escape his nearly all-encompassing grief, Jason had spent thinking of microcircuits and sound waves. The success of Intuner was the best legacy he could give I'Kiti.

Jason Curran reached into his navy blue backpack and pulled a red plastic bag. Right before returning to the Kairaku Inn to collect his belongings and spend the night, he had made a stop in one of Hanga Roa's numerous souvenir shops. He carved "*I'Kiti Vapui*" with a chiseled stone on a wide wooden tablet laden covered with indecipherable rongorongo glyphs, then placed it at his feet. One item was still missing, however. Jason pulled out one of two identical replica moai built of the same stones and coral as the originals and set it on a mound of earth facing towards the solitary statue on Ahu Ko Te Riku. This was exactly as I'Kiti would have liked it, Jason thought, with a view that could never get old and no artificial confines walling him from the earth.

Jason took one final look at I'Kiti Vapui's burial site, then at the moai with eyes, as the miniature moai could view it. He was about to head to the airport when he remembered the one last thing he had to do. Jason drew out his cellphone and photographed the lone moai at Ahu Ko Te Riku and the ones on the nearby ahu. It seemed almost anticlimactic to be taking pictures right now, but he had just come out of the greatest crucible of his life.

He definitely wanted his family to see this.

PART IV

22. COME WHAT MAY

MONDAY, MAY 6, 2013

PRINCE STREET, SYDNEY

Jason forced his eyes open as the taxi turned onto Prince Street. The seemingly interminable odyssey from Easter Island to Santiago to Auckland to Sydney was even harder when Jason grieved over the sudden death of his mentor, I'Kiti Vapui.

Nevertheless, Jason also knew the value of his desperate decision to seek isolation. He had learned more about life in four weeks on Easter Island than in nearly four years of a Northport education. He was coming home a wiser man.

Jason Curran looked out the window as the taxi drove through Mosman, the homeland he had fled, and finally parked in front of the Currans' orange-roofed house. As he walked over to the porch to ring the doorbell, Jason attempted to erase the memories of the last time he had been right here. At least today he could tell his parents the truth about his return.

As he stood in front of the door, Jason suddenly remembered that the house would be vacant on a weekday morning.

Jason dialed his mother's cell number. The phone on the other line rang four times, then played an automated, "You have reached Elektra Kananaskis Curran at Kananaskis Architects. Please leave a message—"

Instead, Jason tried her office phone. He guessed that she would storm out of a rushed meeting with clients if it meant hearing from him for the first time in nearly a month.

"Hello, Mami," Jason greeted her.

"Jason!" she shouted, sounding startled yet overjoyed. "You can't believe how happy I am to hear from you! Where are you right now? Are you safe? Do you need any help?"

"It's good to hear from you too, Mami. I'm back in Sydney, waiting at home."

"Wait, you just came back?"

"Yes, about a minute ago. I'm sorry I didn't tell you until now," he apologized in advance.

"Where were you? We were so scared!"

"You didn't have to, Mami. I knew what I was doing." Well, that was a rather flagrant lie, Jason thought, pinching himself. "It's a long story."

"I'll come home right now! I'm in the middle of a meeting, but I'll say that Chloë is sick and I need to pick her up from school immediately. That should excuse both of us."

Jason chuckled in his head at his mother, the eternal pragmatist. "Thank you, Mami."

"Did you call Dad yet?"

"Not yet, but I will right now," he replied, dialing his father's office number. "See you in a bit. Don't go anywhere!"

For the next half hour or so, Jason reran the plan for the Intuner in his head. His next objective was to reach out to a venture capitalist to support his project as both an investor and a business mentor. He knew in which direction to go to finish the necessary scientific research, but he needed logistical and capital help. Plus, now that Derek Park had inevitably excommunicated him, Jason had no one to help him network. Once he found someone to guide him, he would put I'Kiti's idea to good use.

It was then that Jason realized how wrong he had been about the whole Northport fiasco. It had been an unbearable trauma yet a tremendous opportunity. Without the devastating email from President DiTancini, he would never have fled to Easter Island and found the secret to Intuner and his place in the world as its creator.

Suddenly, a beige Volvo XC90 pulled into the driveway. Jason ran over, then threw himself into his parents' and Chloë's arms. He stayed in the group hug for a few seconds until his father broke the silence.

"We're glad to have you back, Jason," Liam Curran began. "We were so worried for you! Where were you, and what happened with Northport?"

Clearly, in the month since Jason had been gone, his father had tempered his usual outbursts of anger. "I'm sorry, Dad. I should have told you what had happened earlier, but I was more confused about it than anyone else."

"You should tell us inside, Jason," his mother suggested before he could explain.

For an hour, Jason recounted everything, from his initial shock upon hearing the allegations of international espionage to the cave of eternal night to his philosophical discussions with I'Kiti Vapui. "I know it sounds far-fetched, but it's completely true. You know how rarely I lie."

"Actually," his mother began, "We did call Northport's president, but he refused to answer any of our questions about what had happened to you. What you tell us about how they treated you seems in character."

"You spoke to President DiTancini? I wasn't allowed to speak to anyone but Dean Washington!" Jason responded with dread. "But you know, I've finally decided that I'll never retry my terrible hermit experiment. Also, if I want my project to succeed, I need someone, or several people, to guide me through the entire process."

"Well, Jason, it's good to hear that you've been able to rebound," his father told him. "As far as we're concerned, you're finished with Northport. We're not giving another cent of our money to those pricks! And I mean, you already received all the education you needed from there. It doesn't matter at all if you don't complete the last three months, and besides, employers today care about skills and experience, not diplomas. I recently read that dropping out of college to create a startup company was now the new thing on American campuses."

"Thanks, Dad." Jason began to scratch his eyes, then said, "Now, all this talking is making me tired. I didn't have much time for shopping, but I did get some tiny gifts for Chloë. Here," he said, facing his younger sister, "I bought you some plush toys."

Jason ran over to his backpack, then removed the replica moai he had bought for himself and placed I'Kiti's dolphin necklace around him. He handed out the three remaining souvenirs to his sister, explaining, "I got you a moai from Easter Island and two kiwis during my layover in New Zealand. I didn't know which one you'd prefer, so I got you both a kiwi bird and a kiwifruit."

Chloë Curran giggled. "More soldiers for our war! Hey, we never filmed it, remember?"

"I'll be sure to do that with you later," Jason said to Chloë, who rushed up the stairs to add the three new arrivals to her zoo of plush animals.

"Well," he said, facing his parents this time, "I'm going to get something to drink and then sleep a little. I'm exhausted." He lifted his body from the living room sofa, then stared at the table for a second.

"Actually, I was wondering something. Do you remember when I was young and had that Easter Island phase, the one where I built that?" Jason pointed to the gray LEGO moai on the tabletop.

"Oh...that," his father responded, "You had a lot of those phases when you were younger. You're not going to tell me your trip to Easter Island was because you got back into it, was it?"

"Well, it was because I'd always wanted to go there. There's something about the moai's gaze that always spoke to me. But I was just curious to know something. I remember that after I built the LEGO moai, there was a woman from Singapore, or maybe it was Hong Kong, who came here with her husband. I spent the whole afternoon talking to her about my creation."

Elektra Curran looked around for a few seconds, then said, "Oh, right! Wong Sam Ting! That was a long time ago, though!"

"Wong Sam Ting was her name?"

"No, that was her husband. I met him during an architectural internship in Sydney before you were born. When you were a kid, he came back to Sydney with his wife for a project and stopped here for an afternoon tea."

"Oh, so is his wife an architect too?"

"No, actually. I can't remember what she did before or what she does now. I think Sam divorced his wife after a few years, but I haven't heard from him in ages. Here, you know what, Jason? Come with me. I'll search through my old emails to find his wife's name—I think I still have my conversations with him."

Jason followed his mother to her desktop computer, then looked as she searched for *"Wong Sam Ting"* in her email archive. After combing through a few old messages together, they noticed the phrase "*my wife, Han Cha Seng*" in the text of one of them.

"Nice, thanks! Here, I'll google her," Jason said energetically. "She was so nice to me, so I'm curious to see who she is." Jason opened his own computer, then read out loud to his mother, *"Han Cha Seng, venture capitalist in the field of technology—"*

Jason locked his eyes on the flashing screen for a few seconds. "Mami! My project!"

"What do you mean?" his perplexed mother asked.

"Don't you get it? I'm looking for a venture capitalist to help me with my project! She's exactly the person I need!"

"Wait, Jason, take some time—"

"No, Mami! I don't have a minute to lose! This is fate, or rather the Mana!" he yelled gleefully, the energy he had lost during the long transpacific voyage suddenly flying back into his body. "I'll check her work address and go buy a ticket to Singapore! I still have all my stuff in my backpack, so I'll just take it and leave in the next ten minutes!"

Before she could protest, Jason unplugged and stored his laptop, then fetched his toothbrush and razor from upstairs and charged down as quickly as the last time he had fled Sydney the last time. As he landed on the ground floor, he nearly crashed into his mother.

"Sorry, Mami! I didn't see you." His head began to fall onto his shoulder. "I must just be so tired...so tired..."

Oh, no, it was coming back. As a child, every so often he had fainted when he was a treacherous combination of tired and hyperactive. Instead, he sat down on the steps and told his mother, "You know, I think I'll rest for a couple days and then fly over there. It seems like I haven't been in an actual bed for a decade."

His mother's eyes lit up. "Jason, you've come back to reason!"

"Thanks, Mami. Come what may, I'll let you know what I'm doing this time."

Jason hugged her again, then walked up the stairs. Pretty soon he would unpack the few supplies he had taken with him but only keep them out of his backpack for a few days. Now that he knew where he was going with Intuner, he did not have a minute to lose.

Just as he was about to close the door of his room, he kept it open for just a few seconds to hear the conversation that transpired.

"Mami, if Jason's staying, can we finally film our stuffed animal war?" Chloë asked her mother as she walked in.

"Of course, Chloë! But only for a couple days, because then he's going to Singapore!"

"Wait, Mami, Jason's going to leave *again*? Like, seriously?"

"Yes, but this time, I'm not worried. I have faith in him. I actually think he knows what he's doing."

✈ ✈ ✈

SUNDAY, MAY 5, 2013

PIKEROP ICE CREAM AND FROZEN YOGURT, FALLS CHURCH

Lars Børgensen parked his silver Toyota Camry in front of the expansive strip mall. The streets were relatively busy at this time, with many of the Northern Virginia suburb's dwellers returning from a day of dining and visiting museums in the adjacent metropolis of Washington, D.C. Even on Sunday evenings, the rainbow-colored interiors of Pikerop and Falls Church's five other frozen yogurt joints served as the temporary headquarters of middle and high school students. The distracting giggling explained why the name Pikerop was said to be a modified spelling of "Pick her up."

While Lars Børgensen was not in the mood for frozen yogurt, he found it much less intimidating to meet here rather than in the eerie silence of the one-person apartment he had moved to after losing his wife, Lena, to lung cancer almost four years ago. For the parent of a college student, it was either a tremendous honor or a terrible disgrace to have the university's Dean of Students request a face-to-face meeting, and knowing his daughter, Lars had no doubt that it would be the latter.

What had Melissa done this time? Lars could still recall the moment when she was still his and his deceased wife's pride and joy: captain of the debate team, lead in the musical, lacrosse star, to name a few. When had she completely changed into someone almost unrecognizable as his daughter? If he remembered correctly, though a father's grasp of time was always likely to be off when it involved his child growing up, it was in the middle of her senior year of high school. Right after her early admission to Northport University, Melissa had apparently decided that she had earned the right to party as hard as she worked.

In half a year of high school, Melissa had gone through a red shift in social circles, somehow ending up with those who shunned academic excellence and cycling through nearly half a dozen boyfriends. Once she entered Northport, Melissa justified her constant hooking up with different males by the fact that she felt too busy with her college work and extracurricular activities to commit to a relationship and would find the time to do so later—as if she would by some miracle be so much freer when she managed the stresses of an actual job!

At first, Lars Børgensen had refused to stand and say nothing while his daughter disgusted him. However, a heated argument about her behavior over Thanksgiving of her freshman year had led her to essentially excommunicate him over Winter Break and instead go to Miami Beach with her friends to do heaven knows what. As a result, he had decided, at the cost of great pain to himself, that a father could only do so much to control his adult daughter. Come what may, Melissa would always be his baby girl, but to the world she would be someone unrecognizable.

On most days, Lars wondered what had gone wrong, what he would change if he turned the flow of time backwards. Had he pushed her too far, prioritizing her chances of college admission over her sanity? Had he been too engulfed in his own work to show her the affection she so badly needed during the grueling decline in her mother's health? She had held together very courageously, even rescuing Lars himself from the brink of depression. Then again, perhaps the trauma had eventually caught up with her, shattering her previously firm sense of right and wrong. Some people surmounted haunting experiences by recalling their best memories. Melissa had probably taken the opposite path at the crossroads, changing her way of living to the point that what had happened before was not the same lifetime. Maybe...

"Good evening, are you Mr. Børgensen?" a deep female voice asked him.

Lars never thought he would have felt so relieved upon meeting Northport's disciplinary enforcer, but he could finally focus on something other than an unchangeable past.

Rising from his chair, Lars looked up at her and said, "Yes. Nice to meet you, Dean Washington."

"Please, call me Nathalie. We were once colleagues."

Lars chuckled. In this situation, he felt more like a current Northport parent than a former employee. "Thank you, Nathalie." He folded his eyebrows down. "I assume the circumstances for your visit are not too positive."

"Really, it's nothing bad," she told him, not wanting to stress him unnecessarily.

He breathed a sigh of relief. "Good, I thought Melissa had been suspended, or something of the sort."

"Oh, no, not at all. Don't worry. I mean, if she had been, we would not be able to contact you under the Family Educational Rights and Privacy Act."

"Well, that's encouraging, isn't it?" he replied, laughing nervously.

"Of course. Now, if you'll excuse me, I'm rather hungry. My flight was delayed by an hour, and you know what onboard meal services are like today—nonexistent. Do you mind if I go grab something?"

"No, not all. Please, go ahead."

Nathalie looked at the pristine white table. "I take it you've eaten already, right?"

"Oh, no, Nathalie. I'm not a big fan of frozen yogurt. I just thought it would be a simpler place to meet than my home," deliberately omitting the embarrassing facts that he was too stressed to eat anything and would feel uncomfortable meeting her in the disorganized mess that was his apartment.

"Okay, I'll be back soon, I promise. I don't want to make you wait more than you need to."

As she left the table, Nathalie walked across the light green tiled floor to the dispensers, then pressed the metal handle to squeeze out a few swirls of strawberry lemonade sorbet into a cylindrical paper cup. She garnished her pink mound with chunks of mango, strawberries, and blueberries. Hoping for a culinary experience, she placed a few Japanese mochi rice cakes as well and some coconut granola flakes while she was at it. After weighing her nearly full cup on the scale, she drew her credit card and selected a purple spoon from the rack.

Nathalie saw Lars Børgensen sitting patiently on his fuschia stool as she returned and began eating spoonfuls of sorbet. "I have to say in advance, I'm sorry I had to contact you on such short notice. If you could only meet at ten on a Sunday night, I'm sure you have better things to do right now, so I'll get to the point quickly."

"If it's important, don't rush it."

"All right. Does the name Jason Curran sound familiar? He came to your talk at Northport two months ago and discussed nanotechnology with you."

Lars looked at the glowing lights for a few seconds, thinking it highly improbable that Jason was a member of the same social circles as Melissa. "Yes, I do actually, and quite well! He's such a bright and motivated young man. Speaks thirty languages, I think."

Nathalie smiled. "That's him."

Suddenly, a long-extinguished fuse in Lars's brain lit up. "Shoot! I never answered his messages!"

"Which messages?" she asked.

"Oh, he sent me a very long list of technical questions on implantable devices. I got the emails and promised myself I'd respond as soon as I could, but then things got crazy. I had to give a talk in the Netherlands and attend a conference in Costa Rica, so the emails fell to the bottom of my inbox. Then, about a month ago, there was a security breach at Bechtel. We had to delete all of our emails in a certain date range, so I probably don't have his coordinates any more. Ah, such a shame! What a bright young man."

Nathalie lifted her head at the revelation. "Was he ever pushy?" she asked, recalling one of the most prevalent traits of those with Asperger's.

"Well, he was intense about his passion, that's for sure, but whoever isn't is a fake academic," he replied, causing both to chuckle. "So, why did you come so far just to tell me about Jason?"

"It actually turns out he's gone through a big change in his life," she responded, thinking carefully about how to avoid damaging Jason's reputation.

"I remember he was working on a breakthrough project. Will I hear about these developments in the news anytime soon?" he asked eagerly.

"We'll see. Anyway, I must head back to my hotel. I have a very early flight back to Kennedy tomorrow."

"That's it? That's all you want to ask me??" Lars asked, perplexed. It seemed like a tremendous amount of trouble for such a nondescript interview, Lars thought. "You didn't want to tell me anything about Melissa?"

Nathalie made sure not to cause him any undue stress by linking Melissa Børgensen to Jason. "No, not at all."

"Oh, all right," he responded awkwardly. "Sorry I asked—I'm a father. Primordial instincts, I guess."

Nathalie laughed, then shook his hand. "It was great meeting you, Mr. Børgensen."

"Please, call me Lars."

"Good night, Lars!" she told him, pushing the glass door and returning to the parking lot.

"You too, Nathalie."

Lars looked back at her as she left the room. Was that really all she had wanted to talk about? It still seemed like so much hassle for such a banal conversation. Had she wanted to go to Washington for another reason and needed an excuse to have her trip paid for by Northport's administrative staff travel office?

Oh, whatever. Lars had no reason to worry about her personal issues. He had enough of his own, after all. He walked over to the dispensers, then filled and purchased a cup of frozen yogurt. For the first time this weekend, he could actually eat.

23. YOU'LL NEVER WALK ALONE

THURSDAY, MAY 9, 2013

CHANGI INTERNATIONAL AIRPORT, SINGAPORE

The tires screeched as the gargantuan Boeing 777-300ER touched down on the runway. "Ladies and gentlemen," the pilot announced in a strong English accent, "Welcome to Singapore. If you are in transit to London, please take all your hand baggage with you. If Singapore is your final destination, we hope you have enjoyed your time flying with us. Thank you for choosing to fly British Airways."

Jason Curran raised his head from his somnolent position, pulled his backpack out of the overhead bin, and followed the other passengers exiting through the jet bridge. He was among the only ones on the aircraft disembarking in the city-state at the tip of Malaysia rather than continuing onto London, but he did not need to follow a crowd to find his way through the massive terminal building. It was far easier for him to navigate an airport than a social scene.

For someone used to the dilapidated facilities at New York's Kennedy Airport, the inside of Changi International Airport was a sight to be seen. Jason could see his own reflection in the white floor and smell the orchids growing from the flower pots. After advancing through the immigration line, he presented his blue-and-gold Australian passport at the desk.

The officer scanned his photograph, staring intermittently at him.

"Sorry, madam, it's an old picture. I haven't had it retaken in many years," he explained.

"That is fine. Are you visiting for business or pleasure?"

"Business," replied, smiling as he pronounced the word.

Unfortunately, he had fallen on an officer who found her normal job of processing passengers quickly through too boring. "You look a bit young for business. Are you here as an intern?"

"No, not quite. I'm here to launch a project."

"Well," she said with a pleased look on her face, "Thank you for what you're doing. It's people like you who keep us growing."

Jason smiled, realizing that he had struck her finest chord. "The pleasure's all mine," he responded.

He heard a soft clanging sound as she pressed a stamp on an empty page. "Welcome to Singapore."

Unfortunately, Jason had never actually crossed the border during his earlier transits, and in his soporific state, even reading signs required effort. He would have to be quick in determining the optimal mode of transportation to Han Cha Seng's address. He blew his nose, then accidentally dropped the tissue. He dove to pick it up and properly dispose of it, recalling the exorbitant penalties for littering, as well as similar misdemeanors such as spitting, chewing gum, and failing to flush public toilets in the "Fine City."

Jason scanned large groups anxiously yet excitedly waiting for family and friends, then saw a line of men in suits, probably limousine drivers, holding signs with various names. He would just have walked by had his eyes not happened to drift to a sign that read *"Han Cha Seng."* Jason stopped for a second, then moved his head away. It was probably a common name, after all.

A slim woman with long black hair in a leopard-print jacket walked through the passageway and handed her four-wheeled suitcase to her chauffeur.

"Welcome, Ms. Han. How was your trip in from Manila?"

"Great, thanks for asking, though the city itself wasn't so enjoyable. The traffic and chaos made me kaput."

"Sorry to hear, Madam. Will you be heading directly back to Robinson Road?"

"Yes, please. I've had quite a tiring day."

Jason chuckled. Coincidences were a funny thing. She was a near-perfect incarnate form of his quarry's photograph, at least as far as he could remember. Suddenly, he could feel a jolt of vigor in his whole body. He intentionally backed up into her, nearly knocking her handbag off, then caught it in a miraculous gesture he could not have consciously executed.

"I am so sorry, madam. Here you go," he said, passing her the handbag before staring at her for a second. "Are you...are you Han Cha Seng?"

As the woman frowned for a few seconds, Jason wondered what he had done wrong. Had he grossly mispronounced her name? Were the hands he had placed on her handbag too sweaty? However, she merely smiled and asked, "Do I know you?"

"I'm Jason Curran," he introduced himself, shaking her hand.

"Pleased to meet you, Jason Curran. How do you know of me? Are you one of the local young entrepreneurs?"

"Well, no. Not yet, at least."

"Oh. Do you just read *The Straits Times* often? They published a picture of me the other day before I could say anything about it."

"I haven't, but I should soon, you know? I always like reading the local press to know what's happening around me."

"Wait," she asked with a puzzled glance, "Where do you know me from, then?"

"It turns out, Ms. Han, that you're an old friend of my family. Well, I mean, not old in age," he added in the hope that he would not offend her, "But from a long time ago! You came to our house in Sydney about fifteen years ago. My parents are Liam and Elektra Curran. Your husband and my mother interned together in an architecture company."

Seeing that Han Cha Seng was hesitating for a few seconds, Jason continued, "It's fine. I wouldn't expect you to remember. But maybe," he said, pulling the LEGO moai out his backpack, "This'll help."

She stared at the intricate creation for a few seconds, then looked up at him and opened her mouth wide. "Of course! Now I remember! My, you made quite an impression on me at the time! What a charming young man you've become! What have you been doing in the past, well, two decades?"

"I actually started at Northport University almost four years ago," he answered. Even if he failed to graduate, the fact that he had been accepted there was commendable and marketable.

"Well, will you look at that. I certainly wasn't lying when I said then that you'd do great things."

"Thank you, Ms. Han."

"Please, Jason, you're a family friend. Call me Cha."

"Thank you, Cha."

"So, Jason," she inquired, "What brings you to Singapore?"

"Well, I'm here to...actually, you. That's why I brought my LEGO creation, since I don't normally carry it around." He paused for a second, attempting not to sound too bizarre in his explanation. "The truth is, I've been working on a tech project for the past couple years, but I've never gotten it past the idea stage. You're the only venture capitalist I know, so naturally I turned to you."

As Cha looked down for a second, Jason asked himself if he had messed up again and done something unacceptable in tracking her down to Singapore. Before he could find a way to edge out of the awkward situation, she replied, "Oh, great! What's your project?"

"It's called Intuner." Jason saw that her driver had been waiting patiently for some time now. "Can I pitch it to you in the car? It'll be more private."

"Definitely! Where are you staying, by the way?"

"Well, I haven't planned that far ahead. I'm looking for a cheap hotel. Do you know any in Changi, or would I be better off asking the visitor information desk?"

"Neither, actually. Why don't you stay with me until you figure out what you're doing? I live alone, but I have a gigantic apartment. A friend of the family—even of my ex-husband—is always welcome."

"Thank you so much for your offer! But really," he said, trying to be as polite as he had learned to be, "That won't be necessary. I'll just—"

"No, Jason. You look very tired. Come, at least for a few days."

Jason would not refuse such a splendid offer. "Why, thanks, Cha!"

"No problem." She now turned to face her chauffeur. "Kuan, you wouldn't mind taking an extra passenger with you, would you?"

"Why, not at all, Ms. Han! Come along, now."

Jason admired Cha's cerulean BMW 335i as the driver placed their bags in the trunk. In a country whose exorbitant automobile taxes encouraged the use of public transportation, even a relatively cheap luxury car cost several hundred thousand dollars.

"What if you could always sing on pitch and never fear that you would make a mistake?" Jason asked Cha. "Never shame yourself in front of a director during an audition, or in front of a demanding audience as a professional? Intuner controls this through the brain, changing the pitch you emit to the rest of the world." Jason paused for a few seconds. "No pun intended, but speaking of pitch, that was my first pitch! It was hard."

"I can imagine so, but it sounds quite impressive and, who knows, maybe it'll be revolutionary! Are you marketing this to both amateurs and experts?"

"I think there's a demand for both. Now," he told her as they drove on, "I'm sorry if I seem really tired. I flew back from South America just four days ago," he explained, cutting himself off before he inadvertently revealed why he had been there. The whole story of the past five weeks would not place him in the most positive light. Later on, he would make sure he found appropriate excuses for why he had not finished college, why he was pathologically afraid of returning to the United States, and all the other oddities about his recent life.

"I'll probably just look out the window and get a feel for the lay of the land, if I don't fall asleep," Jason said.

"You certainly need your rest. Have a nice nap, Jason."

"Thanks, Cha."

Jason scanned the hazy scene as best as he could. Ficus trees germinated in the medians of what the signs identified as the East Coast Parkway, and residents of the surrounding white apartment blocks patriotically waved the red-and-white national flag. This was the densest nation after Monaco, after all. As he saw all flowers and shrubs dispersed at every minuscule space between white residential blocks, Jason wondered whether that statistic applied to plants as well as people.

About fifteen minutes of that landscape later, Jason spotted a cluster of towering skyscrapers glowing in the night sky. Such a metropolitan scene was not out of the ordinary for someone who had spent much time in Sydney and New York City, but the Marina Bay Sands was another story. He had read about it in online architecture magazines and heard his mother decry it as a revolting abomination, but seeing its colossal form face-to-face almost knocked him into the door. As if the three monstrous blocks and the massive sail perched on top of them were not enough, a vertigo-inducing pool stretched over the top, and an inexplicable hand-shaped bulb lay to the side of the structure.

Finally, they crossed the sloping bridge leading to Singapore's Downtown Core, then turned onto Robinson Road.

Cha's chauffeur pulled out their bags, then opened the doors for her and then for Jason. "Good night, Ms. Han. Good night, sir."

"Good night," both responded in unison.

As the doorman let them into the tall, modernist tower and into the elevator, Cha faced Jason and told him, "Good man, Kuan. He gets me to Changi every time, and trust me, I need to go there rather often. I just spent the day in Manila talking to a bunch of young Filipino entrepreneurs."

"You only use him for airport transfers? So when you go to work, do you use the underground—what do you call it here?"

"The MRT. No, I don't."

"Oh, is it a bit seedy at night? That's surprising—I thought Singapore was as safe as Switzerland!"

"No, it's super safe. I mean, I wouldn't do anything stupid just to prove that point, but I've never felt unsafe in any neighborhood here. I actually like walking the streets at night, since there aren't so many strangers staring at me and judging me. Another problem with the MRT—and what I like the least about being in airports, I should add. That's actually why I felt a bit uncomfortable at first when you recognized me at Changi. But no, that's not the reason. I don't need to actually *get* to work. Jason, I do all of my work from my apartment. I read emails and make phone calls the whole day, and I'm everywhere from Andorra to Zambia for business half of the time."

Jason was sure that Cha would have lots of interesting stories to tell him, but for the moment, he simply replied, "It's great that you've been so successful without even having an office!"

"I promise you'll learn that from personal experience very soon."

"I hope so. When I'm fully awake, though."

The two exited the elevator and entered a sleek apartment with orchids sprouting from a bed on the walls and jungle vines hanging from the ceiling. A large couch laden with a faux cheetah cloth faced on a splendid panorama of the Singapore Strait. "Home, sweet home. Make yourself comfortable. The guest room is on the right. I'm sure Sumi—she's the Bangladeshi caretaker—has made it very comfortable. I'll take good care of you, Jason. While you're here, you'll never walk alone."

Jason smiled when he saw the floor space. He would have space to practice jeet kune do every day here. "Thank you for your hospitality, Cha. Well, it was a great pleasure meeting you, and I'll see you tomorrow," he said, shaking her hand.

"Tell me, Jason. I know you're really tired, but there's just one thing I've been wondering."

"Trust me, Cha, there will be lots of those in the days to come."

"Well, yes, you'll need to explain more about Intuner when you're awake."

"Yeah, definitely. Well, I'm going to go set my stuff up and tell my parents how lucky I am. I promised to let them know when I was settled into my hotel room. Good night, Cha," he replied, looking around for the guest room she had indicated.

"Jason, don't you remember? You haven't let me ask my question."

"Oh, right. Sorry about that."

"You didn't know I was flying into Changi, did you?"

Jason hissed almost silently, hoping this would not turn into yet another slipshod accusation against him. "No, not at all. It was just a coincidence."

"That's fine. I mean, I basically live in Changi, so the chance of finding me there is pretty high."

"All a day in the life, right?" Jason asked, laughing softly.

"But Jason, if you hadn't found me with my chauffeur, what would you have done?"

"You said only one question." Jason saw Cha's face turn from a brief smirk to a pronounced frown, so he decided he was best off replying.

"To be perfectly honest, I don't know. I only planned my trip here three days ago. I guess I would have stood at the foot of your tower for a few hours, waited for your doorman to open the door for someone of my age, snuck in behind, and knocked at your front door?"

Han Cha Seng slapped her palm against her forehead. "Jason Curran, it seems I have to teach you more than how to start a business."

24. NOTHING TO LOSE

FRIDAY, MAY 10, 2013

MALACCA PANTRY RESTAURANT, SINGAPORE

It was a perfect complement to the glowing blue and pink lights of Orchard Road's interminable high-end malls. Modernist glass sculptures lined the teak wood walls and muted glass panels subdivided the massive dining area of the chic Tamarine Hotel's restaurant, a recent acquisition by the Sultan of Brunei. The bustling crowds, apparently a fraction of what they were on Ramadan evenings, managed not to infringe the slightest on each other's privacy. No one came to Malacca Pantry for the atmosphere, though.

Even if he had not spent much of the last month surviving on bananas and taro, Jason Curran would have thrown himself headfirst at the endless buffet of food from almost every country in Asia. His eyes watered at the expanse. He could see a Burmese table with a spread of fragrant curries, a Taiwanese rice noodle bar, a palette of rainbow-colored fruit juices, and twenty or so similar tables.

After fifteen minutes, or maybe twenty, or thirty, Jason returned to the table, holding a large stainless steel plate in each hand and balancing a glass of dragonfruit juice in the crest of his left arm.

"Well, Jason," Han Cha Seng told him giddily as she raised her eyes from her cellphone, "It seems like you're enjoying yourself here."

"Oh, yes, Cha. Thank you so much! I could live here forever."

"The pleasure's all mine, Jason."

Jason tasted a few spoonfuls of a bamboo shoot and lentil soup. "Have you tried the Nepalese food? I think it's my favorite so far."

"Actually, no," she replied, picking a few leaves of steamed spinach with her chopsticks. "I'm just eating some vegetables."

"They have lots of vegetarian options. That stew with rice and lentils looks particularly appetizing."

"Well, I'm avoiding carbohydrates at all costs."

Jason looked incredulously at Cha. Her body had the height-to-width ratio of a Manhattan skyscraper, so he wondered how much further she could actually go. However, Jason found it wise to change the subject—an unfortunate experience in high school had taught him that it was a potentially explosive topic.

"Oh. Well, thanks so much for investing in Intuner!"

"You're welcome, Jason, but you're also wrong."

Jason stared at her quizzically. Had his sojourn on Easter Island made him senile? He was almost sure he had just heard that she had not invested in his project. "I'm sorry?" he asked.

"As far as the rest of the world is concerned, I never invested in Intuner. Solo Holdings in the Seychelles is the sole investor."

"I see. May I ask why you keep your funding a secret then?"

"No, I prefer to keep my life a secret—well, to the extent that it's possible when you're a venture capitalist, of course. As the French say, 'To live happily, let's live hidden.'"

Jason nodded. That had been his exact philosophy at Northport before it had spectacularly backfired.

"I'm not worried for my safety or anything," Cha continued. "It's not like anyone is going to try to assassinate me and steal my predictions on real estate prices in Bahrain, or something as crazy as that. Actually, I don't have a problem meeting a few clients in person in random countries. No, I'm just afraid to walk down the street and go to my office."

"Wait, why?" asked Jason.

"Because I know I'll be judged."

That was ironic, Jason thought, looking at her as he drank his dragonfruit juice. She was stunningly beautiful, finely intelligent, and extremely successful in her profession. Besides, in a metropolis like Singapore, everyone was far too busy with a myriad of issues to even stare at any strangers. Even if they did, how would they even evaluate Cha, or anyone else? They would never be able to gauge whether or not she fit in, because the very concept of fitting in was nonexistent. In a large city, as Jason saw it, it was impossible to be different from the norm, since there was no norm. There was always someone richer than the local tycoon, dumber than the village idiot, and more socially awkward than the weirdo.

Having grown up in a city of four million, Jason had been shocked when he had stepped into the far smaller Northport environment. For all its cosmopolitan outlook and emphasis on diversity, the Northport community held a rather rigid view of how its inhabitants should go about their lives. The few times he had actually ventured to New York City, Jason had marveled at the dissimilar types drawn to the so-called "center of the universe," from the eccentric financier with his hair and mustache dyed lime-green to the anarchist protester in a cartoon character disguise. If he could redo his college years, Jason would definitely find the time—he did not know how, but somehow he would—to make far more frequent trips there.

In spite of this, why was she morbidly afraid of being evaluated? She probably just had her issues, like him. No, like everyone. It was the only logical explanation.

"And really," Cha continued, "It's not like I'm being paranoid. I'm being judged all the time. We all are. My husband left me because he couldn't deal with the fact that I couldn't bear any children. Later, when I earned much more money in real estate than he ever did, it made it harder for me to find a partner. Show the typical Singaporean male a self-made woman who's single past the age of forty, and he'll think there's something seriously wrong with her. Why? Because Confucian societies say that it has to be that way. See, Jason, I was born only three years after Singapore became an independent country, so everyone in my generation's a product of the national educational system. With our test scores, others think we have better schools, but there's something very important that we don't have in our system."

"What's that? I've seen the rankings, and Singapore nearly always comes up first in the world."

"Art."

"How so?" Jason asked, perplexed.

"It's just missing. It's not part of our conformist educational system. I'm not saying that schools in Singapore never have art classes or that artist's ever come out of here, but there are very few, because we don't encourage creativity. Not even that, actually. We *repress* creativity. We can mold our youth into the best and brightest businessmen and administrators, or anything that involves playing within the rules of the system. But when it comes to following our passions and creating what doesn't already exist, that's where we fall behind. It doesn't only mean we can't paint great pictures or write great novels; it makes it very hard for us to invent anything new, technology or otherwise."

Jason nodded. "You know, Cha, I'd probably use up your whole paper supply if I wrote down a list of everything I hate about America's so-called "values." I can't stand all the hypocrisy in everything they do. But I have to say, though, I've never seen a country that encourages people to innovate that much."

He thought back to Fan Weixiong, the first Chinese high schooler he had met on Northport's campus this past Winter Quarter, when the route to one of his classes crossed the tourists' scheduled path. Though Jason regretted that Weixiong had first told him the superstition about leaving watches in rooms, something that had formed part of Nathalie Washington's allegations of suspicious behavior, he had later had a great email conversation with the young visitor from Qingdao. At one point, Jason had mentioned the electronic circuitry laboratory he had built in his attic as a hobby. In a way so obsequious that, despite his clouded social vision, Jason recognized he was being worshipped as a god, Weixiong had applauded Jason's creativity, saying that a student in a Chinese high school would lack not only the time, but the very idea to undertake such an unconventional project in a universe where creativity was foreign.

"You're right, Jason. I really loved my experience living in Silicon Valley a couple years ago, though Singapore will always be my home. But actually, there's one thing that "makes the Lion City roar," as they say. Talented people from all over the world come here and bring their creativity. Amazing people like you."

Cha paused for a few seconds, then asked, "You know, Jason, I've just been wondering. You have all these amazing ideas and you come to me so I can help you put them in action. Why do you trust me?"

"I'm sorry?" Jason asked, thinking he had been too focused on determining the spices in his Thai curry to hear her correctly.

"Seriously, how do you know I'm not a crook? I might be out to steal your ideas. And why did you come into my apartment in the dead of night? I could do all kinds of things to you while you're laying in bed there."

For a split second, Jason wondered whether he had not been vigilant enough, then brushed aside those thoughts. "I mean, Cha, I know you."

"You *know* me? I'm the ex-wife of an old acquaintance of your mother's. What does 'knowing' even mean in today's world? Do you 'know' someone you've exchanged a hundred messages with on an online dating site? And before you try telling me that it does, meeting someone face to face doesn't fix the whole problem. There are people who've been duped by their spouses of thirty years."

Jason pondered that question for a moment. "I know exactly why," he responded. "If you tried to do anything to me, I would write about it online, and immediately the whole world would know." Still, the explanation did not satisfy him. He cared nothing for Cha's reputation. Digging dirt on her would not make him go further. He still had to figure out the reason why he trusted her so much to open up so much.

"Very good, Jason. See, reputation and image go a long way in getting mind share."

"Mind share?" Jason asked, perplexed. "What's that."

"You know, when people immediately think about your product. Like when I think about luxury hotel chains, I immediately think of Four Seasons, Tamarine, Park Hyatt, and the like."

"Oh, I see. But I really don't care about reputation, Cha. Actions speak louder than words."

"Except when the words speak first. When you're selling a product, most people will figure out who you are before figuring out what you do. If you appear unprofessional or untrustworthy, it doesn't matter how great your product is. Rub people the wrong way, and you're screwed."

Not so long ago, Jason would have resisted hearing words like these, but now he dug through his earwax with a napkin to make sure he heard every syllable. "All right, Cha. So which image do I have?"

"Oh, I don't know. A genius who's sometimes uneasy in society? A little boy who's all grown up and trying to find his place in the world? Don't worry, I'll rub that off of you."

He did not know whether he was interpreting it correctly, but it sounded more like a compliment than a reprimand. "Thanks, Cha. Now, I'm going to grab some dessert."

As Jason brought back copious servings, he announced to Cha, "So when I was scooping some tapioca pudding, I had this idea for Intuner's logo. Maybe—"

"Slow down, Jason."

Jason nearly dropped his plates of sweets. Had he done something wrong again? Was the way he was carrying his plates a vulgar gesture in the local culture? Or was she merely telling him to speak more slowly?

"You talk too much. You're definitely not shy like the entrepreneur I met in Mountain View all those years ago who showed me this new programming language he had designed but could barely look me in the eye and hold a conversation about the weather in California. You're the other extreme. You don't listen enough and say too much about yourself. You barely ever ask any questions, except for when you're trying to clarify tiny factual details. Are you not interested in me? Do you not care how I feel, how I've been doing today?"

Jason reprimanded himself, then picked up on her hint. "So how's your day been, Cha?"

"Oh, come on, Jason. You're smart. You can do better than that."

Jason hesitated for a few seconds. What would be acceptable to ask? He should not inquire into whether she wanted some dessert, since she had mentioned her obsession with her diet. Figuring out if she also listened to Rodrigo Oliveira and had downloaded his new compilation album, *Tenor Classics*, might be a good icebreaker. Maybe he should take that route, holding the same conversation with her as he would with Aurélia. As he opened his mouth, though, he wondered why he was even trying to invent a new question. He could copy the exact ones she was asking to him. Conversational questions were not patented, after all.

"All right, Cha. Why do *you* trust *me*?"

"Well, Jason, my job's all about risk. Do you know how many startups fail? I've heard figures over ninety percent."

"Scary stuff."

"Cost of doing business," Cha replied matter-of-factly. "But besides that, I just get good vibes from you. You don't seem like a charlatan. You look more excited about your idea than the money it can bring you. Even if the market isn't going to stand behind your project, I know you'll keep on going until you get it right."

Cha placed her hand firmly on Jason's shoulder. "That's why I always like a nice guy."

It was funny, Jason thought, how easily the words could have come from Aurélia's mouth. And then, right as he started eating his durian sorbet, he finally understood. Maybe the dessert, despite its pungent odor, was helping him think more clearly. He knew exactly why he had been so quick to trust Cha.

While in the cave on Easter Island, he had concluded that he could never trust anyone because anyone could harm him, even unintentionally. After I'Kiti Vapui had explained to him that he needed to rely on others, Jason had struggled to reconcile that idea with the evident danger of being overly trusting. Now, though, he understood that trust was not a question of absolute certainty, but rather of calculated risk. It was not like he knew Cha's intentions were benign, even though he had learned enough about reading people lately to assume that they were. If she was actually trying to harm him, though, did he really care? After falling so low since that fateful letter from President DiTancini, he doubted that he did.

He just had nothing to lose.

✦ ✦ ✦

WHITE DOLPHIN CAFÉ, NORTHPORT

Juan Ravénto sipped his double strawberry-coconut mochaccino. He made sure to enjoy every drop of it—after all, he had never drunk anything of the sort, and he could not guess the next time he would on the Office of the Dean's expense account. He could not yet see the woman who had called him to the White Dolphin Café, but while relaying her message to him, Juan's supervisor had reassured him by mentioning that this interview was completely unrelated to Juan's work performance and that Juan would not be penalized for the shifts he missed as a result. As he finally finished the exotic drink he had ordered from the endless menu, he stared at the table and wondered when she would come, hoping that her questions would not be too challenging.

Nathalie Washington scanned the sides of the room. The café was a hub of activity for everything from casual dates to job interviews to book clubs. The red brick walls displayed photographs of tourists wearing White Dolphin Café t-shirts in front of monuments labeled as Tajikistan's Fann Mountains, Bolivia's Madidi National Park, and Mali's Great Mosque of Djenné, among more conventional destinations such as the Eiffel Tower and Disneyland. Posters advertised a local indie rock band's concerts and the launch party for a coming-of-age novel recently written by a Northport student. Nathalie recalled reading about a Romanian modern artist's new exposition of environmental activist paintings in *The Daily Deer*, so that was the most likely explanation for the surrounding depictions of burning forests and gray clouds of smog. Missing from the scene, however, was Elena Zarabić.

To pass the time, Nathalie went to the counter and purchased an espresso from the eccentrically bearded barista. By the time she returned with her white cup, a woman in a blue dress sat on the opposite chair.

"Oh, sorry I'm late!" Nathalie told her. "I went to grab some coffee. So, you must be Elena Zarabić!"

"Not a problem," Elena answered, standing up to shake her hand. "So nice to meet you, Dean Washington."

"You too, Elena."

"Now, I am glad you told me I was not in trouble. It is always stressful to be convoked by the Dean of Students."

"Yes, I'm sorry if it worried you to read my name." Following her stress-inducing encounter with Lars Børgensen, she had notified her two interviewees today

310

that they were not called as a result of any problematic action on their part or that of their kin.

"Everyone does what they have to do, I guess," Elena responded, brushing her short brown hair to the side.

"Of course. Now, let me get straight to the point. I hear that all the time, you see trios of Chinese visitors exchanging weird objects with a Northport student, is that correct?"

"Yes, it is."

"What kinds of objects were they?"

"Oh, I could not tell very well. There are flasks blocking the window in my laboratory. However, I think I once saw a piece of paper and several watches. I was suspicious since I saw the same kinds of objects being exchanged every time."

That was interesting, Nathalie thought. It would explain the collection of watches in Jason Curran's room. "Was that student's name Jason Curran, by any chance?" she asked Elena.

"I have no idea, really. My undergraduate laboratory assistant, Vanya Lakshmi, handled all of that. Vanya knows the university so much better than I do—she has been here for longer, and as a graduate student I do not interact with as many different people. She talked to her friend—I don't know to whom—so that he could look into it. Then, she told me that he had told her to warn the administration about the strange exchanges."

"Do you know who this friend of hers was?"

"No, sorry. I put Vanya in charge of the whole thing, so I have no idea."

"I should really ask Vanya, then, but where is she? I haven't been able to get in contact with her."

"That could be difficult. Regrettably, Vanya has been at the university health center for the past week!"

"That's horrible! I'm really sorry for her. Was this for mononucleosis?" she asked, guessing a very common cause for trips to the Arlen Health Center.

"No, not at all. This was for sleep deprivation and mental exhaustion, since she is so absurdly busy. You could never guess how many things she does at Northport. The hours she spends with me are nothing compared to the rest. To give you an idea, she just finished writing a musical play!"

"She was Arlened for a lack of sleep?" Nathalie asked incredulously. Every year she worked at this job, the students seemed more skilled not only at competing on the global scale, but also at nearly destroying their lives in the process.

"Pardon?"

"Oh, right, I'm sorry I used that term. It's an undergraduate thing, probably. It's what the students say when someone gets sent to the Arlen Health Center."

"Ah, I understand. However, I know nothing more about the strange trios of visitors and their contact. Vanya knows all the details, and I'm sure she'll be happy to discuss them with you. Unfortunately, it may be a while before she recovers."

Clearly, Nathalie would not learn any more details about the process from Elena Zarabić, and frankly, with all the misinterpretations involved in Jason's story, she doubted Vanya would be of more help. "Well, I'm so sorry to hear about Vanya! Send her my best wishes. Thank you for being so open, and good luck with your research. Have a nice day!"

"You too, Dean Washington," Elena responded, walking out of the White Dolphin Café.

Nathalie walked through the relatively exiguous yet packed space. At the end of the room, she approached the man she took to be her second interviewee.

"Good morning! I am Nathalie Washington, Dean of Students."

Juan Ravénto put down his nearly empty coffee cup. "Nice to meet you, Mrs. Washington."

"And you are Juan...Rurvénto?"

"*Ravénto*," he corrected.

"Oh, I'm sorry about that," Nathalie replied, ashamed of her blunder.

"Is fine, Mrs. Washington."

"Thank you for your understanding. Now, I just have a few questions for you, if you don't mind."

"Yes, Mrs. Washington."

"And like I said, you're not in trouble."

"Thank you, Mrs. Washington."

"Now, do you work in Mancini Hall on Mondays, Wednesdays, and Fridays?"

"Yes."

"In the basement?"

"Everywhere."

"Do you ever see anything bizarre in the basement restroom?"

"I just do my job, Mrs. Washington. Everything is normal."

"Sorry, I should rephrase my question. Have you seen or heard anything bizarre in the basement restroom?"

Juan thought back to the serial hand-washer. How could he ever forget someone who had done so much to impede his job? "Yes, but not now. Couple months ago, I think. But it estop now."

Nathalie smiled. This would probably end up being an easy interview. "Like what?"

"Well, there was one estudent who I always hear espeak in the restroom."

"Do you know who that student was?"

"No, sorry. I only know he make a mess of soap and water every time."

"What was he speaking?"

"Not English, and certainly not Espanish. I think he espeak Chinese and North Korean. But I only hear that from other estudent. I no espeak them myself."

That was interesting, Nathalie thought. She had very well doubted that someone had told Juan Ravénto, though it would be typical of a surreal place like Northport to employ a janitor who was secretly a master linguist. "From whom did you hear this?"

"Well, I no remember his name, but one day I estand in the restroom and clean, and the estudent who espeak the languages walk in with other estudent. When the first estudent speak in the estall, I ask the other one which language he espeak. He just listen for a couple seconds. He come back few days later and tell me his friend espeak Chinese and North Korean. I ask him how he know, and he say he estudy Chinese at Northport, and he is Korean, so he know how to hear North Korean language. I think the estudent in the estall is just annoying for espending so much time there, but the Korean estudent tell me to complain to the administration, because he might espy in hiding."

Nathalie Washington thought for a second. "You don't know his name, do you?"

"No, sorry, Mrs. Washington."

"It's fine. You've been very helpful, Mr. Ravénto. Have a nice day!"

As she rose from her wooden chair, Nathalie inadvertently spilled what remained of her espresso. Immediately, Juan ran and fetched some paper towels, then wiped the liquid off the hardwood floor.

"Oh, thank you so much!" Nathalie replied, flushing with embarrassment. "That's really nice of you, but really, you didn't need to do that! I could have cleaned it up myself."

Juan Ravénto smiled. "Is part of job."

25. TAKE ME ALONG

WEDNESDAY, MAY 15, 2013

GARDENS BY THE BAY, SINGAPORE

"Happy birthday, Jason."

"Thanks, Cha. You couldn't have picked a more perfect setting."

Jason Curran and Han Cha Seng walked on the gray pedestrian bridge over to the recently completed Gardens by the Bay. It might be a mere stretch of reclaimed land next to the main island of Pulau Ujong, but it could not look more otherworldly. Two massive sky blue domes in the shape of tortoise shells, their white sails jutting out like the ice rings of Saturn, stood in the middle of an endless jungle. Interspersed among them, the neon yellows and purples of alien-looking supertrees glowed in the night sky. Behind them, the lights of the imposing Marina Bay Sands and record-height Singapore Flyer Ferris wheel monopolized the field of view, covering the clustered skyscrapers of Singapore's financial district.

"Tell me, Jason. How would you have spent your twenty-second birthday if you hadn't left Northport to work on Intuner?" Cha inquired.

"I don't know. I try to plan most things on the day of." Jason had long stopped adhering to the routines that had dictated his early life.

"Really? You wouldn't have done this?"

"Come to Singapore? No, my family travels often, but we still can't afford frivolous trips."

"Don't be a wisecrack, Jason. You know exactly what I mean."

Jason wondered whether he had managed to hear every word right while completely missing her point. "Actually, I don't, sorry."

Cha let out a heavy sigh. She had quickly realized that he was often slow to pick up on her intended meaning, as she had learned every time she had attempted a double entendre. "You know, go on a quiet stroll under the shining moon, the city lights right behind you."

"Not really."

"You're telling me that you don't have a beautiful girlfriend to spend your birthday evening with, instead of an old businesswoman?"

Oh, so that was what she had meant, Jason thought. It would have been so much simpler had she said it directly.

"Well, I very briefly had a girlfriend in sophomore year, but no one since then."

"Not in two years? Jason, you know very well that I'm not going to believe that."

Where was she going, though? Was she somehow interested in him romantically and checking to make sure that there was no competition? No, that was too far-fetched. Being a businessman did not give him the right to be haughty.

"Why not?" he inquired.

"Oh, come on, Jason. You're intelligent, successful, cultured, and though it's certainly not the most important quality for a partner," she told him, opening her black eyes wide to get a good look at him in the nighttime light, "You're very handsome."

"Handsome? Nothing compared to you," he replied, drawing from her suggestion that he pay more attention to her. "And to be honest, I'm not that successful. I won't have a college degree, and look, Intuner isn't going be the next Microsoft."

"All right, Jason. Cut the fake modesty. I know very well that you have a sweetheart, if not more than one."

"Well, this year I had a female friend, but not a girlfriend."

Cha wondered why Jason was always obsessed with the little details. "Is there really a difference?" she asked.

"I mean, we didn't get physical or anything. But yeah, I did enjoy her company."

Jason might be inexperienced, but at least he had his values straight, Cha thought. "Good for you. Emotional intimacy matters more than anything physical."

"Sure. I mean, we were pretty close."

"You *were*?"

"Yeah, she left me. Actually, I left her. Well, sort of."

"Jason, did she leave you, or did you leave her? I don't see how it's so ambiguous."

"Well, she stopped talking to me," he admitted, "So then I stopped talking to her."

"Was this after you chose to leave Northport, since you weren't seeing her every day anymore?"

Jason grunted. By focusing so much on responding appropriately to her questions, he had shot himself in the foot and revealed way too much. He had to stall, a conversational skill he barely possessed.

"Not right away. We talked a lot for a few days after I left. But like I told you, she stopped talking to me after that, so I blocked her email."

Cha's eyebrows dropped. "What did you do to her, Jason?"

Even at night, the heat of the tropics was intense, so Jason's face began to drip with sweat. "I didn't do anything to her!"

"Look, I might not think like young people today, but I know very well that no one would just stop talking to a friend out of the blue. Besides, you definitely don't seem like the kind of person who would intimidate anyone else."

That was ironic, Jason thought, since that was exactly what had happened. Unfortunately, if he did not stay on his guard, she would figure that out soon enough. For now, his only hope of concealing the truth was to be mysterious. "I think I know what happened, but it didn't involve her."

"Please, Jason, stop being so mysterious."

Oh, that was just *great*, Jason thought. She was not letting him be enigmatic in his replies, so he would have to resist in a more straightforward manner. "No, Cha. I can't tell."

Cha moved from Jason's side and stood right in front of him, blocking his way as he moved to the side. "Jason, I'd like to know more than the culinary tastes of the person whose project I'm pouring so much money into."

"*You* are? I thought Solo Holdings was," Jason replied with a smirk.

"Please," Cha said, frowning deeply, "This is no time for jokes. And come on, I thought you trusted me. You know very well how much I hate being judged. I'd really be a hypocrite if I started being so judgmental myself."

Jason hesitated for a few moments, blowing his nose loudly and then fixing his shoelaces to buy himself some time. If he refused to tell her anything, she would certainly pull out all her anonymous funding for his project, and

Intuner would be no more. Cha would be able to pierce through any of his lies with her X-ray vision, so he had to tell the truth.

Now, if he admitted the truth and she felt horrified, she would not be able to alert anyone. She had no proof, only a possibly falsified oral confession, and she would not send a tipoff to anyone—after all, she had made it clear that she would never tell anyone that she knew him. Besides, why would a Singaporean businesswoman want to protect American national secrets? The worst that could happen would be for her to stop funding his project, leaving him in no worse a situation than if he stayed silent.

However, if Jason revealed what had truly happened, he would likely be in a better position than if he said nothing. Others had truly believed that he was a victim when he had told them the story. His parents loved him unconditionally, so they did not count, but Orosz Sólyom and I'Kiti Vapui had agreed with Jason's assessment of the situation as fundamentally unjust. Perhaps he could learn as much from Cha.

Finally, Jason let out a heavy sigh. "The truth is, Cha, I didn't *choose* to leave Northport."

"Because you felt that you needed to go work on Intuner immediately, so you forced yourself to go?"

"No, Cha. Because *Northport* forced me to go."

Cha took a few steps away from him, then covered her mouth with the palm of her left hand. So *that* was the reason why he had left Northport so close to the end.

What else was he hiding? She exposed her mouth to say, "Jason, I want the full story."

"Oh, you'll get it, Cha. You haven't exactly given me a choice." He paused for a second, wondering in how much excruciating detail he should recount his life for the past few months.

"Jason, tell me exactly what happened. I don't care what crime you were kicked out for, but if you tell me a single lie, you'll regret—"

"All right, all right," Jason said, letting out an exasperated sigh.

"Good. I always appreciate honesty."

As far as Jason could judge, Cha did not look like she was bluffing. He was best off not even trying to sugarcoat any details. "It didn't have to do with my good friend, Aurélia, at all. Ironically, it all started because of Intuner."

Cha stared at him with an odd look on her face, so Jason clarified, "But don't worry, it's nothing about Intuner itself. One day, I went to this talk by a former Northport professor contracting for the U.S. government, Lars Børgensen. The talk was great, and I felt that Professor Børgensen could help me with some really hard technical stuff for Intuner. I spoke with him for a long time after his talk. He had to go, so I sent him an email with a ton of detailed questions. He didn't respond after I followed up, which wasn't surprising since he lives such a busy life, but I knew that I desperately needed his help."

If Jason was interpreting it correctly, Cha seemed less suspicious already. "So what did you do?"

"During his talk, he had mentioned that he had a daughter, Melissa, at Northport. I thought that if responding to an audience member from one of his talks wasn't high on his priority list, responding to his own daughter was. So, I got in touch with Melissa and asked if she could contact her father and send him the list of questions. She said she would, but she never did."

"And? Did you ever try recontacting her?"

"On the contrary, I did, and many times. So much that when I got tired of Melissa not answering any of my calls, texts, or emails, I searched for her everywhere on campus. Finally, I found her at a party one night. She promised to talk to her dad, but she seemed upset to see me there. I have no idea why, but she would never do it. Unlucky me, Melissa was friends with Cayley Thompson, this really smart Biology major I'd offered to pay for research on Intuner. She was so busy with all her clubs and activities on campus that she never had the time to do the research. So I kept asking her when she would deliver. Look, I think I was being pushy about contacting them over and over, and I wouldn't do it again. I know better now. But was my behavior justified? Of course! They promised me some favors, and if they knew that they were too busy to do what they said, they could at least have given me the courtesy of asking me to go away for good and apologizing."

"Well, just because it makes sense doesn't mean it's the best thing to do," Cha said.

"Unfortunately not. Okay, so it was the last day of Spring Break. I was at the airport in Sydney, about to fly back to the States, when I got an email from Northport's president, Tony DiTancini, telling me that I'd been suspended due to serious complaints about my behavior. The message was super scary! It told me that I should stay out of the States for a while because the federal authorities were on the case."

Cha let out a gasp, but she continued to listen. She counted herself lucky for having convinced Jason to tell her everything.

"Worst of all," he continued, "I had no idea what it was about! I waited for a few really painful days until Northport's Dean of Students, Nathalie Washington, finally wrote to me. Then I talked with her on the phone. She asked me if I'd talked to Melissa and Cayley, because they'd complained that I was acting in a weird and possibly threatening way."

Cha shook her head in disgust. "A complaint for *being weird*? That keeps you out of the country? What has this world come to?"

"Well, Dean Washington thought that the issue was more complex. More absurd, if you ask me. She asked me a bunch of other unrelated questions, like whether I ever exchanged papers with Chinese tourists or hid in a restroom to practice foreign languages. At the end of the conversation, she dropped the bomb on me: it was a complaint of international espionage. No, I'm not kidding. Me, a *spy*? Meet Jason Curran, the new Julius Rosenberg—ridiculous, no?"

Cha was not sure what to believe. She knew that she had to listen to reason and tread carefully, yet her instincts told her that Jason had really been victimized. His story seemed like the plot of a thriller, yet it sounded plausible. While Jason had a penchant for sly humor, he did not come off as someone who would find it funny to make up such a story. In her career, she had maneuvered enough legal systems to see procedures go awry. This definitely seemed like one of those cases. Plus, she could see where everything was coming from. Unlike her, those who stuck to the system would not be attracted to Jason's nonconformist behavior. Was she certain that he was telling the truth? No, but she would assume so. As analytical as she could be, sometimes she just had to trust her gut feeling rather than picking out the evidence that would best disprove it. That had served her quite well in business.

Before Cha could even open her mouth to react, Jason continued his story. He had learned long ago not to interrupt those who were speaking, especially when they were in a position of authority, but this time he had to make an exception. She was probably not convinced that he really been victimized, so he had to prove that to her quickly. Explaining his story in the way that was factually accurate while painting him in the most positive light possible was tricky enough; having to respond to whichever remark she decided to make would be overkill.

"In my later emails," he recounted, "I asked Dean Washington if I could see the words of the complaint, but she never let me, because it was always about the 'Northport system' and its ludicrous policies. Then, Aurélia just stopped talking to me, probably because she had heard rumors about me getting suspended."

"So did you ever talk to Aurélia again?"

"Not after that. It was very painful to realize that she believed the rumors instead of trusting me. I ended up blocking her emails so I'd think less about her."

As Cha saw it, Jason still had feelings for Aurélia, but he was fighting a battle with himself to repress them. "You've gotten over her, then?"

Jason thought back to those haunting nights in the cave on Easter Island. He had quickly abandoned all thoughts of his project, reputation, chances of employment, and shelter from the police, but he had never erased Aurélia from his mind. He had practically convinced himself that she was dead. In barely a week in Singapore, Jason had played in his head countless scenarios by which he could get in touch with Aurélia, often times as outlandish as his earlier dreams of returning to Northport in disguise. Jason looked up at Cha, now standing there with a confident smile on her face. He was past trying to recreate what he had once had. Was he over Aurélia?

"Yeah."

"That's good." If he was not an emotional wreck, her work would be far easier. "So what did your parents say about everything that happened?" Cha asked.

"Are you kidding? I didn't tell them! I was way too afraid!"

"I mean—"

"Cha, do you have any idea how they would have reacted?"

"But don't they love you, Jason?"

"Of course they do!" he replied, wondering if he had not made a mistake in taking that fact for granted his whole life.

"So don't you think they would have defended you? Fought tooth and nail to save their son?"

"You know, you're right. But back then, I thought that having others help me was a weakness. If I didn't fend completely for myself, I lost. I told myself that I was afraid my parents would do something terrible to me if they found out, but I think I was lying to myself. I get it now. My real fear was that they'd help me, and that was a failure I couldn't accept," he recalled.

"So did they ever find out?"

"Of course. My mom always finds out. Well, actually, this time it was my sister."

"You have a sister? How come you never told me about her? How old is she?"

"Eleven," Jason replied, wondering why he never thought to share any details about his family with anyone he met.

"She must be so cute! What's her name?"

"Chloë."

"Nice name."

Now it was Jason's turn to play her game and ask questions. "Do you have any siblings?"

"No, my parents would have been crazy to have two kids. I was already high-management enough. But wait, how did your sister find out?"

"You know how little kids are. She was fooling around with my phone to see if I had a secret girlfriend or something, and she saw a message from Dean Washington. Right when I was washing my hands!"

"Classic," Cha said, chuckling. As much as Jason's story saddened her, the hand-washing reference was just so typical of Jason.

"Okay, I get it. I shouldn't spend so much time at the sink. Anyway, to get back on topic, I freaked out when I saw her with it, so my mom wondered what was happening and read the message. I couldn't build up the courage to face them and ran away instead."

"That's horrible, Jason," she replied in a way that sounded genuine. "That's not why you came to Singapore, is it?"

"Come on, do I really look like I ran away from home just a week ago? You have no idea what I looked like when I did. It was bad. I went to Easter Island, the most remote settlement on Earth, to try living like a hermit in a cave. I saw what had happened when I had tried to deal with others, so I never wanted any of that ever again. It was just a phase, though. I couldn't survive that way for long."

Cha chuckled again as she imagined Jason away from clean bathroom conditions for more than an hour, though she would probably not fare better than him in that environment.

"After the two darkest weeks of my life, figuratively and literally," he continued, shuddering at the eternal dark night in the cave, "I was rescued by a local shaman called I'Kiti Vapui, who taught me his philosophy, a combination of native Polynesian beliefs and modern physics. I told him what had happened to me and explained Intuner, and he suggested the internal loop idea. But before I could learn more from him, he was killed accidentally in a political protest," Jason explained, reprimanding himself for getting the exact details of the chronology wrong. He was still unable to believe that I'Kiti had given his most valuable advice not before, but right as he died. It seemed like something right out of a dramatic movie.

"I'm really sorry you had to go through all this pain. It seems the world hates you, Jason!"

"At least you don't, Cha, and oh am I glad of that," he responded with raised eyebrows and a crooked smile, doing his best to imitate one of her mannerisms.

Cha barely stopped herself from giggling. Jason's attempts at flirtatious banter were quite entertaining.

"But anyway, after I'Kiti died," Jason resumed, "I figured that I had nothing more to do on Easter Island, so

I decided to go back to Sydney. I was reenergized and ready to find my little niche in the world. I also figured that if the FBI hadn't given me any trouble yet, I was safe. I told the whole story to my family. Once we were done bashing Northport's administration, we talked about Easter Island. I noticed the LEGO Easter Island statue just standing in my living room, so I asked them about the woman who had complimented me on it when I was a kid. While digging up information on who you were, they learned that you were a venture capitalist, so I thought you'd be perfect for Intuner. This was fate, and I didn't have a moment to waste, so I left for Singapore as soon as I could get some rest and a plane ticket. And then…well, that's pretty much when you joined my life."

"Wow, this whole story...I can barely believe it, Jason!"

"I know, right? Sure, my ancestors might have been convicts, but being a criminal isn't genetic! And I mean, I don't deserve a kangaroo court just because I'm Australian!"

"That's cute. If you ever write a novel about your story, you should also say that social awkwardness is not a crime."

"'Social awkwardness is not a crime.' I like it."

"I have to say, though, you fooled me. Look, I've noticed that you don't live your life like everyone else," Cha remarked. "And I certainly wouldn't suggest that you do otherwise, because that's what I love about you," she added. He seemed to have taken all of her helpful advice to the letter, so she should not inadvertently give him harmful advice.

"When I looked at you before, I always thought you had this sort of fear of being too social inside you. But it's funny, I always assumed that it was because you were inexperienced. You hadn't seen enough of the world—not geographically, of course, but socially, in terms of your relationships with others—so you were afraid of venturing out. Everyone's afraid of what they don't know. It doesn't matter how educated you are, there's always going to be some things that are a mystery to us, and we'll avoid them like the plague. Whatever we can't imagine is scarier than the scariest thing we *can* imagine. That's why everyone fears death so much."

Jason's mind flickered back to that dreaded cave. The memories still frightened him every few nights, but at least he could visualize that hell clearly.

"But I never would have guessed that you'd been through something like that. I'm telling you, it takes a whole lot of effort to hide such an important detail of your life from the people you meet. That's why it's so hard to connect with the people who work with you. Remember what I told you the other day about keeping a good image? In business, you always need to be invulnerable. As far as everyone sees you, you have absolutely no, uh, garbage, for lack of a better term. You're able to use all your energy towards your work. Yet when you look at it, everyone has their issues. When we talk about them with others, that's how we learn."

Cha thought back to the self-consciousness she had revealed to Jason right as he had first come into her apartment. "For as long as they were alive, my parents judged me for everything. So did my teachers, employers, and my husband. I was never good enough, smart enough, pretty enough. Trying to live with all these expectations made me worry about how even a stranger on the MRT would evaluate me."

Well, that made more sense, Jason thought. Everyone had a backstory.

"After I got divorced, a story that's nowhere near as interesting as your recent adventures," she recounted, "I wanted a change of scenery. I moved to Silicon Valley, which made sense since I had studied engineering, like you. Tech was the new thing. And while I was there, I don't know, I just didn't feel comfortable. I know I told you I'd loved it there, but apart from seeing so much creativity, it was dreadful for me. When you move to a place, people don't have any preconceived ideas about you, so they judge you from day one. I knew that they'd see my anxiety, but as I told you it's not something you can show in work. So at some point, I just gave up. I told myself that if I couldn't hide my insecurity from others, I would just hide *myself* from them. That's why I don't have a physical office."

"I've always been wondering, but I thought it would be impolite to pry too much into it," Jason said. "How do you manage when you go to meetings with entrepreneurs and other investors?"

Cha sighed. After all the unfortunate personal details that Jason had revealed to her, it would be unfair for her not to admit that she had also lied to him. "Jason, I should really tell you something. Apart from this one, I don't invest in technology projects."

"Is this another one of those things where it's not you, it's Solo Holdings?" Cha had pulled that technicality on him more than enough times.

"No, Intuner's the first project I've invested in since Silicon Valley. It's been over ten years. I did it with Intuner just because of you, because I knew you and felt attached an immediate connection to you when you came here, but it's really not my thing anymore. Everything about me online, like my biography and damn picture of me that I can't remove, it's a cover, just like my story about the young entrepreneurs in Manila. See, when I was in Silicon Valley, I figured out where the real future was: real estate speculation. No matter what people are creating, they need to find a place to live. That's why I travel so much. Manila was one of those places where I went to browse which properties are the best investments. I'm going to Honolulu for a scouting trip in two weeks, actually. While I was there on vacation some time ago, I realized how much growth potential that city has."

"So when you're on vacation, don't you feel like people are judging you?"

"I mean, when you're swimming at the beach in Hawaii, do you really think you're going to focus on sticking to your principles? But really, though, I just try to lay low, find a good balance. I don't want to take anything to the extreme, you know? I don't want to live like a total hermit."

"Like me in the cave?"

"Oh, come on."

"Hey, it's true. You wouldn't have wanted to see me there."

"Who knows? Maybe I would have."

"Well, I don't think you could ever be more isolated than I was."

"We can test that theory out someday, Jason."

"Deal."

"Anyway, like I was saying, I'm glad I have Kuan to drive me and Sumi to take care of the apartment, honestly. No company would make me insane. But that's really as far as I figured I could go in my daily life. With that insecurity hovering over me, I couldn't survive in any business that wasn't completely solitary like the one I have. But you, you can help me get past that. You've learned to bury all of those worries behind you. You've done what I could never do. That's why you're my better half, Jason."

Cha brushed Jason's hair playfully, then paused for a few seconds. "Ah, well. I've talked way too much. I don't like hearing my own voice."

"I wasn't going to say it, but it's pretty hypocritical of you to talk so much judging by what you told me the other day—you know, the whole thing about not talking and listening," he told her with a smile.

"Hey, I make mistakes too, okay?" she told him, chuckling.

"Oh, really? I thought you weren't allowed to, being such a perfect, successful woman who's molding me in the image of her perfect, successful man."

"Stop it." She began brushing his hair, then caressed his cheek.

As he felt the palm of Cha's hand, Jason copied her. In some cases, it wasn't just easier to reciprocate what the person in front of him was doing. It was actually quite pleasurable.

After a few seconds, Jason asked in the cryptic questioning style he had absorbed from I'Kiti Vapui, "Cha, when you're alone at night, do you ever count the stars?"

"Not really, why?"

"I was just thinking about how much our lives really matter. Do you ever wonder if each one of those far-off star systems might have its Northport, and the Northport we know is the worst of a million Northports? If we'll never have the technology to find the other Northports, and their procedures are so cumbersome that they're too busy to ever find us, so we'll be kept in the dark about it forever?"

"I've never thought of it that way, Jason," Cha replied. "But maybe I should."

Cha stared up at the stars for a few seconds, then back at Jason. He was still so fragile. She needed to help him, strengthen him against a world that had beaten him up. Now was the time to tell him.

"Oh, by the way," she told him, "I forgot to tell you something. I need to fly out to London tomorrow. I'm going to seal the deal for something."

"Take me along, Cha," Jason replied with a smile, then looked at her unmoving face. Clearly, he had overstepped his boundaries. "I'm sorry. I should have made it clearer that I wasn't serious."

"Oh, Jason," she replied, keeping her stiff face. "You don't need to joke about going there with me. I wasn't planning otherwise. Did you really think I'd trust you to stay here alone?"

26. THE POINT OF NO RETURN

THURSDAY, MAY 16, 2013

JEMAA EL-FNAA SOUQ, MARRAKESH

When Nathalie Washington had accepted her job as Northport's Dean of Students, she had never read a poster saying, "Join the Office of the Dean, See the World". As much as she loved interacting with students as opposed to corporate stakeholders, even when it meant confronting troubled students and their infuriatingly overprotective parents, for seventeen years she had held a certain jealous envy for her colleagues who crisscrossed the globe to give seminars and attend lectures. If the whole affair with Jason Curran had brought her anything positive, however, it was that she could now hang such a sign on her office door. Today, since she was conducting her investigation in her own time, she had better take advantage of the opportunity to visit Morocco.

Camels trotted through the sandy alleys of the Jemaa el-Fnaa market, where salesmen hassled tourists to sell them curios. Spice stalls displayed a palette of reds and yellows reminiscent of paint color chips in a hardware store, and storytellers entertained turbaned locals and baseball-capped visitors.

Nathalie stopped for some temporary refuge from the afternoon heat. Under a tent, rows of oranges from local groves stood stacked next to a sign offering freshly squeezed orange juices at one-fifth of what they cost at the White Dolphin Café in Northport.

"I'll have one orange juice, please," Nathalie told the salesman, wishing she had taken a bit of time on the flight to learn a few words of Arabic, or at the very least French.

Orange juice in hand, she continued on to the resplendent Oulde El-Kahlouche Hotel, where she walked up the stairs to the terrace for a view of the Koutoubia Mosque's minaret among the snow-capped Atlas Mountains. As much as she wished she could stare at the view indefinitely and pretend she lived in that postcard-perfect universe, she had a mission to complete.

She descended into the hotel lobby, a magnificent atrium with a large fountain in the middle and blue and white tiles on the surrounding walls. She walked under the beige arches to the reception and asked the concierge, "Good afternoon. I am the Dean of Students at Northport University in New York, and I have come here to check on the program."

Technically, that was true. This spring, one of Northport's Near Eastern Studies professors had launched a one-week seminar class by the name of "NEA 241: Using Art To Transcend Cultural Boundaries in the Arab World." In order to revive a moribund department, the professor had offered a free one-week voyage to Marrakesh.

On paper, the goal was to analyze the Berber, Arab, and French influence on the city's architecture, mosaics, and music. In reality, though, if similar past programs were any indication, most participants would probably spend their week swimming in the Oulde El-Kahlouche Hotel's magnificent pool, riding camels, and shopping for jewelry in the Jemaa El-Fnaa souq.

Nathalie Washington was spending Wednesday to Saturday evaluating Marrakesh as a potential location for Northport's renowned and costly Gibb Study Abroad Program. Two years before, a music course with a week-long trip to the Czech Republic had proven so popular that the Gibb Program had added an entire summer of study in Prague, though this time for nearly an entire academic quarter's tuition price.

At least, that was what Nathalie had told Northport's administrative staff travel secretary last Friday when she had asked for a ticket to Casablanca on the Office of the Dean's expense account. Nathalie could not care less about Tony DiTancini's new mercenary phase of founding overseas programs in whichever location would be sufficiently profitable.

Instead, she had come to visit the two lone participants who had not had to apply for one of Northport's most selective courses. The process by which these lucky students were selected was very opaque to all but a few members of the administration. In this case, they had benefited from a secret university policy designed to appease students who had complained about something at Northport—for instance, whistleblowers who reported cheating on a test, since students were supposed to monitor themselves under the Northport Honesty Code.

In most cases, the administration extended the plaintiffs' meal plans or gave them preferences for housing the next year. This time, however, the remuneration had been infinitely larger because the two concurrent complaints had uncovered much more than a plagiarizer: an alleged international spy and potential danger to campus security, Jason Curran.

Nathalie Washington looked at the hotel's receptionist. "Could I please see the list of Northport students on the program and their rooms?" She looked at the directory and said, "Please tell the guests in Room 95 to come down to the lobby immediately. It concerns a slight change in plans for tomorrow." The concierge did as instructed, and Nathalie sat on a red silk-draped couch across from the fountain. Soon, the two women she had been expecting walked in.

"Melissa Børgensen, Cayley Thompson. Please, have a seat. I won't be long."

Nathalie took a good look at the blonde and brunette sitting across from her. Their revealing mini shorts and skin-tight, cutoff tank tops suggested that they had been too excited by the prospect of a free trip to pay attention to the section of the program coordinator's memo urging the participating students to respect local customs by not dressing as they might for a party in Elton Hall.

"I trust you're enjoying your time in Marrakesh," Nathalie began. "How've you been since we last talked about a month ago?"

It was the blonde, Melissa Børgensen, who spoke first. "Much better! Thanks so much for getting that weird creep Jason kicked out of Northport!"

Nathalie Washington let out an exasperated sigh. When Melissa Børgensen and Cayley Thompson had written their complaint to her in mid-March, they had mentioned that he behaved suspiciously and that they feared that he was dangerous to the campus community. Unfortunately, Melissa Børgensen's dismissive attitude and Cayley's similar face suggested that their motives had included annoyance as well as fear.

Not taking Melissa's comment as a compliment, Nathalie replied, "What about Jason made you most fearful?"

"Just the fact that he had all these weird obsessions, he approached us at random times to ask for help on that mysterious project of his, and he didn't seem to care about making friends and having fun. You know, he just seemed so out of tune with the rest of us."

"So because he was different from the typical Northport student, you thought he was dangerous?" Nathalie asked dubiously. Even though she did not doubt Jason's innocence, she had until now assumed that there was one piece of the puzzle over which she had glanced, one final element that would have made their fears more grounded.

"Well, it wasn't only that," Cayley Thompson pointed out. "Jason's a loner, and lots of campus gunmen are loners. That creeped us out."

"Just as lots of criminals are black. Does that mean that because I'm black, you can just assume I'm a criminal?" Nathalie asked.

"I'm sorry! I really didn't mean to offend you," Cayley responded, her face showing obvious traces of shame. "Still, though, he could do all sorts of things, Dean Washington."

"Like what?"

"Well, we don't know, and we sure don't want to know."

"You have no idea what Jason Curran was suspended for, do you?"

Cayley kept her mouth shut, but Melissa answered impulsively. "Um...being a weird creep?"

"My, oh, my, honey. No, it wasn't that at all. My investigation led me to believe that Jason was actually an international spy selling secrets to foreign governments. All the pieces of the puzzle seemed to fit together. With the widespread fear of the Chinese and other governments stealing our knowledge and endangering our national security, the Northport administration was even more thoroughly convinced than I was."

"Wait, so that was true, the spy thing?" Melissa asked. "I heard rumors about it on campus, but I thought they were a joke. I guess that when we went around telling our friends that we had gotten that creep Jason kicked out, some told different stories."

Nathalie Washington was becoming angrier by the minute. "You bragged about it? Consider yourself lucky that Northport doesn't have policy on slander, because right now, I really feel like I should suggest an amendment to—"

No doubt trying to defuse Nathalie's irritation, Cayley asked, "Dean Washington, what exactly were the pieces of this puzzle?"

"Well, there were too many to count. Jason called the number of the Chinese-owned Port of Piraeus in Greece. A janitor in Mancini Hall heard Jason repeatedly speaking foreign languages to his telephone while hiding in the bathroom stall. A medical graduate student who did not know who Jason was saw him exchanging objects with Chinese visitors almost every other day. Jason often receives money from China and sends flash drives back. He keeps a pile of old watches and a map of Russia and Mongolia with names in a coded language written on them. He never let anyone at all into his room."

"Convinced yet?" Nathalie asked. "He was desperate, Melissa, to get in contact with your father, an engineer doing some work for the CIA and other federal agencies. Jason stays up late in the neuroscience lab on most Thursdays and Saturdays. Add this to the fact that he had taken a First-Year Seminar called, if I remember the exact name, 'Enigmas: Using Computers to Code and Decipher Secret Languages', and you'll understand why I believed it at first."

"Wow. So Jason wasn't a creep but a *spy*?" Cayley inquired.

"It's convincing, no? Especially if you're paranoid. But one day, under circumstances that are so strange that you would never believe me if I told you," she explained, doing her best to suppress the smile forming as she recalled the allegedly conspiring dolphins on television, "I wondered if I wasn't jumping to absurd conclusions. Think about it, honey. What if all of these things were purely coincidental?"

"Come on," Melissa said with an estranged face. "How could they be?"

"Well, what if Jason wasn't exchanging trade secrets with the Chinese running the Port of Piraeus? What if he was simply calling the Greek manager who mentions on his online biography that he is a first cousin of the famous architect, Elektra Kananaskis, who happens to be Jason Curran's mother? What if the money he was receiving from China was payment for translation services he was doing for a software company and sending to them on flash drives?"

Nathalie paused and stared at the two students, trying to gauge their level of interest.

"Well, that doesn't seem too likely." Cayley said.

"Trust me, there's more."

"Go on," Melissa told her laconically.

"What if he was learning Korean and all the other languages on a phone program with audio and repeating the words for practice, all while hiding in the restroom because he didn't want his Portuguese professor to hear him learning Arabic in his class? Really, I could convince you for all of these examples, but I'm sure you'd rather be shopping in the souq right now. The thing is, everyone I've interviewed agrees with the facts, including Jason. No one disputes that he wanted to speak to your father, Melissa. Yet, no one's ever testified that his goal was espionage."

"No one of who?" Cayley asked.

"Everyone who was involved. But even then, there's still one missing piece. Someone else is involved."

"Someone doing what?" Melissa asked.

"Someone tying all the threads together to make this whole thing look like a conspiracy. I didn't stumble on all these puzzle pieces by chance. Someone saw Jason making the phone call to Piraeus and traced the number, someone told the janitor in Mancini Hall who was speaking which foreign languages in the bathroom stall, someone anonymously reported that Jason was receiving funds from China and putting flash drives in the packages he was sending back there, and someone told the graduate student's assistant that Jason was the one exchanging objects with Chinese visitors every other morning."

Nathalie paused for a few moments to catch her breath. "Shall I continue, ladies?"

Both had now shifted their facial expressions to appear very stoic. "Sure," they said simultaneously.

"Someone suggested that Jason was trying to talk to a computer scientist working for the CIA in order to steal government secrets, someone gave us an anonymous tipoff to check his room for suspicious objects, someone related the mystery of Jason's project to the fact that he took a class on coding enigmas in freshman year, and someone spread the rumors that Jason had been suspended for espionage. Now, if I've put the pieces of the puzzle together correctly, this individual is the same someone who made you fearful of Jason Curran's lifestyle and encouraged you to complain to the administration. The question remains, ladies, who is this shadow figure?"

"Dean Washington," Cayley said smoothly. "No one ever made us afraid of Jason."

"Well, no one except Jason, obviously," Melissa clarified.

"Is that really true, though? Didn't someone else plant the idea in your minds and encourage you to complain?"

Cayley pulled her lips apart, but before any words came out, Melissa stared at her from the corner of her eye. As Cayley returned to silence, Melissa yelled, "That's not fair! You can't ask us to tell on our friend! Do you have any idea how uncomfortable I feel about doing that?"

"Ladies," Nathalie said in an authoritative voice, "I'm getting very tired of your little game. If you continue to be uncooperative, you'll go on the first flight back to the States. Say goodbye to your free vacation. Does this friend—if you can even call someone who manipulates you this way a friend—mean that much to you?"

Melissa and Cayley looked around at the Oulde El-Kahlouche Hotel's magnificent atrium for a few moments. "All right," Cayley conceded, "It was our friend—"

Right before Cayley could finish her sentence, Nathalie had answered her own question. Of course! It was almost too obvious. How had she not pieced the elements together earlier?

"Wait!" she blurted. "It's fine, honey. You don't need to tell me. I already know who it is—well, I think I do, at least. Your reaction puts me one step closer to absolute certainty."

The two students turned their heads towards each other and made a puzzled face, but clearly they had no intention of volunteering any information if Nathalie was not trying to pry it from them.

"Will that be all, Dean Washington?" Melissa asked, regaining some of her confidence.

Nathalie Washington sighed. The part she told anyone she interviewed about enjoying her job because it allowed her to interact with the students at Northport was truer than they could ever imagine. With one of her sons off producing records in Nashville and the other a U.S. Army lieutenant in Stuttgart, Nathalie had very little time to see her children every year. Whenever she talked at length to any male students, she saw a bit of her sons in them. She always tried to see the female students as the daughters she never had, but this time, she failed to do so.

"Almost. You know, I just want to say this. You ladies disgust me! Do you know that?"

Melissa and Cayley began to shiver, then looked at each other but seemed to find no reassurance. "H-how so?" Melissa asked meekly.

"Because of how you live your whole lives. My generation did so much for feminism. We pushed to pass and, more importantly, *enforce* rape laws so that students like you could walk down the Boulevard at night without being afraid you'd be grabbed and thrown to the ground by a stranger. We lobbied for sexual harassment laws so that if you had an internship, you could be certain that you'd get the job without having to with your boss. We crafted all these date rape laws so that you could get into healthy relationships without worrying about abuse. We went childless, working twice as hard as men because we hoped to break the glass ceiling. Now, you feel like you can just take all of this for granted."

Nathalie caught her breath for a second. All of these interrogations were taking a heavy toll on her. "Instead of taking advantage of the fact that you can be more than housewives," she resumed, "You waste away your nights behaving like wild animals at parties. You freak out when someone calls you three times for help with a project, yet you don't have a problem with guiding a complete stranger around your most private places in the dead of night, when you're too drunk to even notice. As if being drunk was an excuse for bad behavior! We tore ourselves apart so that you could have a better future, free from fear, and what have you done? You've been so content with patriarchy being gone from your lives that you've replaced it with something just as damaging: yourselves."

After a few seconds, Melissa finally managed to push out a simple, "Look, we're not doing this to be evil, just to—" then glanced at Cayley as if probing her friend's approval. Cayley, however, turned her head back and forth between Melissa and Nathalie, seemingly judging each in turn.

However, the two girls could sort out their issues, Nathalie thought. She had gotten what she had come to find in Marrakesh, so she no longer had to deal with them.

"Good day, ladies."

Nathalie Washington left to return to her room, hoping to get some well-deserved rest before her flight back to New York the next day. Then, she would extract the information she could from her suspected culprit and hopefully right at least a small fraction of the wrongs she had inflicted on Jason Curran. If she failed to convince the administration of Jason's innocence, her job would be at stake, but at this point she no longer cared. If President DiTancini could not be redeemed in her mind, she would no longer call herself his servant. She could not promote a system she was convinced was corrupt.

Nathalie Washington walked through the gate to climb the stairs and then shut it behind her. She had reached the point of no return.

27. THE WINNER TAKES IT ALL

FRIDAY, MAY 17, 2013

FATIH DISTRICT, ISTANBUL

The lights of the Hagia Sophia shone Istanbul's night sky, brighter than the so-called "genuine Ottoman" jewels the local merchants sold in the city's bazaars. From its arched windows, the once-basilica-turned-mosque had seen the rise and fall of one of the world's most powerful empires, a violent conquest that had greatly rocked its shell while ultimately leading to its recovery, and swaths or tourists of every religion who now swarmed from dawn to dusk into its belly and treated it as a photographic subject. Yet, it had never seen the spectacle taking place ten thousand meters above its dome, Jason thought as he gazed at the map zooming in on the label *"Istanbul"* as part of the Singapore Airlines Airbus A380's real-time flight path from Singapore to London.

"Jason? Jason!" Cha called out to the passenger to her left, since he had evidently not registered her taps on his shoulder every few minutes. "What are you doing?"

"Just staring at the moving map," he replied matter-of-factly. "I'm surprised we're flying so far south. We should be over Ukraine, not Turkey."

Cha was not surprised. It was typical Jason Curran to focus on such minute details. "Tell me, Jason," she asked, "Do you want any more champagne?"

"I'm fine. I don't drink. Remind me why we're going to London?" Jason asked Cha curtly, silently reprimanding himself for not being more careful with his tone of voice.

"Just walking around and looking at some properties," Cha replied in her usual calm voice, taking a last sip from her third glass of champagne before placing it gently on the seat's armrest. "The high rollers from the UAE love spending their oil money for townhouses in Mayfair, so I want to figure out which places are the best investments. Then we're getting on the first flight back to Singapore on Sunday morning."

"Great, how can I help you though? I don't know much about real estate." Jason asked, still focused on the screen.

"Oh, I didn't take you so you could help my business. I just wanted you to see this," she said, gesturing at their seats in the cabin. "See it as an...expansion of our close business relationship."

For the first time since he had woken up from a solid seven hours of sleep, Jason removed his eyes from the map and looked at his seat, or rather, his bedroom. He had certainly not grown up in a life of squalor, but he could nevertheless not hold back a scream of childlike amazement from sitting in the aircraft's Suites cabin. The sliding doors around his and Cha's seats had been shut tight, and the adjacent seats themselves had been folded together into a double bed laden with rose petals. With only the individual reading lights above them offering a contrast to the pitch-black cabin, it really felt as if they were all alone.

"You only said we would 'seal the deal'," Jason said in a calm but stoic voice."You never gave me all the details."

Cha signed. She had seen Jason grow up from a six-year-old genius who could spend three hours discussing his latest LEGO creation to a handsome, mature young man whose apparent inability to perceive or express emotion always masked deeper rational analysis. Yet now, she could not for the life of her decide whether to interpret Jason's stoic comment as a flirtatious or a clueless response to her overture.

However, the lights would only be off for a few more hours before the dawn arrival into London-Heathrow, and soon the flight attendants passing breakfast and passengers sleeping until the last minute would be walking up and down the cabin. If she wanted to do this in an environment where she could corner and supervise Jason, she had to do it right now, and she would be as straightforward as she had to.

"Trust me, this is a very good return on your investment. You really have much to learn, young one— you're what they call a 'virgin in business'." As she prepared to switch off both reading lights, Cha pulled off her pajama, then shot Jason a suggestive look that he guessed to be more than a suggestion for him to do the same.

"But hopefully, Jason, at the end of this flight," she said as she moved to lay on top of him, "You'll only be a virgin *in business*."

✈ ✈ ✈

SARTORI THEATER, NORTHPORT UNIVERSITY

The evening had been a massive success. Crowds of Northport students had taken a break from their multivariable calculus problem sets and essays on the causes of war to view the premiere of *Aunt Vanya*. Sophomore Vanya Lakshmi had adapted Anton Chekhov's nineteenth-century play about a Russian professor and his young wife into that of a Northport professor and her much younger companion, composing songs to turn the story into a musical while she was at it.

After greeting everyone else, Derek Park congratulated and wished a good night to the playwright, his friend—yes, his friend with benefits, perhaps, but no more than that. If he tied himself down to a single girl, at some point the others would stop pouring their approval on him. The talk of him and Vanya was having the effect he had planned: increasing his popularity, if that was still even possible.

No matter who she was to him, Vanya deserved the applause. The premiere had been flawless, despite the fact that Vanya had returned only last Friday from Arlen Health Center, where she landed after years of piled-up sleep deprivation had finally caught up to her. The Northport student was truly a magical creature, Derek thought, and it felt very satisfying to rule over such a glorious dominion.

As he began pulling the handle on the door out of Sartori Theater, a voice called out his name.

Derek turned back and smiled. "Dean Washington!" Derek told the approaching figure. "So great to see you!"

"You too, Derek. How did you enjoy the show?"

"It was awesome, Dean Washington. My friend Vanya Lakshmi was actually the one who wrote and directed it, and what she's done is even more amazing when you consider that she was Arlened for weeks."

"I heard about that, actually! I'm really sorry for her, but I'm glad she was able to accomplish this. Honestly, the talent the students have here…"

"It's amazing. I'm really proud to call myself their president."

"Speaking of that, I'm glad I ran into you, because I wanted to congratulate you on the stellar job you've done as Student Council President. Of course, I can't vouch for everyone in the student body personally, but you're extremely popular among the entire administration."

"Thank you, Dean Washington. The compliment means a lot to me."

"It's my job, isn't it?" she asked him, laughing. "How does it feel, though, to be leaving in only a few weeks?"

"Honestly, it's bittersweet, but I believe in my successor. She's a very sharp woman."

"Speaking of which," Nathalie began, "I've been wondering something lately. What will Northport look like in, say, thirty years' time? Or rather, with massive online courses becoming so popular, will there still be universities in thirty years?"

"I really hope so, Dean Washington. Even if we can learn everything online, it would be such a shame to lose our community spirit! It's such a unique experience. I mean, will we really be able to 'live and learn' online. And even if we're still around, our admit rate will be what, half a percent?"

"You know, I should consider myself lucky if I don't get to see the day when that happens." Both chuckled.

"Well, it was great talking to you, Derek. If we don't run into each other before Commencement, I'll congratulate you now on almost being done with your time at Northport. I'm sure it was a hectic four years for you, and you deserve the reward at the end."

"Thank you, Dean Washington. It was nice seeing you. Have a good night!"

"You too!" Nathalie Washington began walking in the direction of the door, then stopped and turned to face him again. "Oh, one more thing. Do you know what impressed me most about the play, Derek? "

"Let me guess—the fact that the students at Northport are even more amazing every year?"

"Well, Derek, you're one of the most gifted students I know, but with the admissions process being harder and harder every year, that's bound to happen, isn't it? But I wasn't thinking of that, though. Don't you find it wonderful that no one today sang a single note even slightly out of tune?"

That was a funny coincidence, Derek thought. "Well, thankfully it didn't happen tonight, but every once in a while you'll hear an a capella soloist sing a bit off-key. However, with the product I'm developing, that shouldn't be the case anymore."

"Oh, you're going to train people in singing? I guess it shouldn't be a surprise for me. I know you're a star musician—didn't you play at the San Francisco Symphony when you were fifteen?"

"I did, but that's nothing big for a Northport student, is it?" Before she could laugh at his fit of self-deprecation, however, he added, "But no, I'm not doing any training at all. Rather, it's a nanotech startup. I want to sell the idea to investors soon, hopefully to Mazamadou Perikaélé. He gave me his contact information after I went to his talk here a few weeks ago, so I hope to write to him over the summer. Here, I know you need to head out, Dean Washington, so I'll tell you about it next time I see you."

"Oh, how exciting! Are you working on this alone?"

Derek wished that he was, but he regretted the fact that the stray notes he had found regarding Intuner in the neuroscience laboratory, while very informative, left out a critical element that none of his neuroscientist or engineer friends could figure out. The few times when Jason Curran had requested the help of his limitless social network,

Derek had naïvely assumed that Intuner was ready for marketing. What a shame! Derek had originally hoped only for a gracious compensation from Jason, but when he had run into his friends Melissa Børgensen and Cayley Thompson and heard them complain about Jason's strange behavior at that fateful party in Elton Hall, he had decided that instead of picking up a small part of Intuner's profits, he could claim them all for himself. How could he pass up such a wonderful opportunity?

Knowing everyone certainly had its benefits. He was the undisputed hub for all the information on campus, from Vanya's report of a strange shadow figure who perfectly matched Jason's description exchanging strange objects with Chinese visitors to a janitor's questions over why Jason was speaking foreign languages in the restroom to Jason's own description of his funds from a Chinese technology to Derek. He was the supreme voice of authority among the student body; when Nathalie Washington had interviewed him as Jason's only publicly acknowledged friend, Derek had voiced his opinion that Jason was not a potential gunman, leading her to the theory he intended her to have: international espionage.

Now, though, Derek had finally given up on trying to decipher any more information about Intuner. His whole scheme, from turning Melissa and Cayley's annoyance and fleeting fears into paranoia about his "creepy acquaintance" Jason being a potential gunman and likely danger to the campus community to convincing a janitor that someone was secretly communicating with foreign governments, had been useless now that Derek did not have a final product to sell under his own name.

"Well, I have some help," Derek began, "But the ideas behind it are all mine."

"That makes sense. You don't need to dilute your success when the winner takes it all."

"Why do you ask, Dean Washington? Are you just curious?" he asked, still keeping his calm.

"I'm just wondering. I know everyone at Northport has so many different talents, but do you really have the skills to undertake a nanotechnology project when your major is Economics and not, say...*Neuroscience and Engineering?*"

Immediately, Derek's heart sank to the bottom of his gut. She knew.

"Good night and good luck."

Derek Park stared at her in wide-eyed horror as she left the building. Never had he felt so utterly helpless.

Well, there had to be a first time for everything, no?

✤ ✤ ✤

TUESDAY, MAY 21, 2013

LLOYD HALL, NORTHPORT UNIVERSITY

Nathalie Washington only had a few minutes before meeting her boss, so she only combed through the six emails with the "Urgent" label.

"From: Zagel, Rick

To: Washington, Nathalie

Dear Colleagues,

I regret to inform you that this morning, I fell down the staircase on the way to my garage and fractured my hip bone. While the doctors have informed me that I should recover in a few weeks' time and be able to continue some of my functions as Provost by working from a distance, I am in no condition to travel for a while. Therefore, I will not be able to appear at the planned alumni events in Hong Kong on Saturday, May 25 and Melbourne, Australia on Thursday, May 30.

I hope that one of you can fly to those events on such short notice to replace me. The alumni in Hong Kong and Melbourne have been extremely loyal to Northport over the years, and it would be a pity to have to inform them of the events' cancellation. Please feel free to contact me if you have any questions about how to prepare.

Sincerely,

Rick Zagel

Provost of Northport University"

As much as Nathalie did not want to disappoint the university's second-in-command and had gained a new appreciation for traveling, she would have to pass on that offer. As if she did not have enough issues to take care of already, the affair with Jason Curran had drained much of her time and energy. One of her colleagues would hopefully be able to take on the trip on short notice out of either generosity or wanderlust.

She skipped down to the next flagged message.

"From: Savage, Marianna

To: Washington, Nathalie

Dear Nathalie,

I know you must be more than busy as the year comes to a close, so I apologize for having to involve you in this affair.

As you can see in the thread below, Northport senior Chris Garvey was caught for possession of cannabis at the beginning of the month."

Nathalie stared at the student's name for a few seconds, then remembered. When she had conducted her investigation into Jason Curran's past, Chris Garvey had been too high on drugs to provide her with any useful information. Did he do anything all day but smoke?

"As you know," the email continued, *"The university does not take these matters lightly. However, the Commission on Substance Abuse is unsure how to proceed in this case. Our investigation of Chris Garvey's profile reveals that his drug use may be connected to his Rastafari spiritual beliefs, and the last thing we want right now is a religious discrimination lawsuit. Besides, there is no evidence that Chris was involved in dealing drugs to anyone else."*

There was the good news, Nathalie thought. After the whole mess with the Slovak, the last thing she wanted to deal with was another dealer.

"Due to the potential issue of religious discrimination, suspension is off the table, but we have considered a viable alternative. On Friday, Chris is slated to win the Lauper Award for Self-Expression for his visual arts installation, Babylon: Politricks of

Downpression at the Schönberg Center for the Creative Arts. As you can see in the thread below, the director of Schönberg has reluctantly agreed to rescind Chris's award and give it instead to the runner-up for her epic poem. The winner will be notified and invited to Friday's ceremony tomorrow (Tuesday), so this would allow us to punish Chris without possibly dealing with a religious discrimination lawsuit.

As Dean of Students, it falls to you to make an executive decision as to whether this course of action is appropriate, or whether Chris's religious motivations and lack of dealing do not justify a demerit. Please let me know by tomorrow morning how you wish to proceed.

Best regards,

Marianna Savage

Chair, Commission on Substance Abuse"

Nathalie Washington reread the last two paragraphs to make sure she was not becoming delusional. Was the seemingly good-for-nothing Chris Garvey about to win Northport's most coveted artistic prize? How she had underestimated him!

Then again, why was she so surprised that Chris was such a talented artist? Such was the nature of Northport. Everyone was queen or king of something. It was not just conceivable but extremely likely that Chris had created his best artworks while under the influence of drugs, and she did not have the right to deprive anyone of his or her potential. Chris certainly deserved his award, and he would keep it—just as soon as Nathalie could scan the remaining urgent emails to check if any of them were more urgent. Two down, four to go.

"From: Serburg, I. E.

To: Washington, Nathalie

Dear Nathalie,

This message is to follow up on the suicide attempt by one of our students of which I informed you two weeks ago. At this moment, we are still unsure what the Section VIII.C.ii.b.(4) of Northport's Administrative Guide stipulates in this very unique case. Even as the Head of Psychological services, I do not believe that I have the responsibility to decide whether—"

Nathalie lifted her eyes from her phone as she heard Tony DiTancini's voice through the door. "Please come in, Nathalie, if you're there," he told her.

She walked in and took a seat in front of Tony's. "Good afternoon, Tony. So you were able to read all the messages I sent you about Jason Curran this morning?"

"Yes, and was I shocked! With these new revelations, I think we should reconsider our decision. After you came to my office yesterday, I spoke to the university's Board of Trustees, the Provost, the Head of Public Safety, the Head of Disability Services, the Head of Psychological Services, and the General Counsel, and they've all expressed agreement with your verdict: that Jason Curran is not guilty of international espionage in any way. We didn't think outside the box when we tried to figure out what he was doing. As a result, I believe we can readmit Jason Curran to Northport."

Nathalie Washington breathed a sigh of relief. The long road was over. She had finally reversed the enormous injustice for which she had been overwhelmingly, though not intentionally, responsible. How much easier it would have been to achieve this result if she had merely allowed Jason to explain himself! When the Kafkaesque proceedings of the administration under the restrictive Northport system had failed her, she had resorted to the faith she still had for the human race—well, that and, once or twice, deceit and intimidation.

"Now, I hope we can delay writing to Jason for a few days, at least. I wanted to take care of something first."

"Of course. You know what, Nathalie? Could you contact Jason this time? I need to meet with some alumni in Liechtenstein on Thursday anyway, so just do it at your own pace."

"Great." That would let her speak to the only important person in the whole affair whom she had not yet found. Still, one crucial question remained in the nude on the table. "What are we doing about Derek Park?" she inquired.

Tony DiTancini breathed a very long sigh. That could only mean one of two things, Nathalie thought. "Nathalie, there's really nothing we can do."

Unfortunately, Tony had chosen the second option. "What do you mean?" she asked.

"Nathalie, you and I both know there's no way we can press any charges against Derek Park."

"Why? I told you, he tried to sell Jason's project idea to me as his own, and his reaction to my trick question made it clear he was behind everything. Don't you see? He wanted to steal the idea from Jason! Plus, there's no one else it can be, since he's the only person who knows enough students to manipulate everyone in question. It's not like when we were dealing with Jason, where not everything was clear. I see no other angle we can go at it from. Derek can't have developed the same project with the *same name* as Jason's by himself. We have the means, motive, and quasi-confession."

"I'm not denying any of these facts. Personally, I'm convinced, and so is the rest of the administration, that Derek Park is guilty of conspiracy to libel, intentional infliction of emotional distress, and, worst of all, plagiarism."

"Then why can't we send him an official letter like we did to Jason in March? As I've said, Tony, I know he's guilty. His reaction proved it."

"Oh, please stop being so naïve, Nathalie. We'll never be able to mount a full case against him. What you told me still doesn't count as proof."

"Because it did with Jason?" Nathalie asked in shock.

"Should I remind you of the way the Northport system works, Nathalie? It's very different if the students are the one to initiate the complaint. No one would ever accuse Derek of anything independently, and once Jason returns, he won't be allowed to know about Derek's involvement, since the administration cannot guide a

365

student into making any accusations. Do you imagine what a public relations disaster that would be?"

"Well, maybe the system needs to be reformed!" She caught herself for her potential heresy and added, "I'm sorry if I offended you."

"No, it's fine. I certainly didn't invent all these proceedings, and neither did my predecessor or his predecessor. But that's not it."

Nathalie wondered what he was waiting to pull out. "Then what is it, Tony?"

"Look, Nathalie," he began didactically, "I know how strongly you feel about the whole issue, but I still don't understand why. Jason Curran is merely one brilliant student among fifteen thousand brilliant students. We've already spent enough time with this whole fiasco. I certainly don't want to have to deal with him or Derek Park any longer. Commencement is in a few weeks, and the last thing I want to do during that time is be stuck in endless meetings with our General Counsel and his legion of lawyers."

Tony stopped for a few seconds and finished his cup of coffee. "And really," he resumed, "Can you imagine the irreparable damage to our reputation if we don't just settle behind closed doors and the lawsuit becomes public? It's damn if you do, damn if you don't. If he wins based on the fact that there's still no written proof of his crimes, then we appear as a biased cabal. And though everyone tells us not to pick on black or Latino students, picking on an Asian is actually worse, I think. Everyone knows we and the other Ivies are using affirmative action to keep lots of them out of our gates. And if we win based on a forced confession on his part, we look like a bunch of morons for letting such a conspiracy happen under our noses. We don't want everyone here to play the blame game."

Of course, Nathalie thought. "Lawsuit" and "reputation" were the top entries in Tony DiTancini's personal dictionary, right after "donor" and "gift."

"Besides," Tony continued, "We don't want to upset Derek Park in any way possible. He may be dishonest, but at least he knows how to get what he wants. He'll go far in life, and we want to make sure he gives a small part of his hopefully large earnings back to his alma mater."

Of course, Nathalie thought. Especially if the next few decades took him to Wall Street or Silicon Valley, Derek was already a potential donor even before graduating. She breathed a heavy sigh. Sometimes, it was better just to give up. "Well, I guess you're right, Tony. Have a good trip to Liechtenstein, and I'll send Jason the letter soon."

"Thank you, Nathalie. I knew you could come to your senses. Goodbye, now."

Nathalie shook her head as she left Lloyd Hall. Maybe there really was no hope at all for the human race.

28. YOUR SONG

MONDAY, MAY 27, 2013

BOAT QUAY, SINGAPORE

Even to perspicacious eyes, the pastel-colored shophouse on the side of the winding Singapore River looked like any on Boat Quay. All the other nineteenth-century warehouses, originally built for storing rubber and coffee from plantations in Malaya, had since been reconverted into hip cafés, innovative restaurants, and overpriced art galleries. The interior of this one, however, consisted of a tiger-print couch, two rows of plastic chairs scattered around a long wooden desk, a dozen unwrapped computer screens, an exiguous lavatory, and a jungle of violet orchids and snow-white crape jasmines that would one day overtake all the empty space.

The disorderly state of the so-called "office," however, was of no concern to Han Cha Seng. Normally, she would be even more conscious of the appearance of her workplace than of her own looks, but this was not intended for her. Jason Curran had convinced her to help him set up the initial headquarters for Intuner. She had not struggled to overcome her aversion to physical offices; this was Jason's project, not hers. As soon as everything was on track, the angel would fade back into the shadows.

Jason Curran walked through and set his backpack on the couch. He stared in admiration at the "office" he and Cha had moved into the day before. He had reluctantly conceded that he needed some online presence to give Intuner and its parent company, Manureva Electronics, an air of legitimacy when trying to recruit employees and woo investors who, unlike Solo Holdings's mysterious owner, would appear in public. At first, he had feared the danger of being tracked down by the FBI or another security agency, but he had pushed aside that trepidation quite easily. If they had not stopped him yet, they had probably decided that he was of no concern to them and that they had far more pressing matters to deal with. Besides, his webpage only mentioned his name and new company address but nothing about Northport, Australia, or any details that could distinguish him from anyone else with the rather common name "Jason Curran." Anyone looking for him specifically would have to know the name "Intuner;" anyone interested in Intuner would know nothing about his past.

Cha lifted her eyes from the desk as Jason walked in. "Good evening, Jason," she greeted him. "I trust you had a nice walk along the river. I'm sorry I wasn't able to join you. There was just so much to do to make this office presentable!"

"I missed your company only physically," Jason replied. "You were in here the whole time," he added, placing his hand on his heart.

Well, he deserved an A for effort, Cha thought. "Oh, how touching, Jason." It was even entertaining.

"I try, you know?" he answered with a slight smirk. "By the way, I forgot to tell you this, but it's the best coincidence ever. Do you remember Rodrigo Oliveira, the Portuguese opera singer I told you about the other day? Well, I was googling him yesterday to see when his album Arie di Sorbetti was coming out, and this video of him singing "Amazing Grace" last month pops up immediately. I watch it, and it turns out that he had an embarrassing incident during a concert last month because, hear this, he sang slightly out of tune! I have to write to him once I'm done interviewing the developers. Can you believe it? My favorite singer might be our first customer!"

"That's great, Jason! You know, sometimes I feel like I'm getting too old to take any initiatives myself anymore."

"Oh, stop it. But come on, tell me about your ideas."

"To be honest, I think Intuner is just one of countless opportunities for Manureva. We can do far more than a little thing like improving people's singing pitch. Think about the possibilities!"

"Funny, we must be sharing thoughts now. I told myself the same thing when I was in the shower yesterday."

"Oh, you were thinking then? I only heard you struggling to sing some opera aria."

"Music helps me concentrate, I guess. So I told myself that if we get some mind share with Intuner, we can conquer the neurotech market. We could block ourselves from thinking about what we want to ignore. We could

370

force ourselves to fall asleep instead of dealing with insomnia. I mean, we could even forget all our bad memories!"

"I hope I don't qualify as one of those memories," Cha told Jason, raising her eyebrows slightly.

"I don't think so. Definitely not now," Jason replied, pressing his lips tightly on hers.

Only a few seconds into her kiss with Jason, Cha heard a knocking on the door. "Oh, does it really have to be right now? Just forget it, Jason."

"Let me get this. I have a hunch that this isn't the FBI or some passerby who thinks we're some, I don't know, counterculture pub with plastic wrap on the storefront and wants to know when we're open," Jason replied. "No, it has to be an overeager developer trying to get ahead of the others. He probably can't wait until the open house tomorrow, or maybe he just got the dates confused. Speaking from experience, that tends to happen when you're in the lab for too long."

In order to have them hit the ground running, Cha had convinced him to list job postings for Intuner on their website. As much as he wished he had the time to do all the engineering, coding, marketing, and legal work himself, Jason had accepted that hiring full-time employees and strategic partners was a necessity.

Cha hissed softly through her teeth. Someone would see her before she was ready! She planned on being absent when Jason interviewed the developers tomorrow, but she had no idea any of them would be coming today. She needed to think of something quickly.

As Jason pulled the door open, a woman asked, "Jason Curran?"

His eyes nearly burst out of their sockets. "Oh, my."

"Yes, I know I look too old to be a summer intern. As for you, I have to say, you look very different from your university ID picture."

It was strange for Jason to live in a world where he could so easily recognize someone he had never met face-to-face. "Funny, Dean Washington, because you don't."

"I'm impressed you can recognize me only from the old picture on my webpage!"

"That's how things work today," Jason said laconically, doing his best to remain calm. What was she doing here? Had new allegations against him just surfaced, perhaps in light of a new search of his room by the campus police? Were the shades of turquoise and orange most common in his clothing drawer the colors of a newly discovered terrorist group in Bosnia, leading them to think he was in charge of their cell at Northport? Did they think the bottle of teriyaki sauce Jason had often brought into the dining hall contained poison to kill the other students? He almost laughed at the idea, then began to shiver. It was his life, not that of a character in a comedy show, that was at stake. A life that he had gone to great lengths to put back together piece by piece, no less.

Cha remembered exactly who Dean Nathalie Washington was. The way the conversation flowed, it did not seem that Jason was in trouble. The Dean of Students was not trying to intimidate him or assert her authority; she stood with her palms flat on her pants and left the passageway to the door clear instead of blocking it. Just in case, though, Cha lifted her eyes from the paper she was pretending to read and took out the earbuds she had put on quickly in order to buy him a few seconds.

"Oh, by the way, Jason," Nathalie Washington added as she turned her head towards Cha, "You haven't introduced us."

"This is Han Cha—"

"His secretary," Cha interjected, wanting to keep things looking as simple as possible.

"Oh, should we move to another room?"

"No, it's fine, Dean Washington," Jason said. "She has some business transactions to look over, and we don't have another room in our office."

Cha turned her eyes back to her alleged "transactions." While she put her earbuds back in, she played no music so she could listen closely to the rest of the exchange as it transpired.

"So, Dean Washington," Jason began, "Did you fly all the way to Singapore just to find me?" Why did Northport's administration care so much about taking him down? Did they even have the jurisdiction to do anything to him here, on the other side of the world from Northport?

"Well, yes and no, Jason. I'm going to receptions for Northport alumni in Hong Kong and Melbourne, so when I saw your address was in Singapore, I thought it'd be a logical place to stop along the way. But as you can imagine, you were the reason I accepted this assignment. After treating you so badly, the least I could do was come to see you in person."

Cha almost gasped as she understood, then stopped herself. She was supposed to be an oblivious secretary, after all.

"Dean Washington," Jason said, "I don't understand."

"Jason, you told me only to recontact you if Northport took you back. Now, that's exactly what I'm doing."

It took Jason a few seconds to digest the words, to look at her expression and use his practice in reading faces to realize that Nathalie Washington was serious. She had harmed him so much that he had never imagined that she would ever come back for an apology.

"D-D-Dean Washington, I can't believe...but why now?" he asked. This seemed so random, coming over a month after he had last spoken to her. Besides, was she even allowed to do such a thing? "Doesn't this defy the 'Northport system'?" he inquired.

"I'm going to be honest with you, Jason. After this, I don't give a damn about the Northport system. There were two events that changed my mind about you, really. First, I watched a political show making fun of conspiracy theorists, and I wondered if I wasn't a conspiracy theorist myself. What if I'd put together pieces of completely different puzzles to make up a wacky story? Later, I met up with a French family visiting Northport whose son had Asperger's. That really convinced me that you were innocent."

Jason wondered how she had discovered his neurological condition, which he had perennially refused to disclose to Northport's Arlen Health Center or Albinoni Center for Disability Services, but he thought it imprudent to ask.

"I'm sorry," Nathalie Washington said. "I'm really a rambler, aren't I?"

"You know, Dean Washington, I don't care if you ramble. I spent so much time waiting for this response, so a few extra minutes won't make a difference." Maybe justice had been served, he thought. A few random encounters had thrown him out; a few others were bringing him back in.

"Oh, it'll be conclusive, I'll tell you that. After I interviewed everyone who'd complained and learned that you hadn't done anything wrong, I spoke with President DiTancini. He's generously agreed to reinstate you, recognizing that we were too narrow-minded in judging your life, and he's really sorry for any harm we did to you."

"Thank you, Dean Washington," Jason said in relief. Despite all the ill will he had towards Northport's administration, Jason knew very well that without the years he had benefited from the university's generous faculty and quasi-unlimited resources, Intuner would still be a great idea, but it would only be that, an idea.

Something was still bothering him, though. "I still don't understand what happened to bring about all these complaints about me. Could you please explain? Did these events—these various complaints, I mean—just...happen?"

Nathalie Washington looked at him with a frown on her face. "Nothing ever happens by itself, Jason."

"So there was someone pulling all the strings behind the scenes, so to speak?"

"Yes."

"Who?"

"I'm sure you can guess easily enough."

So someone had been manipulating Melissa, Cayley, and the rest? "I don't understand. Only one person at Northport really knew me—this girl in my grade, Aurélia Chitour—and I honestly don't think she had a reason to do anything so horrid."

"Did you really have only one friend on campus, Jason? I feel like I know your social life better than you do."

"Well, no—oh, well, there was Derek Park. But he doesn't count."

"What do you mean, Jason?"

"He wasn't really a friend. I mean, he was nice, but he didn't do it because he liked me, like Aurélia. He just wanted all the votes he could get in the student council elections."

"Was that the only reason, Jason?"

"What else could it be? He wouldn't associate with someone as 'uncool' as myself out of pleasure. I didn't even pretend to care about parties or gossip when we spoke. All we ever talked about was Intuner." Jason thought back to his inopportune discussion with Derek on the way back from Williams to Lauderdale, when he had revealed the basics of Intuner. He had been very secretive about the whole thing, not telling more than generalities even to Aurélia, but he had told Derek enough for the latter to agree to help him. Jason had not minded having to give Derek a fraction of the profits if Intuner actually took off; getting money from Intuner was secondary to accomplishing a project he had so relentlessly pursued. But perhaps a fraction had not been enough for Derek.

"Oh...*I told him about my project.* Shoot, that was pretty stupid of me."

Cha's hand tensed into a claw around her flimsy earbuds. How had Jason made such an egregious mistake and not even noticed it? Such blunders were too typical for Jason. They were already fighting an uphill battle to develop Intuner; how could they manage running against a competitor who had a good head start and a nearly infinite social network? Had Jason really been that clueless?

"Well, I should be glad it was incomplete back then. He won't be going anywhere with the notes I left on campus."

Cha's pulse slowed down drastically. There was only going to be one Intuner on the market. Things could have turned out very differently, though. She just wished she had actually known Jason at the time to teach him the value of discretion, a principle he had applied quite arbitrarily for Intuner. Jason had not been very perceptive when he had tempted his "friend" to steal the idea, but he had been lucky, and often that mattered more.

"Yes," Nathalie concurred, "In this case, you were lucky this whole drama didn't happen a few months later, when your notes were complete."

"That's for sure. So is that what happened, then? Was Derek really behind everything?"

"Pretty much. The behaviors were yours, of course, but he's the one who told others how they should interpret them. He turned Melissa Børgensen and Cayley Thompson's annoyance with you into a paranoid fear. He told them that you might be threatening because of your awkward behavior, portraying you as a possible gunman, then manipulated everyone from a janitor to myself into thinking that you were guilty of some horrendous crime."

Jason had to say, he was impressed—not with his gullibility, but with Intuner's value. All his life, he had been used to others denigrating his outlandish ideas, so the fact that someone would concoct a Machiavellian scheme to steal his idea seemed like a bigger accomplishment on his part than anything else.

"Well," he told Nathalie Washington, "I'm certainly glad I won't be seeing him again!"

"Unfortunately, Jason, you'll be seeing him at Commencement. President DiTancini refused to take any disciplinary action against Derek. He said it would cost us financially and damage our reputation, which is all he ever talks about."

"Why am I not surprised?" Jason hesitated for a few moments. "But actually, that's not what I mean. Even if he's at Commencement, I won't be seeing him."

"I'm sure you can avoid him in the next month or so. It's a pretty big class, and if you really, really want to, you can cover your ears while he makes the speech at Commencement."

"No, Dean Washington. That's not it."

"What is it, then?"

For so many agonizing nights, Jason would have moved heaven and earth to set foot on campus again. Now, all he needed to do was pack his bags and get on an airplane, with the ticket probably provided by the Office of the Dean. He looked over at his backpack, wondered how soon he could get back if he flew out the next day, and what he would do as soon as he stepped into his room. Hopefully, the map of Dnålkčïrb had not been confiscated yet, and even if it had, he could redraw it in two minutes. Then, he looked at the orchids and jasmines sprouting up around the walls of a new office, at the various technical readouts for Intuner, and at his "secretary" sitting at her desk. Would I'Kiti Vapui be proud to see him here? As his Mana had faded away, had his last thoughts had been to hope—no, to know—that Jason would one day build all this? There was no choice to make.

"I'm not returning to Northport."

"B-b-but, Jason!" she replied, clearly flabbergasted. "Is it because of Derek?"

"No, though it certainly isn't helping either." While Jason had temporarily entertained thoughts of rejoining the community that had shunned him, he had known, even if he had never really admitted it to himself, that he had a reason for never going back as a student.

"Then why? Everything's ready for you! It's all been cleared with the campus police and the FBI, and no one's been talking about you in weeks! And look, considering how you've done academically in the past four years, you can definitely graduate without any classes this quarter. Enjoy yourself for the next month! Impress us all by learning a fifty-first language!"

"I really don't think that's going to work out."

"Do you think you can't get your old life back, Jason? I told you, everything's back to normal—"

"No, Dean Washington. I don't want to get my old life back. Not anymore. I've gained far too much in my new life, and I would never give it away and just pretend that nothing happened in past two months. My life isn't some fairytale where all the bad spells get overturned and everyone lives happily ever after. It's a vast world out there, but in a way it's also a simple one. Once you remove all the useless garbage on the surface, it's not that complicated. But it's only when you're at the ends of the earth, in the belly of the beast, so to speak, that you realize how few things in life matter so much."

Nathalie Washington stayed silent for a short moment. "Jason, if you want to reconsider, we'll also be sending you an email and a letter—"

Jason placed his palm upright in front of his chest. "No, save the time and shipping costs. A flexible first class ticket back to New York won't tempt me back either," he recommended, though a part of him thought it would be funny to see how many resources they would expend to bring him back. Was President DiTancini already on a flight to Singapore? "My decision is final."

"Well, good luck, Jason," Nathalie Washington said, letting out a resigned sigh. "I'd say farewell to you, but I'm certain our paths will cross again someday. It's a small world out there."

"I never thought I'd say this, but it was nice to meet you in person."

"You too, Jason. I'm sure you'll do great things. Goodbye."

"Goodbye, Dean Washington." Jason showed her the way to the door, then returned to the large wooden desk in the center of the room.

"You chose well, Jason," Cha congratulated him.

"Thanks. It wasn't a hard decision, really. I saw no reason to pretend I was hesitating and waste her time. Look, I'm really grateful for all the classes I took at Northport, but I think it's part of my past. Anyway, I need some peace of mind. I'm going to go wash my hands."

That was another typical Jason move, Cha thought. Perhaps she should adopt his uncanny ability to find pleasure in the most esoteric things.

Still, she wondered if she would have made the same choice in his position. Returning to a known world would probably have been too tempting. As she had told him the other day, "unknown" was a synonym for "terrifying." Had he decided to go back to Northport, following his life path would have been like building from an IKEA booklet. He just had to follow the curriculum, follow along during his interview for one of the firms recruiting heavily at Northport, and follow orders from his boss to rise through the ranks and live a happy life.

Now, though, Jason was going through uncharted territory. As much as she believed in Intuner and the possibility for future neurotechnological developments, startups were a crapshoot. More times than not, advertising failed, technology malfunctioned, competitors emerged, and teams fell apart. She just hoped he had not opted to stay in Singapore because of her. She truly loved the man who deviated from the crowds and did not repudiate her for her insecurity, but rather embraced it as his own. Of course she egotistically wanted him to stay with her forever. But that was not what love was. Since she truly loved him, she wanted him to succeed and enjoy his life, not take a dangerous risk so he could stay with an insecure, sterile woman twice his age. It was cliché, she told herself, but it was funny how often clichés turned out to be true.

After a few minutes, Jason returned from the sink, then stood in front of Cha. "Do you know what irks me most about all these universities, Cha?" he asked. "It's their obsession with diversity. They can get as many Asians and Hispanics, Buddhists and Bahá'ís, legacies and first-generations, and golfers and saxophonists as they want, but that's only superficial. They'll never have real diversity if they make a bubble where everyone tries to conform to a social mold."

Cha smiled. It was typical of Jason to express his veiled anger through rational analysis. Then again, if he washed his hands for that long every time, he probably had time to think all of those ideas out.

As she prepared to concur, a soft voice replied, "Jason, just be glad that not everyone appreciates conformity."

Tilting her head to the side, Cha noticed a young woman walking from behind one of the overgrown orchids. Most likely, she had walked in and hidden while Cha had pretended to be busy looking at the papers on the desk and Jason had actually been busy talking to Dean Washington. Could she be—

"Aurélia?" Jason asked in shock.

"Hey, Jason," Aurélia told him. "I missed you."

Jason looked straight into Aurélia's eyes, and then Cha understood. Nathalie Washington had convinced Aurélia of Jason's innocence and brought her to Singapore to also apologize to Jason face-to-face, and probably motivate him to return to campus. Now was the time to see if he had been telling the truth when he had said he was completely over her.

Of course, if he walked into the sunset with Aurélia, there was nothing she could do about it. Aurélia was actually his age, after all. Was that really a weakness for her older self though? Not only could Cha navigate a still-confused Jason, she suspected that only an older woman like herself had the maturity to look past the uncool image Jason probably displayed to his classmates. Whatever happened, she would go with the tide—ironic, she thought, for someone whose profession as a real estate speculator hinged on going against it to win when others lost.

"Am I surprised to see you here, Aurélia."

"Well, I actually met Dean Washington by chance during one of the campus tours I was leading, and we talked about you at some point in the conversation. Later, she asked me if I wanted to come to speak to some alumni and readmit you, so how could I refuse? Like Dean Washington, I wanted to give you the dignity of hearing my apology face-to-face, especially since you didn't respond to my messages."

"Which messages?" Jason asked with incredulity.

"To be honest, at first I thought the rumors on campus might be true, so I felt betrayed. I ignored you for a while, but then I realized what a fool I'd been for ever believing them. I started to get worried for you, so I wrote to you several times. You never responded."

"That's because I blocked your email not long after you removed yourself from my Skype contacts," he reluctantly admitted, "But I'm really sorry. I need to fix that very soon."

"Don't worry about it! I did something way worse. I didn't trust you. I hope that wasn't too hard for you."

It had been a very hard time indeed, but Jason had rebounded nonetheless, as Cha could testify.

Aurélia scanned the office. "Wow, it looks like you're getting all your stuff set up here! How's your project been going?"

"Oh, it's moving forward for sure. That thing I told you about being able to sing in tune, it's all true. You know, it wasn't just about the money. I wanted to fix my own errors when I sang. Soon, I'll be able to sing the song I've been preparing for years: your song."

"Oh, Jason," she said, smiling.

Jason smiled back at her, then looked up at the ceiling. What was he going to do? No matter what lies he had told himself, he had never moved past Aurélia, and here she was. But was he letting himself get carried away? He had promised himself that he would not return to Northport, to an approximation of the life he knew before. Could he find another way? Did he have to make that decision today? Why was everything always so confusing?

"How long are you staying in Singapore?" Aurélia asked, interrupting his thoughts at the right moment.

"Honestly, as long as it takes for Intuner to get finished and launch, and who knows what'll happen after that. I'm setting up my office here, and Cha's really been helping me out in lots of ways."

"Who's Cha?" Aurélia asked.

"My secretary," he replied.

"Nice to meet you!" Aurélia said in a friendly voice.

"Equally," she answered. "Here, I don't want to intrude, so I'll go back to reading over the interview questions for tomorrow—your friend's such a busy young man!"

"How about you?" Jason asked. "How long are you staying here?"

"I know it sounds super weird, but I'm flying out with Dean Washington tomorrow night. We're going to Melbourne to speak to some other alumni, and then both have a ton of stuff to take care of before Commencement."

"Well, look at you, you little jetsetter."

"You know, I was thinking you could maybe show me around. Dean Washington needs to talk to me about stuff for Melbourne tonight, but I'd love to come back in the morning."

"Yeah, I mean, um," he said, wondering what Cha would think of him reconnecting with his past crush, "I don't think that's going to work out, sorry. We're having a huge meeting with some developers tomorrow morning."

Cha smiled slyly. Jason had definitely been a good investment. He knew very well that the open house was in the mid-afternoon. Should she be proud or ashamed of herself for teaching someone once so fixated on honesty to lie so convincingly?

"But definitely shoot me an email and we'll be in touch. I'll be sure to unblock you before then."

"I'd love it if you had the time, but if it doesn't work out tomorrow, tell me if when you're in New York for work or anything. Who knows, maybe I can come back here over the summer. I start my job with an NGO in Brooklyn in September, but I'm free for a few months before then. It's always so nice to see you."

"Yeah, we'll figure something out."

As she headed for the door, Aurélia gave him a hug and a quick kiss on the cheek. "Keep being you," she whispered, then left into the sunset-drenched quay.

Jason slowly reciprocated the kiss, then waved goodbye to her. As she left the door, though, he looked back at Cha. Had he made a mistake in kissing Aurélia? Was that something acceptable when his lover sat three meters behind him? Was it less awkward because he had known Aurélia for longer? Should anything stop him when he had never really stopped loving Aurélia? Did it matter?

He looked at Cha, now standing next to the desk with her arms crossed, wondering whether she would admonish him. Yet he saw only a smile, which he copied.

"Oh, Cha. It's been an exhausting day, and tomorrow shouldn't be much more relaxing with all the developers coming in," he told her, collapsing in her warm arms and raising his head for a kiss. "I think I'm going to crash."

"You should get some rest. I'll wake you up when I start feeling lonely."

Cha released him from her embrace, then sat back at her desk. It had been a confusing day for her too. Right now, there was nothing she wanted to do more than bury herself in cumbersome paperwork and forget everything else. She grabbed the tax forms for the office and began reading all the fine print.

A few minutes later, she glanced over at the tiger-print couch. Jason was sound asleep, his feet lodged on the rim and his head tucked on his shoulder. Before dozing off, though, he had taken the time to place something on her desk. First Aurélia, and then this. People got way too much past her radar while she was reading papers.

Cha looked down at the LEGO moai, then stared into its white plastic eyes.

TO BE CONTINUED…

ICELATED

(AN UPCOMING NORTHPORT SAGA TITLE)

DIRK BECK

THE MOVIE IN MY MIND

The images beamed from Tom Nilson's headset. He focused on the upper right-hand corner of the screen projected in front of him, where his avatar stood on in a harbor near a town. Around him stood a forest of deciduous trees, their leaves turning to red and yellow. Sailboats in the harbor bobbed up and down next to a few anchored yachts. Past the marina, a town lay among the groves of trees. Gothic towers poked out of the landscape. Tom pressed his joystick, and the avatar Tom sprinted across the marina to the town.

He soon entered the town and its neat grid of streets lined with red-roofed townhouses. Due to strict architectural codes, only the electric cars omnipresent in the streets differentiated the contemporary town from its appearance a hundred years ago. Tom weaved through visitors walking among rows of clothing stores and ethnic restaurants. He approached the downtown as the ten minutes wound down. On the map, the green and the red dots were almost touching now. He was nearing the target.

While he was not one to make precipitated judgments, Tom was sure that this college town was his very own Northport. Why were the owners of Base Camp Alpha taking him here?

Soon enough, the answer had found him. The screen displayed the words, *"Terrorists have invaded Northport's campus. Rid all the buildings of them. Watch out: they may be dressed as tourists and employees, or even Northport students. Look out for anyone with their eyes hidden by their turquoise Northport hoodie."*

Tom noticed a small map on the corner of his quadrant, where green dot indicated his location. The map provided a basic street plan of the city. On one end, a red spot marked what Tom knew must be his target. Beside the map, a timer counted down from ten minutes. In only ten minutes, he had to reach that location. Tom noticed the machine gun concealed in his avatar's pocket.

He pressed the joystick forward and ran across Northport's main thoroughfare, Garvarentz Boulevard, to his target. He immediately recognized the fancy brick lodge. After all, every Northport student knew some version of the high-profile incident that had led to the hotel's opening, a scandal involving the rambunctious fraternity Iota Nu Alpha a decade or two ago.

The way Tom had heard the story, Iota Nu Alpha had set up an underground nonprofit strip club to enhance its hazing process. Northport's president had heard the word about it and, after attending multiple peep shows incognito, shut down the fraternity. Afterwards, the university's administration had made the much-decried decision to take over the privately run organization's headquarters and sold it to a real estate company turning it into the luxurious Turquoise Deer Lodge.

Tom pulled the ringed handles on the wooden doors. In the large lobby inside, tourists relaxed on sleek turquoise couches, a deliberate contrast with the old wooden floorboards and brick-and-mortar walls.

A message flashed on the screen. *"You have reached your target. Eliminate the enemy."* Tom had never studied Japanese at Northport, but it was common knowledge that the videogame's name, "Kamikaze," meant "Suicide." There was no question that he would die before the round was up. His goal was to inflict as much damage as possible before then. He would never raise a hand against anyone in real life, but in the videogame world, his reflexes were lightning-fast.

Tom pulled out his machine gun and shot the receptionists. One fell immediately, his head slamming on the marble desk. The other was smarter in his decision to swerve to the side, under the impact of the shot knocked the desk lamp onto his cranium. Screaming erupted from the lobby as tourists ducked under furniture and rushed out of the room. Blood sprayed in the air as Tom rapid-fired. He chased the fleeing tourists as they escaped the room.

The screen now showed the message, *"Do whatever needs to be done to liberate the campus. Ignore the collateral damage."* Following the instructions, Tom guided his avatar through the hotel's main dining room and sprayed bullets all over. As bodies fell, the red drops of blood morphed with the disguised terrorists' turquoise sweatshirts into a color Tom could not name. A chandelier burst, its crystals spattering all over the floorboards. Ignoring the faint sound of a siren in the distance, he ran outside to the hotel pool. A large group of wealthy-looking Chinese tourists sipped bottles of whiskey and mingled. As the avatar Tom brought out his machine gun, they looked at him, their faces frozen in horror as their bodies floated in the pool.

For a second, Tom paused. He didn't know why he hesitated. After all, he was merely in a simulator. He had never felt this way in a videogame before. No one would actually die if he pushed a button on a joystick. But here, everything seemed so realistic. It was probably because of the location, just the fact that he knew the place so well and was laying waste to it.

He was about to shoot when a bullet whizzed past his ear. He ducked, but then a pair of bullets from one of the hooded terrorists hit him in the back. Suddenly he felt a jolt in the bar holding his chest. A horrible electric shock vibrated through him. He twitched violently as pain enveloped his nerves. As his avatar collapsed on the screen, he fired into the crowd blindly. The electricity in his veins grew and finally subsided as his avatar joined the dead Chinese tourists in the pool. The screen faded to black. Tom looked up at the screen, his muscles still twitching. *"Round 1,"* it said in bold red letters. *"Time alive: 12:14. Kills: 17."*

Panicking, Tom tried to escape from the chair. But the more he squirmed, the tighter it held him. *"Beginning next round in 10, 9, 8..."* the message on the screen counted down. The intense pain must come whenever his avatar in the simulator died. Could he avoid being shot somehow? Maybe he could avoid the target altogether.

ICELATED

But there was a built-in mechanism to prevent him from fleeing the city—Tom was sure of it. The game had only allowed for ten minutes between downtown and the hotel on the last round. Taking longer than ten minutes could only mean death.

He knew there was only one option. He could not hesitate next time. To stay alive, he would just have to play better.

The new landscape appeared before him. Now he stood right at the center of Northport's campus, on Menken Memorial Plaza. Tom's avatar picked up his gun and jogged out of the building and onto the main campus, heading towards the red dot.

His new target was Northport's Legrand Stadium. He reached it with five minutes to spare. He mixed in with the lower-level crowd watching Northport's long-awaited game with its Ivy League rival Princeton, then whipped out his machine gun and fired. The spectators next to him tried to escape, but they were out of luck. The stadium was completely full, and the cheer of the crowd as the Northport Deers scored an equalizing touchdown muffled the victims' screams. Bodies fell down the stadium stairs, one tumbling onto the football field.

Now the crowd noticed, screaming in horror. Tom's avatar shot a few football players, Northport Deers and Princeton Tigers alike. After all, anyone here could be a terrorist. People pushed and shoved, trampling one another. A bloody red mist hung in the air. Suddenly, a bullet struck him in the shoulder. Like last time, electric shocks washed through his body. He ducked down, joining

6

the mob trying to leave the square. He shot around wildly while screaming in pain. Bodies fell like rain, and bullets from Department of Public Safety officers—probably disguised terrorists as well—whizzed past his head.

Then, mercifully, one struck his head. He felt a sudden burst of electricity, and then a soothing absence of pain. The screen went black.

"Time alive: 7:04," the screen read. *"Kills: 120."*

✈ ✈ ✈

Tom Nilson walked out of the simulator room, his whole body shaking. Each death had been more painful than the previous one. He had advanced through more than ten stages on Northport's campus, and in each city he had racked up many more kills than in the previous. Now, as he exited the room and squinted in the bright light, his senses were in disarray. He felt like he was still in the video game world, plotting how to kill the mob around him. His legs still felt like they were vibrating from the electric shocks, and his sense of balance was off.

The whole mission had been so strange. He and a group of other Ivy League students had the study abroad trip to Iceland to study Jupiter's moon Apollonia, not to find themselves on Apollonia itself, under the control of unnamed captors who forced them to play violent viodegames.

Deciding not to ask any questions for the moment, Tom followed the tide of captives to a giant hallway with screens instructing the male and females to continue in separate directions. He dropped his khakis and his shirt in a huge mound of clothes and followed more arrows to a large showering room. Huge shower heads rained lukewarm water down from the ceiling. He flinched instinctively, his nerves on hyper-alert. Then he closed his eyes, trying to calm himself, letting the water wash over his naked body. The water stopped and a giant blow drying system kicked in, warming him and making him feel less tired and hungry, even in only for an instant.

Still damp, Tom followed the crowd to another conveyor belt, which dispensed clothes that did not look like they had been washed recently. But what choice did he have? He snatched one up that looked his size and made his way back to the eating room for dinner. He placed his hand in his pocket as he walked. He still had a flashlight. Everyone had to have one.

He walked out of the hallway and into the dining area, where he finally gave in to his hunger and slurped the mysterious red soup. He stared out the window at the bleak rocky landscape of Apollonia. It had begun to rain heavily, the drops crashing on the eerily blue lakes.

Why, he wondered, had so many bright young students been brought here, and by whom? Whoever had taken them here was probably not trying to exterminate them. Placing them all into a gas chamber or blowing up the spaceship flying them over from Iceland would have been so much simpler. No, the unnamed owner of Base Camp Alpha was using them for some purpose.

The instructions on the simulator screen had mentioned the mission as a counterterrorism operation, but Tom did not buy that. Instructing students to gun down "terrorist" visitors on their own campuses—he assumed that the Princetonians and Yalies had fought the simulated battle on their home turf—seemed unnecessarily brutal. Or maybe, on the contrary, the government was testing them to see if they could withstand such a psychological challenge? Counterterrorism was not for the faint of heart, after all. But that was still not a believable explanation. The government was completely broke. There was no way they could afford such frivolous spending. Why not just train them on campus, just like all the recruiters who ran interview workshops at Northport?

Base Camp Alpha had to be under the control of terrorists, their very own training camp. In recent years, shady organizations around the world had amassed amazing resources. They had taken control of airplanes enough times; maybe seizing a mission to space was their new ploy. And why not attack an Ivy League campus? Terrorists always looked for something showy, and a takeover of Northport or Harvard would certainly make the headlines. Besides, security in airports and government buildings made any sort of attack there impossible. Anyone could sneak a gun or a bomb onto a campus, however. And who better knew how to infiltrate a campus than its own students? Tom had killed many more enemies in the game when he had entered Waxman House through its underground corridors than through the front door.

But would these terrorists really bother with building a base on one of Jupiter's moons and sending the abducted students this far? Earth had many areas more secluded than a moon that had come up on so many front pages of newspapers. The Papua New Guinean highlands were such a place, if that was the only thing Tom took away from his dreadfully boring First-Year Seminar in sociolinguistics. Had Iceland not been the location of the spaceport for missions to Apollonia, the terrorists could easily have hidden there as well.

It was pretty clear now: the terrorists were aliens. With no life on the moon besides a few scattered fungi and bacteria, these aliens had to be foreign as well. If they were coming from a different solar system, Apollonia was a logical stopping point on the way to Earth, and the Ivy League was equally logical for a first assault.

But what were the aliens looking to do? Were they looking to invade Earth? Were they looking for natural resources, or maybe living space for their population? Or were they religious fundamentalists looking to spread their beliefs to humans, following the trend on Earth in the past few decades? It was almost amusing to imagine what would happen once they came in contact with the religious fanatics already on Earth. There would be fewer crazy people in the solar system, that was for sure.

So what was the best thing for Tom and the other captives to do? Should they dance to the tune of whatever crazy plot the aliens had in mind? Those who resisted were never heard from again. In that case, when would Tom and the others escape back to safety?

Tom turned back and stared into the nearly empty dining hall, wondering how to solve this puzzle. Suddenly, his train of thought ended as he saw the only captive who had not yet retreated to the sleeping quarters. He had been meaning to talk to Lilly Schönberg tonight, but he was unsure exactly what to tell her.

After hesitating for a little bit, he opened with, "The movie in my mind finally came. You know, the one those weird robot voices were telling us about."

"Me too!" Lilly answered. "What was it like?"

"Not bad. I was able to kill a bunch of terrorists," he told her, not wanting to bore her with his analysis of who controlled Base Camp Alpha and all the college students here, or why.

"Oh, and Lilly?" he added.

"Yeah?"

Tom thought for a second, wondering how to phrase his question. He was attracted to Lilly, that was for sure. But now, faced with an opportunity to say something, he froze.

"See you around," he told her before walking away.

"Yup, good night!" she shot off.

At least Tom had chosen the right moment to chicken out. The all-too-familiar mechanical voice began chanting, "Ten second warning." Pretty soon, it had finished ticking down to zero, and the lights were out.

Tom felt the familiar wave of exhaustion hitting him. For once, he welcomed it. He had survived his first day on Apollonia.

COMING SOON!

ACKNOWLEDGMENTS

Without the help of so many people, this book would have been like Intuner without the help of Northport University: just an idea. Thank you to my family for encouraging me to bring this project to fruition. Thank you to my grandparents: Bernard Meunier, for giving me my taste for storytelling; Paule Meunier, for helping out at brainstorming sessions over Thai and Indian food; Rachid Aït-Sahalia, for helping with character names; and Nadia Aït-Sahalia, for introducing me to my musical namesake, Idir. Thank you, Yacine Aitsahalia, for taking me to Sydney, Singapore, and Easter Island. Thank you, Ines Aitsahalia, for showing me what cute younger sisters are like and that a girl's love of stuffed animals does not fade with age.

Thank you to everyone who inspired some characters and storylines: you know who you are. Thank you to my guides through the byzantine publishing process: Elisabeth Scharlatt, Victoria Skurnick, Jean Hanff Korelitz, Eileen Kennedy-Moore, Kimberlee Phelan, Shayna Gunn, Karen Bao, Edmund Immergut, and Mary Fan. Thank you to everyone to read my work in its unpolished state: David Myers, Nannerl Keohane, Soo Yeon Kim, Ben Dattner, Judith Weinstein, Milosh Popovic, Gabriella Chu, Valeria Mazarakis, Alex Costin, and Nadira Aitsahlia. Thank you, Menelaos Mazarakis, for suggesting the idea of the many Northports; Drew Oros, for teaching me about mindshare and startups; Gary Gao, for working on the novel's Chinese translation; and Apollonia Kang, for acting as my publicist.

And finally, Sophie Meunier, thank you for being such a supportive editor, cook, cheerleader, and mother throughout the whole process.

ABOUT NORTHPORT BOOKS

Northport Books® is an independent publishing house based in Princeton, New Jersey, with an array of fiction and nonfiction works related to college.

From the adventures of students trying to fit in a daunting campus, to practical how-to guides for those trying to cook for the first time in a tiny dorm room, to satires of every aspect of daily life in the campus bubble, we have it all here at Northport Books®.

With the motto, "Publishing to the college bubble and beyond," we strive to share the experiences of college students and their families with other students, those preparing for college, and readers interested in the unique cultural phenomenon that is the American college campus.

Our books are available in electronic and print formats on Amazon.com®. We are always on the lookout for original ideas, so please feel free to send us any works you have written.

Enjoy and happy reading!

https://twitter.com/northportbooks
https://www.facebook.com/northportbooks
http://www.northportbooks.com/

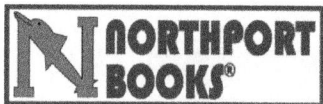

UPCOMING TITLES

Icelated

By Dirk Beck

Cooking in Your Dorm Room: Fast, Easy, and Cheap recipes for the Busy College Student

by E. Q. Roy

Mocktails in Your Dorm Room: An Alcohol-Free Guide to College Bartending

by E. Q. Roy

Cowboy Classes

by Gary Gao

ABOUT THE AUTHOR

Idir Aitsahalia's first name means "life" in Kabyle, a native language of North Africa's indigenous Berber people. Born in Chicago to a French mother and an Algerian father, Idir grew up in an academic family and knows a thing or two about college campuses. He has traveled to over fifty countries and speaks nine languages. In his spare time, he enjoys collecting vintage LEGO models, discovering new ethnic foods, and singing opera in the shower. He lives in Princeton, New Jersey and has worked in several startup companies before going to college—not to Northport, but to a university very much like Northport—where he plans to study economics.

www.ingramcontent.com/pod-product-compliance
Lightning Source LLC
LaVergne TN
LVHW041313080426
835513LV00008B/443